Cliat

59

59

SANTRY BOOKSTORE
DUBLIN CORPORATION PUBLIC LIBRARIES

26.

E0000000001864

New Italian Architecture

Alberto Galardi **New Italian Architecture**

The Architectural Press London

Leabharlanna Co
Áta Cliat
R
Acc. 67 67003
Inv. - 2328-
90/=
Dept.
Class. 720.945

85139 480 9

Published in the U.K. and Commonwealth by
The Architectural Press London 1967
Copyright by Verlag Gerd Hatje Stuttgart 1967
Printed in Germany

Translation into English by E. Rockwell

Contents · Inhalt

Introduction   6

Examples

Houses for one family, and holiday houses   22

Houses for several families, blocks of flats and housing estates   36

Tourist centres   56

Community and welfare buildings   60

Schools   78

Churches   88

Cultural buildings and restaurants   100

Sports buildings   106

Exhibition buildings   132

Department stores and office buildings   144

Buildings for industry, traffic and transport   168

Bibliography   193

Index   203

Einleitung   7

Beispiele

Einfamilien- und Ferienhäuser   22

Mehrfamilienhäuser, Wohnblocks und Siedlungen   36

Touristenzentren   56

Sozialbauten   60

Schulen   78

Kirchen   88

Kulturbauten und Restaurants   100

Sportbauten   106

Ausstellungsbauten   132

Kaufhäuser, Büro- und Verwaltungsgebäude   144

Industrie- und Verkehrsbauten   168

Bibliographie   193

Index   203

Introduction

1

In Italy, too, the second half of the 19th century saw a general revival of the arts. The most appropriate point in time to mark the transition between the two cultural eras which dominated the first and second halves of the century, respectively, is the year of national unification.

In 1866, Italian positivism finds its expression in Pasquale Villari who established the historic method of cultural appraisal. Taking its cue from mathematical terminology, philosophy assumes a new language, and scientific and technological research begin to play an exceedingly important part.

Romanticism is now opposed by a new and realistic spirit. In the wake of the Risorgimento — rather late compared with other more advanced nations — Italian industry and capital begin to conglomerate in the large cities. As a result, the urban population begins to increase abruptly, and the desertion of the countryside commences. But the conditions, already present in other European countries, favouring a rapid promotion and co-ordination of urban development are still missing. It is only later, after the consolidation of national consciousness, that the social structure begins to develop organically.

Architectural Romanticism in Italy has derived inspiration from the wide range of earlier building styles and has mainly been influenced by Italian regional architecture, from Lombard Romanesque to Siennese Gothic, from Florentine Renaissance to Piedmontese Baroque, blossoming into a surprisingly great variety of "Neo-styles".

Prominent examples are the Villa Favart (1857), the Loggia at the Piazzale Michelangelo in Florence (Fig. 1), designed by Giuseppe Poggi in Cinquecento style, the monumental Campo Santo in Milan (1863) by Carlo Maciachini (Fig. 2) in Pisa-Gothic style, the pseudo-medieval Palazzo Valentino in Turin (1884) by Alfredo D'Andrade (Fig. 3), the Savings Bank at Pistoia (1905) by Tito Azzolini (Fig. 4) in Florentine Renaissance style, and the monument to Victor Emmanuel II in Rome (1885—1911) by Giuseppe Sacconi (Fig. 5) in Greco-Roman style. This monument, no doubt a borderline case in the stylistic aberrations of eclecticism, clearly demonstrates the dubious character of an entire school of architecture solely bent on dusting up and composing the architectural forms of earlier epochs. The motley mixture of stylistic contrivances and the obvious dishonesty of an architecture which ceases to be an expression of its time are the essential features leading to the final climax of 19th century eclecticism, which had first arisen towards the end of the 18th century with the birth of Neo-Classicism.

The need for a new style and, in particular, for a renewal was stressed by Camillo Boito: "Even in art, a lie is an ugly and unnecessary thing as it never, or hardly ever, succeeds in its deception. If architecture ceases to be a liar and becomes a

2

3

4

Die zweite Hälfte des 19. Jahrhunderts ist auch in Italien durch eine allgemeine Erneuerung der Künste gekennzeichnet. Treffend bestimmt der Zeitpunkt der nationalen Einigung die Grenze zwischen den beiden Kulturperioden, die die erste und die zweite Hälfte des Jahrhunderts prägten.

Im Jahr 1866 findet der italienische Positivismus in Pasquale Villari seinen Ausdruck; mit ihm wird die historische Methode in der Kulturbetrachtung begründet. Die Philosophie nimmt — indem sie sich an der mathematischen Terminologie orientiert — eine neue Sprache an, und die wissenschaftliche und technologische Forschung beginnt eine überaus wichtige Rolle zu spielen.

Dem Romantizismus stellt sich nun ein neuer und realistischer Geist entgegen. Mit der nationalen Einigung entstehen in Italien, gegenüber den anderen, fortgeschritteneren Nationen beträchtlich verspätet, die Industrien und Kapitalballungen in den großen Städten. Die Umschichtung in den Städten führt zu einer plötzlichen Bevölkerungszunahme; die Landflucht setzt ein. Es fehlen jedoch noch die Voraussetzungen zur Förderung und Koordinierung der städtischen Entwicklung, durch die zu dieser Zeit die Gesellschaft in anderen europäischen Ländern rasch umgeformt wird. Erst später, nach Festigung des nationalen Bewußtseins, entwickelt sich die Sozialstruktur in organischer Weise. Der architektonische Romantizismus in Italien hatte aus dem umfangreichen Reservoir der vorhergegangenen Baustile geschöpft und sich vor allem von der regionalen italienischen Architektur beeinflussen lassen, von der lombardischen Romanik bis zur sienesischen Gotik, von der florentinischen Renaissance bis zum piemontesischen Barock, wobei er überraschend zahlreiche und ebenso verschiedenartige Blüten im »Neo-Stil« hervorbrachte.

So entstehen in Italien die Villa Favart (1857) und der Pavillon des Michelangelo-Platzes in Florenz (Bild 1) von Giuseppe Poggi im Stil des Cinquecento, der Monumentalfriedhof in Mailand (1863) von Carlo Maciachini (Bild 2) in gotisch-pisanischem Stil, das mittelalterliche Schloß des Valentino in Turin (1884) von Alfredo D'Andrade (Bild 3), die Sparkasse in Pistoia (1905) von Tito Azzolini (Bild 4) in florentinischem Renaissance-Stil und das Denkmal Viktor Emanuels II. in Rom (1885–1911) von Giuseppe Sacconi (Bild 5) in griechisch-römischem Stil. Dieses Monument, zweifellos ein Grenzfall des Eklektizismus, macht die Fragwürdigkeit einer ganzen Architektur deutlich, die einzig auf dem Wiederhervorholen und der Komposition von Architekturformen anderer Epochen beruht. Das Durcheinander der Stilmittel und die Unehrlichkeit der Architektur, die nicht mehr Ausdruck ihrer Zeit ist, sind die wesentlichen Ursachen für den Eklektizismus des 19. Jahrhunderts, der gegen Ende des 18. Jahrhunderts mit der Geburt des Neoklassizismus aufkam.

Über die Notwendigkeit eines neuen Stils und vor allem einer Erneuerung schrieb Camillo Boito: »Die Lüge ist auch in der Kunst eine häßliche und unnütze Sache,

5

6

revealer of truth, such conversion can already be regarded as a foundation for the modern style . . . The architect must thus be a highly skilled expert; he must have a thorough knowledge of the habits of the society to which he belongs; he must know not only what is necessary but also what is useful and beneficial in the buildings erected by him; finally, he must be a clever and ingenious artist. If only one of these qualifications should be absent, he may be an engineer, an ornamentalist, a decorator; but he is not an architect."

Because of his historical awareness, Camillo Boito (1836—1914) — architect, architectural historian, theoretician of the restoration of buildings, man of letters, critic and teacher at the Milan School of Architecture — is the most acknowledged architect of his time.

Even more than his architectural creations, the moral fervour typical for Boito's teachings and writings bears witness to his search for the renewal of architecture as a live expression of its time. As to the restoration of buildings, Boito is a true reformer: he can justly be regarded as the founder of the science of restoration in its modern sense.

In his book "Practical Problems of the Plastic Arts", Boito has this to say: "If restorations are based on the theory of M. Viollet-Le-Duc, which may be regarded as the romantic theory of restoration and was, up to the day before yesterday, accepted as omnipotent and followed by many if not most people in Italy, I would prefer poor restorations to good ones. Whilst the blissful ignorance displayed by the former enables me to distinguish between the old and the new part, the admirable ingenuity and cleverness of the latter, which make the new appear old, tend to confuse my judgment to such an extent that the pleasure in viewing the building dissipates, and surveying it becomes a highly onerous task."

As an architect, Camillo Boito belonged to the school of eclecticism, and his work, though honest and controlled, never excelled the standard of the architecture of his time.

The hospital at Gallarate (1871), the Palazzo Debite (Fig. 6) in Padua (1873), the school at the Via Galvani in Milan (1888), and the Giuseppe Verdi Convalescence Home for musicians (Fig. 7) in Milan (1899) bear witness to Boito's architectural activities, and reveal the limitations of his creative capacity, giving no indication of the reforming ardour so fervently proclaimed from the pulpit and in his writings.

The architect who, in Italy, made a significant contribution to the promotion of a new expressive language and of the renewal desired by Boito was Gaetano Moretti (1860—1938).

Moretti was a disciple of Boito's whom he succeeded in the chair at the Milan School of Architecture. His teaching method differed greatly from that of his predecessor. Thus, Moretti advocated a more liberal use of imagination as a basic means of reforming architecture, whilst Boito saw the possibilities of renewal in the synthesis of humanistic and technological findings alone.

About the coming architectural style, Boito wrote as follows: "If we are not deceived either by history (in which we have great confidence) or by reason (in which we have less confidence), the new architecture cannot spring from the head of an architect. It can neither be totally novel nor can it be composed of a blend of several styles — it must freely develop into an integrated Italian style which, though steeped in the past, must shed its archaeological character so that it can become wholly modern."

Later, Gaetano Moretti wrote about his teaching in the following terms: "From the day on which I had the honour of becoming Camillo Boito's successor, I have always carried out my duties with conscientious respect for artistic and scientific trends, with a sure eye on the future."

As an architect, Moretti was particularly interested in major town planning tasks.

The monumental Campo Santo (Figs. 8, 9) at Chiavari (1894), the study for the remodelling of the Piazza De Ferrari in Genoa, the power station (Fig. 10) at Trezzo d'Adda (1906), and the redevelopment plan for the City of Chiavari (1934) are among those works which bear witness to Moretti's creative faculties over a period of 50 years includes the turn of the century.

7

denn eine Täuschung gelingt ihr nie oder fast nie. Wenn die Architektur von der Lügnerin zur Verkünderin der Wahrheit wird, dann ist damit schon die Grundlage des modernen Stils gefunden . . . Der Architekt muß also ein sehr erfahrener Fachmann sein; er muß die Gewohnheiten der Gesellschaft, in der er lebt, gründlich kennen; er muß wissen, was bei den Bauten, die er errichtet, nicht nur notwendig, sondern auch nützlich und vorteilhaft ist, und außerdem muß er ein kluger und einfallsreicher Künstler sein. Wenn ihm auch nur eine dieser Eigenschaften fehlt, dann ist er ein Ingenieur, ein Ornamentiker, ein Dekorateur, aber kein Architekt.«

Camillo Boito (1836–1914), Architekt, Wissenschaftler der Architekturgeschichte, Theoretiker der Bauwerksrestaurierung, Literat, Kritiker und Lehrer an der Schule für Architektur in Mailand, ist wegen seiner geschichtsbewußten Haltung der anerkannteste Architekt seiner Zeit.

Der sittliche Eifer, der Boitos Unterricht und seine Schriften kennzeichnete, bezeugt noch stärker als sein architektonisches Schaffen die Suche nach einer Erneuerung der Architektur, die lebendiger Ausdruck ihrer Epoche ist. Auf dem Gebiet der Restaurierung war Boito ein wirklicher Reformator: er kann mit Recht als Begründer der Restaurierungswissenschaft, wie wir sie heute verstehen, angesehen werden.

In seinem Buch »Praktische Fragen der bildenden Künste« schrieb Boito folgendes: »Wenn Restaurierungen nach der Theorie des Herrn Viollet-Le-Duc ausgeführt werden, die man die romantische Restaurierungstheorie nennen kann — die bis vorgestern allgemeingültig war und von vielen, ja von den meisten in Italien befolgt wird —, dann ziehe ich die schlechten Restaurierungen den guten vor. Während mich jene dank der wohltätigen Unwissenheit den alten vom neuen Teil unterscheiden lassen, versetzen mich diese durch eine bewundernswerte Wissenschaft und Schlauheit, mit der sie das Neue alt erscheinen lassen, in eine solche Ratlosigkeit des Urteils, daß die Freude am Betrachten des Bauwerks schwindet und seine Erforschung eine überaus lästige Mühe wird.«

Als Architekt gehörte Camillo Boito dem Eklektizismus an, und sein Werk, obwohl ehrlich und kontrolliert, ragte nie über das Niveau der damaligen Baukunst hinaus.

Das Krankenhaus in Gallarate (1871), der Debite-Palast (Bild 6) in Padua (1873), die Schule in der Galvanistraße in Mailand (1888) und das Giuseppe-Verdi-Erholungsheim für Musiker (Bild 7) in Mailand (1899) bezeugen zur Genüge Boitos architektonisches Wirken, bei dem die Grenzen seiner schöpferischen Fähigkeiten sichtbar werden und das nichts von der sowohl vom Katheder als auch in den Schriften so hitzig verfochtenen Erneuerung ahnen läßt.

Der Architekt, der in Italien einen bedeutenden Schritt auf dem Weg zu einer neuen ausdrucksvollen Sprache und zu der von Boito gewünschten Erneuerung tat, war Gaetano Moretti (1860–1938).

Moretti war ein Schüler von Boito, dem er auf dem Lehrstuhl an der Schule für Architektur in Mailand nachfolgte. Seine Lehrmethode unterschied sich wesentlich von der seines Vorgängers. So verfocht Moretti eine größere Freiheit der Phantasie als grundlegendes Element zur Reformierung der Architektur, wogegen Boito allein in der Synthese der humanistischen und der technischen Erkenntnisse die Möglichkeit zur Erneuerung sah.

Über den zukünftigen Architekturstil schrieb Boito folgendes: »Die neue Architektur kann, wenn uns die Geschichte, zu der wir großes Vertrauen haben, ebensowenig täuscht wie die Vernunft, in die wir geringes Vertrauen setzen, nicht dem Kopf eines Architekten entspringen. Sie kann weder ganz und gar neuartig sein, noch kann sie sich aus einem Gemisch von mehreren Stilen zusammensetzen, sondern sie muß sich frei zu einem einheitlichen, von der Vergangenheit geprägten italienischen Stil entwickeln, dessen archäologischen Charakter sie jedoch ablegen muß, um ganz modern werden zu können.«

Gaetano Moretti schrieb später über seine Lehrtätigkeit: »Von dem Tag an, an dem ich die Ehre hatte, Camillo Boitos Nachfolger zu sein, habe ich meine Tätigkeit stets mit gewissenhafter Achtung vor der künstlerischen und der wissenschaftlichen Tendenz mit einem sicheren Blick in die Zukunft ausgeübt.«

Moretti widmete sich mit besonderem Interesse großen städtebaulichen Aufgaben. Der Monumental-Friedhof in Chiavari aus dem Jahre 1894 (Bild 8, 9), die Studie

11

12

13

In his principal work, the Campo Santo at Chiavari, the personality of the young architect became most clearly manifest. This hill-top cemetery, original in its topographical adaptation to the ground as well as in its design, and distinguished by the purity of its architectural composition, represents a novel and unusual creation which, owing to its remarkable intensity, makes an exquisite contribution without historic-stylistic reminiscences.

The year 1906 saw the completion of the Trezzo d'Adda power station which, because of its emphatic formal language, is in keeping with the cultural climate influenced by the Art Nouveau and which, because of the integrity of its design, can be regarded as the most typical product of Italian architecture from the transition period between the 19th and 20th centuries.

The theories advanced by Morris which, in Britain, formed the foundation of the "Arts and Crafts" movement, created on the Continent the climate for the growth of that movement which, known in Belgium as Art Nouveau, in Germany as Jugendstil, in Austria as Sezession and in Italy as Liberty, forms the link between 19th century eclecticism and modern architecture. The International Exhibition for Decorative Art in Turin (1902) thus offered a — somewhat belated — opportunity of vying in this sphere with the countries beyond the Alps. For the first time, the works of Ashbee, Behrens, Crane, Hoffmann, Horta, Mackintosh, Morris and Voysey are seen in Italy and exert a strong influence on architecture which is found to be the branch of Italian culture most receptive to innovations. The overall design of the Turin exhibition (Figs. 11—13) is in the hands of Raimondo D'Aronco who here represents the Italian avant-garde. In addition, Gaetano Moretti (Fig. 14), Ernesto Basile, Giacomo Cometti and Eugenio Quarti exhibit furniture and implements inspired by the new spirit of the Art Nouveau.

To Italy, the Turin exibition — having officially opened the door to the Art Nouveau — represents the beginning of a long flowering season of "Floreal" architecture which — often copied and reduced to a simple play at two-dimensional decoration — becomes a characteristic of Italian architecture for nearly twenty years. This new style is accompanied by persisting eclecticism and by avant-garde movements.

The reforming zeal of the Art Nouveau was, in Italy, hailed by an elite headed by architects such as Raimondo D'Aronco (1857—1917) and Giulio Arata.

Raimondo D'Aronco is the most prominent personality of that epoch; he had met Wagner and Olbrich who had exerted a strong influence on him. He was the only Italian architect receptive to the cultural trends emanating from the countries to the north of the Alps. In 1896, he was appointed court architect to the Turkish Sultan Abdul-Hamid, and from that time on to the collapse of the Ottoman Empire, he resided in Istanbul though he remained in continous touch with the Italian and other European centres of culture.

As he won the First Prize for the overall architectural design, his name is indissolubly linked with the Turin exhibition of 1902. The Pavilion of this exhibition, later destroyed, represents an important landmark in the history of Italian architecture, officially confirming the end of eclecticism. The fan-shaped building, forming part of the entrance rotunda, clearly reveals the architect's intention that the alignments of the concentric galleries should, in the interior, create an effect of continuity.

Another significant work of his is the Pavilion of Plastic Arts (Fig. 15) at the Udine exhibition of 1903 which is reminiscent of the Turin Pavilion although the integrity and consistency of its design already point to new architectural trends.

Those of D'Aronco's works which were planned and executed in Turkey, though rooted in European culture, clearly reveal something of the magic which the Orient exerted on his personality. The Well-and-Tomb Library (Fig. 16) at Yildiz (1903), which is perhaps the most interesting and most integral example among his Turkish works, the mosque at the Karakeuy Square at Galata (1903) and the well at Tophané (Fig. 17) are the most characteristic creations of his more mature years where the structural element cedes priority to preoccupation with architectural details.

über die Neugestaltung der Piazza De Ferrari in Genua, das Kraftwerk (Bild 10) in Trezzo d'Adda (1906) und der Plan für die Neugestaltung der Stadt Chiavari (1934) sind die Werke, die in einer die Jahrhundertwende einschließenden Zeitspanne von 50 Jahren Morettis klare, schöpferische Kraft bezeugen.

In seinem Hauptwerk, dem Friedhof von Chiavari, offenbarte sich die Persönlichkeit des jungen Architekten am deutlichsten. Die sowohl in ihrer topographischen Anpassung wie in ihrer Gestaltung originale Bauanlage auf einem Hügel ist eine, auch in der Reinheit des kompositorischen Ausdrucks, neue und ungewöhnliche Schöpfung, die dank ihrer bemerkenswerten Intensität einen hervorragenden Beitrag ohne geschichtlich-stilistische Reminiszenzen darstellt.

Aus dem Jahr 1906 stammt das Kraftwerk in Trezzo d'Adda, das in seiner eindringlichen Sprache eine Übereinstimmung mit der vom »Art Nouveau« beeinflußten Kulturatmosphäre zeigt und das wegen seiner Einheitlichkeit als das typischste Werk der italienischen Architektur aus der Zeit zwischen dem 19. und 20. Jahrhundert angesehen werden kann.

Die Theorien von Morris, die in England zur Grundlage für die »Arts and Crafts« wurden, schufen auf dem Kontinent die Voraussetzungen für die Entstehung jener Bewegung, die in Belgien als »Art Nouveau«, in Deutschland als »Jugendstil«, in Österreich als »Sezession« und in Italien als »Liberty« das Bindeglied zwischen dem Eklektizismus des 19. Jahrhunderts und der modernen Architektur bildet. So bot — wenn auch mit einiger Verspätung — die im Jahr 1902 in Turin abgehaltene »Internationale Ausstellung für Dekorationskunst« Italien die Gelegenheit, sich auf diesem Gebiet mit den jenseits der Alpen liegenden Ländern zu messen. Zum erstenmal tauchen die Werke von Ashbee, Behrens, Crane, Hoffmann, Horta, Mackintosh, Morris und Voysey auf und nehmen starken Einfluß auf die Architektur als den Bereich der italienischen Kultur, der sich gegenüber Neuem am meisten aufgeschlossen zeigt. Die Gesamtgestaltung der Turiner Ausstellung (Bild 11—13) liegt in den Händen von Raimondo D'Aronco, der die italienische Avantgarde vertritt; daneben stellen Gaetano Moretti (Bild 14), Ernesto Basile, Giacomo Cometti und Eugenio Quarti im neuen Geist des Art Nouveau geschaffene Möbel und Geräte aus.

Für Italien bedeutet die Turiner Ausstellung, da sie offiziell die Tür zum Art Nouveau öffnet, den Beginn einer ausgedehnten Blüte der »Floreal«-Architektur, die — sehr oft kopiert und zu einem einfachen Spiel der Flächendekoration herabgemindert — fast zwei Jahrzehnte lang ein Kennzeichen der italienischen Architektur ist. Begleitet wird dieser neue Stil von anhaltendem Eklektizismus und von Avantgarde-Bewegungen.

Das Erneuerungsdrängen des Art Nouveau fand in Italien die Zustimmung einer Elite, an deren Spitze Raimondo D'Aronco (1857—1917) und Giulio Arata standen.

Raimondo D'Aronco ist die hervorragende Persönlichkeit dieser Epoche; er kannte Wagner und Olbrich, die ihn stark beeinflußten. Er war der einzige italienische Architekt, der sich gegenüber den kulturellen Bestrebungen, die von den Ländern nördlich der Alpen ausgingen, aufgeschlossen zeigte. Im Jahr 1896 wurde er zum amtlichen Architekten des türkischen Sultans Abdul Amid ernannt, und von diesem Zeitpunkt an bis zum Zusammenbruch des Osmanischen Reiches hatte er seinen Wohnsitz in Konstantinopel, obwohl er ununterbrochene Verbindungen mit der italienischen und der übrigen europäischen Kulturwelt unterhielt.

Sein Name ist, da er als Sieger aus dem Wettbewerb um ihre architektonische Gesamtgestaltung hervorgegangen war, unlösbar mit der Turiner Ausstellung des Jahres 1902 verknüpft. Der — inzwischen zerstörte — Pavillon dieser Ausstellung bezeichnet einen wichtigen Abschnitt in der Geschichte der italienischen Architektur, der das Ende des »stilistischen Eklektizismus« offiziell bestätigt. Der dem Eingangsrundbau eingegliederte, fächerförmige Baukörper macht die Absicht des Architekten deutlich, im Innern durch die Fluchten der konzentrischen Galerien fortlaufend wirkende Räume zu schaffen.

Von Bedeutung ist weiterhin der Pavillon der bildenden Künste (Bild 15) auf der Ausstellung in Udine (1903), der an den Pavillon von Turin erinnert, obwohl er in seiner Einheitlichkeit und Geschlossenheit bereits die neuen Architekturtendenzen erkennen läßt.

14

15

16

11

17

18

19

Writing about Raimondo D'Aronco in a contribution to "Emporium" in April, 1913, Piacentini had this to say: "This is Raimondo D'Aronco's paramount trait: his everlasting careful search, his rejection of the past, and his discontent with the present. He is essentially the most sincere, perhaps the most perfect exponent of contemporary architecture. In studying his works, one can sense the organic nature and near-perfection of this evolution."

After his return from Turkey to his native country, D'Aronco virtually retired from the architectural scene: this was undoubtedly a great loss to Italian culture and the development of architecture. Thus, after the disappearance of the main protagonist of the Art Nouveau, its link with rationalism came to an end in Italy; there was no master mind able to mediate between the two movements.

Another architect, Ernesto Basile, was active in a cultural climate very different from that of D'Aronco's, viz. in Sicily and Argentina. His architecture was limited by his provincialism. The Biondo Kursaal at Palermo (Fig. 18) is possibly the best work where, in the words of Carlo Battaglia, ". . . he has been responsible for everything, from the colour schemes to the relief decors, and from the lattice-work of the outer doors to the inner doors and glass doors. And all of it bears the hallmark of his personality in that he created ever-new forms permeated by the live fascination of elegance".

It may be added that Basile's architecture exhausts itself in a play with decorations without ever going beyond these limitations into the realms of a deeper and comprehensive approach to problems.

After D'Aronco, Giuseppe Sommaruga must be regarded as the most prominent personality of the Art Nouveau in Italy. The Palazzo Castiglioni (Figs. 20—22) at the Corso Venezia in Milan is the most important work of Sommaruga's whose influence had a paramount effect on the formation of contemporary Italian taste. In 1917, Luigi Angelini described Sommaruga's Palazzo Castiglioni as follows: "In 1903 when, to the accompaniment of endless public commentary, the scaffoldings were stripped from the exquisite facade of the palazzo built for the Castiglioni family at the Corso Venezia, Milan, this building seemed to us, who were young — indeed very young — like a revelation. In this palazzo, all the fine qualities highlighted by Sommaruga's talent were reflected completely, more organically and more vitally. And it represented a reforming programme and the courageous utterance of a powerful spirit."

Giulio Arata, though professing his allegiance to Art Nouveau, revealed in his works the legacy of 19th century eclecticism which can be traced in his architecture though it is nowhere reflected in markedly unhistoric forms. The palazzo at the Via Cappuccini in Milan (Fig. 19) is the most important example of an architectural creation reflecting the decadence of the new architecture.

At the beginning of the 20th century — hailed as the greatest century of history — Expressionism and Cubism had finally managed to steer the conception of art into a crisis. That is why, during the first decade of the present century, new aesthetic criteria were formulated which primarily emanated from Futurism. The latter, in its turn, with its strict programmatic formulation and its universality (there were specifically futuristic works in every sphere of art), made its own essential contribution to the revolution initiated by the Expressionist and Cubist movements.

The "Futurist Manifesto" published by Filippo Tommaso Marinetti on 20th February 1909 was followed, on 11th February 1910, by the "Manifesto of Futurist Painting" signed by Carrà, Russolo, Balla, Severini and Boccioni.

Futurist ideology, expressing radical rejection of the past, glorification of the naked beauty of the machine, pleasure at the transient, and enthusiasm for rapid motion, opened unlimited horizons for creative forces.

The "Manifesto of Futuristic Architecture" by Antonio Sant'Elia was published on 10th August, 1914 in the literary review "Lacerba", following the publication of a first treatise by Sant'Elia on 20th May of the same year in the introduction to the catalogue of the Milan Art Exhibition entitled "Group of New Trends".

Apart from the Manifesto, the only works left behind by Sant'Elia were his "Architectural Dreams" and a collection of sketches (Figs. 23, 24) as his premature death

20

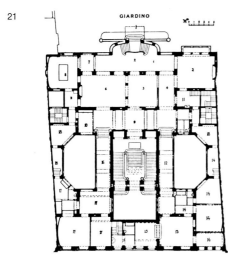

21

GIARDINO

22

Die in der Türkei geplanten und gebauten Werke D'Aroncos weisen, obwohl sie in der europäischen Kultur wurzeln, entschieden etwas vom Zauber auf, den der Orient auf seine Persönlichkeit ausübte. Die Brunnen-Grab-Bibliothek (Bild 16) in Yildiz (1903), vielleicht das interessanteste und einheitlichste Beispiel seines türkischen Schaffens, die Moschee auf dem Karakeuy-Platz in Galata (1903) und der Brunnen von Tophané (Bild 17) sind die bezeichnendsten Werke seiner Reife, bei denen das Strukturelle zugunsten orientalischer Architekturdetails in den Hintergrund tritt.

Über Raimondo D'Aronco schrieb Piacentini im April 1913 in einem Artikel im »Emporium« folgendes: »Dies ist der hervorspringende Charakterzug Raimondo D'Aroncos: das immerwährende, besorgte Suchen, die Ablehnung der Vergangenheit und die Unzufriedenheit gegenüber der Gegenwart. Er ist im wesentlichen der aufrichtigste, vielleicht der vollkommenste Exponent zeitgenössischer Baukunst. Beim Studium seiner Werke spürt man das Organische und nahezu Vollkommene dieser Evolution.«

Nach seiner Rückkehr aus der Türkei in sein Heimatland zog sich D'Aronco praktisch von der Architekturszene zurück, und dies war zweifellos ein großer Verlust für die italienische Kultur und für die Entwicklung der Architektur. So endete in Italien, nachdem der Hauptvertreter des Art Nouveau abgetreten war, die Fortdauer der Bindung des Art Nouveau an den Rationalismus; es fehlte also ein Meister, der es verstanden hätte, zwischen den beiden Richtungen zu vermitteln.

Der Architekt Ernesto Basile wirkte in einer ganz anderen kulturellen Atmosphäre als D'Aronco, in Sizilien und in Argentinien. Sein Provinzialismus zog die Grenzen seiner Architektur. Der Biondo-Kursaal in Palermo (Bild 18) ist vielleicht sein bestes Werk, bei dem er, wie Carlo Battaglia sagt, ». . . alles entworfen hat, von den Farbbis zu den Reliefdekorationen, von den Türgittern bis zu den inneren Türen und den Glastüren. Und allem hat er den Stempel seiner Persönlichkeit aufgedrückt, indem er immer neue Formen schuf, denen die lebendige Faszination der Eleganz innewohnt.«

Wir können hinzufügen, daß sich die Architektur Basiles in einem Spiel mit der Dekoration erschöpft, ohne je dessen Grenzen zu einer tieferen und umfassenden Auseinandersetzung zu überschreiten.

Giuseppe Sommaruga ist nach D'Aronco die hervorragendste Persönlichkeit des Art Nouveau in Italien. Der Castiglioni-Palast (Bild 20—22) auf dem Corso Venezia in Mailand ist das wichtigste Werk Sommarugas, dem eine grundlegende Bedeutung für die Bildung des italienischen Geschmacks jener Zeit zukam. Luigi Angelini schrieb 1917 in einem Artikel über Sommarugas Castiglioni-Palast: »Im Jahr 1903, als unter endlosen Kommentaren des Publikums auf dem Corso Venezia in Mailand die von Gerüsten befreite, wunderbare Front des für die Familie Castiglioni erbauten Palastes sichtbar wurde, kam uns, die wir jung, ja damals sehr jung waren, dieser Bau wie eine Offenbarung vor. In diesem Palast fanden sich alle guten Eigenschaften, die die Begabung Sommarugas in so helles Licht gerückt hatten, vollzählig, organischer und vitaler wieder. Und es war ein Programm der Erneuerung und die mutige Äußerung eines kraftvollen Geistes.«

Giulio Arata brachte, obwohl er sich zum Art Nouveau bekannte, in seinen Werken das Vermächtnis des Eklektizismus des 19. Jahrhunderts mit, der in seiner Architektur spürbar ist, auch wenn er sich nie in ausgesprochen unhistorischen Formen niederschlägt. Der Palast an der Via Cappuccini in Mailand (Bild 19) ist das wichtigste Beispiel seines architektonischen Schaffens, in dem sich die Dekadenz der neuen Architektur widerspiegelt.

Expressionismus und Kubismus hatten zu Anfang des 20. Jahrhunderts die Kunstauffassung des »Jahrhunderts der Geschichte« endgültig in eine Krise hineinmanövriert. So kam es im ersten Jahrzehnt dieses Jahrhunderts zur Bildung neuer ästhetischer Kriterien, die in erster Linie vom Futurismus ausgelöst worden waren, der wiederum mit seiner strengen programmatischen Formulierung und seiner Universalität (auf jedem Gebiet künstlerischer Tätigkeit gab es ein spezielles futuristisches Phänomen) die von der expressionistischen und kubistischen Bewegung begonnene Revolution durch einen wesentlichen Beitrag ergänzte.

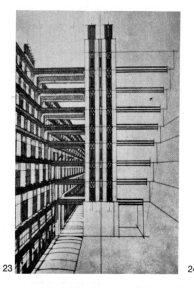

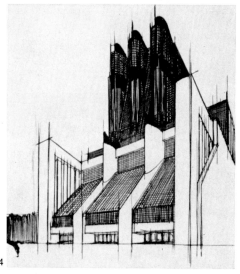

23   24

25

prevented him from realising a single building. In the event, nobody was there to continue the discussion which he began, with the exception of Virgilio Marchi, author of "Futuristic Architecture" and of a series of architectural sketches (Fig. 25). After the end of the First World War, Sant'Elia's prophecies were forgotten. Mainly inspired by the works of Giovanni Muzio, Marcello Piacentini, Piero Portaluppi and, to some extent, Gio Ponti, Italian architecture adopted the path of Neo-Monumentalism without any decoration which, influenced by the classic Roman spirit, represented the official architecture and was opposed to the arising rationalistic trend. The Fascist regime thus recognised in Neo-Monumentalism its own mirror image and the architectural expression corresponding to its own ideology. The houses by Vittorio Colonnese and Giovanni Muzio at the Via Moscova in Milan, the office palaces by Piero Portaluppi at the Piazza Diaz in Milan (Fig. 27), the group of buildings at the Piazza della Vittoria in Genoa (Fig. 26) and the Ambasciatori Hotel in Rome (Fig. 28), both by Marcello Piacentini, are the most typical examples for the new official academicism.

Italian Rationalism dates back to the group formed in Milan in 1926 by Gino Figini, Guido Frette, Sebastiano Larco, Adalberto Libera, Gino Pollini, Carlo Enrico Rava and Giuseppe Terragni who condemned Futurism because of its violent polemics and its strict rejection of all that belonged to the past. They gave rise to an architec-

26

Dem »Futuristischen Manifest« Filippo Tommaso Marinettis vom 20. Februar 1909 folgte am 11. Februar des Jahres 1910 das von Carrà, Russolo, Balla, Severini und Boccioni unterzeichnete Manifest der futuristischen Malerei.

Die futuristische Thematik, die sich sowohl auf die radikale Ablehnung der Vergangenheit als auch auf die Verherrlichung der Schönheit der Maschine gründet, auf die Freude am Vergänglichen und auf die Begeisterung für die in ihrer Entwicklung begriffene Bewegung, eröffnet der gestaltenden Kraft unbegrenzte Horizonte.

Das »Manifest der futuristischen Architektur« von Antonio Sant'Elia wurde am 10. August 1914 in der Literatur-Zeitschrift »Lacerba« veröffentlicht, nachdem eine erste Abhandlung von Sant'Elia am 20. Mai desselben Jahres im Vorwort des Kataloges der Mailänder Kunstausstellung »Gruppe Neue Tendenzen« erschienen war.

Von Sant'Elia blieben uns außer dem Manifest nur noch seine »Architekturträume« und eine Skizzensammlung (Bild 23, 24), da er wegen seines frühen Todes nicht einen einzigen Bau hatte verwirklichen können. Praktisch führte niemand das von ihm eingeleitete Gespräch fort, wenn man von Virgilio Marchi absieht, dem Verfasser der »Futuristischen Architektur« und einer Serie von Architekturskizzen (Bild 25). Nach dem Ende des ersten Weltkrieges waren die Prophezeiungen Sant'Elias vergessen. Die italienische Architektur begab sich, hauptsächlich durch die Werke von Giovanni Muzio, Marcello Piacentini, Piero Portaluppi und nur teilweise durch das Verdienst Gio Pontis, auf den Weg eines Neo-Monumentalismus ohne jede Dekoration, der, beeinflußt vom klassischen römischen Geist, die offizielle Architektur darstellte und im Gegensatz zur aufkommenden rationalistischen Bewegung stand. So erkannte das faschistische Regime im Neo-Monumentalismus sein eigenes Antlitz wieder und den seiner Ideologie entsprechenden architektonischen Ausdruck.

Die Häuser in der Via Moscova in Mailand von Vittorio Colonnese und Giovanni Muzio, die Büropaläste an der Piazza Diaz in Mailand (Bild 27) von Piero Portaluppi, der Gebäudekomplex an der Piazza della Vittoria in Genua (Bild 26) und das Hotel Ambasciatori in Rom (Bild 28), beide von Marcello Piacentini, sind die typischsten Beispiele für den neuen amtlichen Akademismus.

Der italienische Rationalismus entsteht 1926 mit der in Mailand von Gino Figini, Guido Frette, Sebastiano Larco, Adalberto Libera, Gino Pollini, Carlo Enrico Rava und Giuseppe Terragni gebildeten Gruppe, die den Futurismus wegen seiner gewalttätigen Polemik und wegen der strikten Ablehnung all dessen verdammte, was der Vergangenheit angehörte. Sie riefen eine Architektur ins Leben, die sich auf die Logik und auf die Rationalität als natürliche Folgeerscheinung der besonderen Erfordernisse ihrer Zeit gründete. Dem individualistischen Charakter der Architektur der Vergangenheit wurde die Anonymität der in Serie hergestellten Architektur, der futuristischen Unnachgiebigkeit ein solider konstruktiver Wille entgegengesetzt.

Zweifellos trug die futuristische Aktion zur Sache des Rationalismus wesentlich bei, schon wegen der Bedeutung dessen, was Sant'Elia nachdrücklich und apokalyptisch verkündet hatte: »Das Problem der futuristischen Architektur ist nicht das Problem einer linearen Neuordnung. Es handelt sich nicht darum, neue Linien zu finden, neue Formen für Fenster und Türen, nicht darum, Säulen, Pfeiler und Konsolen durch Karyatiden, dicke Fliegen oder Frösche zu ersetzen; es geht nicht darum, ob man die Fassade aus bloßem Ziegelstein aufmauert, sie verputzt oder mit Steinen verkleidet, noch darum, Formenunterschiede zwischen dem neuen und alten Gebäude zu bestimmen. Es geht einzig und allein darum, das futuristische Haus mit gesundem Grundriß zu schaffen, hierfür alle Hilfsmittel der Wissenschaft und der Technik einzusetzen und dabei in vornehmer Weise alle Ansprüche unserer Sitten und unseres Geistes zu erfüllen, alles zu unterdrücken, was grotesk oder schwerfällig ist und zu uns im Gegensatz steht (Tradition, Stil, Proportion), indem man neue Formen, neue Linien, eine neue Harmonie der Profile und des Volumens determiniert, eine Architektur, die ihre Daseinsberechtigung ausschließlich aus der besonderen Beschaffenheit des modernen Lebens bezieht und als ästhetischer Wert unserem Feingefühl entspricht. Diese Architektur kann keinem Gesetz geschichtlicher Beständigkeit unterliegen. Sie muß so neu sein, wie unser Gemütszustand neu ist ...«

27

28

ture which was founded on logic and rationalism as a natural corollary to the specific requirements of their time. The individualistic character of the architecture of the past was contrasted with the anonymity of mass- produced architecture, and Futuristic inflexibility with a solid, constructive will.

The Futurists undoubtedly made a considerable contribution to the cause of Rationalism, if only because of the importance of what Sant'Elia had expressly and apocalyptically proclaimed: "The problem of Futuristic architecture is not one of linear reorientation. The aim is not to find new lines or new shapes for windows or doors, not to replace columns, pillars and brackets by caryatids, thick flies or frogs; it is irrelevant whether the facade is composed of mere bricks, or plastered, or lined with stone, nor is it a question of determining formal differences between a new and an old building. The one and only objective is to create the Futuristic house based on a sound plan. For this purpose, it is necessary to bring into play all the aids of science and technology, thus nobly meeting all the requirements of our customs and our intellect, and to suppress all that is grotesque or cumbersome and is in opposition to us (tradition, style, proportion). This can be achieved by defining new shapes, new lines, a new harmony of profiles and volume, an architecture which owes its raison d'être exclusively to the specific nature of modern life and aesthetically corresponds to our refined senses. Such an architecture cannot be subjected to any law of historic durability. It must be as new as the state of our mind is new . . ."

"Modern methods of stress analysis, the use of reinforced concrete and steel preclude an architecture arising in the classical and traditional manner . . ."

"We must invent and build the Futuristic city — like one gigantic, clamorous building site, swift, mobile and dynamic in all its parts, and the Futuristic house in the image of a gigantic machine . . ."

"And I declare that Futuristic architecture is the architecture of calculation, of foolhardy courage and simplicity; it is the architecture of reinforced concrete, of steel, of glass, of textile fibres, and of all those substitutes for wood, stone and brick which enable us to reach a maximum of elasticity and lightness."

In contrast to the Futurists, the new generation of architects proclaims: ". . . Our past and our present are not incompatible. We do not want to break with tradition; it is tradition which changes . . .". As the position of the Rationalists is politically identical with that of the Traditionalists, the polemics between the two movements are, however, almost wholly confined to fruitless technical-formal questions.

In 1928, a first Exhibition of Rational Architecture took place at the Palazzo delle Esposizioni in Rome when a declaration proclaims the birth of the Italian Rationalistic Movement: ". . . We Italians who devote our entire energy to this Movement feel that this is our architecture because the constructive power is our Roman heritage. And Roman architecture was profoundly rational, purposeful and efficient . . .". In 1931, the second Exhibition of Rational Architecture at the Bardi Gallery, Rome, sponsored by the "Italian Movement for Modern Architecture" gave rise to prolonged and bitter arguments.

A few years earlier, the first examples of rational architecture emerged in Italy, among them an apartment house at Como (Fig. 29) built in 1928 by Giuseppe Terragni and the Gualino office block in Turin (Fig. 30), built in 1929 by Giuseppe Pagano and Levi Montalcini.

In 1933, a group of architects consisting of Bottoni, Cereghini, Figini, Frette, Griffini, Lingeri, Pollini, Banfi, Belgiojoso, Peressutti and Rogers published their comprehensive, nine-point "Architectural Programme" in the first issue of the new review "Quadrante". Points 5 and 6 read as follows: "Affirmation — in relation to European Rationalism — of a clear, straight and unyielding Italian note as recorded in the basic polemics of 'Group 7'."

". . . Definition of the characteristics of Rationalist Italian trends. Affirmation of Classicism and Mediterraneanism — to be understood as an attitude of mind and not as a mere adoption of forms or as folklore — in contrast to Nordism, Baroquism, or the romantic arbitrariness of some modern European architecture . . ."

In an article published in the journal "Domus", entitled ::Finis and da capo for

29

30

31

32

»Die Berechnung der Materialfestigkeit, die Verwendung von Stahlbeton und Stahl schließen eine im klassischen und traditionellen Sinn entstandene Architektur aus...«
»Wir müssen die futuristische Stadt erfinden und bauen — gleich einer ungeheuren, lärmenden Baustelle, beschwingt, beweglich und dynamisch in all ihren Teilen, und das futuristische Haus gleich einer riesigen Maschine...«
»Und ich verkünde, daß die futuristische Architektur die Architektur der Berechnung, des tollkühnen Wagemuts und der Einfachheit ist: sie ist die Architektur des Stahlbetons, des Stahls, des Glases, der Textilfaser und all jener Ersatzstoffe für Holz, Stein und Ziegel, mit denen man ein Höchstmaß an Elastizität und Leichtigkeit erreichen kann.«
Die neue Architektengeneration behauptet im Gegensatz zu den Futuristen: »... Unsere Vergangenheit und unsere Gegenwart sind nicht unvereinbar. Wir wollen nicht mit der Tradition brechen; es ist die Tradition, die sich wandelt...« Da sich die Stellung der Rationalisten auf politischer Ebene mit der der »Traditionalisten« deckt, beschränkt sich die Polemik zwischen beiden Richtungen jedoch fast nur auf unfruchtbare technisch-formale Fragen.
Im Jahre 1928 findet im Palazzo delle Esposizioni in Rom die erste Ausstellung rationaler Architektur statt, auf der eine Proklamation gleichzeitig die Geburtsstunde der italienischen Rationalistenbewegung verkündet: »... Wir Italiener, die wir dieser Bewegung unsere ganze Energie widmen, fühlen, daß dies ›unsere‹ Architektur ist, weil die konstruktive Kraft unser römisches Vermächtnis darstellt. Und tief rational, zweckmäßig und rationell war die römische Architektur...« Die zweite Ausstellung rationaler Architektur, die von der »Italienischen Bewegung für moderne Architektur« im Jahre 1931 in der Galerie Bardi in Rom veranstaltet wird, löst eine ausgedehnte und erbitterte Polemik aus.
Wenige Jahre vorher waren die ersten Beispiele rationaler Architektur aufgetaucht, so 1928 ein Mietshaus in Como (Bild 29) von Giuseppe Terragni und 1929 der Büropalast Gualino in Turin (Bild 30) von Giuseppe Pagano und Levi Montalcini.
Im Jahr 1933 legten die Architekten Bottoni, Cereghini, Figini, Frette, Griffini, Lingeri, Pollini, Banfi, Belgiojoso, Peressutti und Rogers ihr neun Punkte umfassendes »Architekturprogramm« in der ersten Nummer der Zeitschrift »Quadrante« dar. Die Punkte 5 und 6 haben folgenden Wortlaut: »Bejahung — in bezug auf den europäischen Rationalismus — einer entschiedenen, geradlinigen und unnachgiebigen italienischen Tendenz, wie sie in den Grundsatz-Polemiken der ›Gruppe 7‹ verzeichnet ist.« — »Bestimmung der Eigenarten der rationalistischen italienischen Tendenz. Bejahung von ›Klassizismus‹ und ›Mediterranismus‹ — als Geisteshaltung verstanden, nicht als Übernahme von Formen oder als Folklore — im Gegensatz zum ›Nordismus‹, zum ›Barockismus‹ oder zur romantischen Willkür eines Teiles der neuen europäischen Architektur...«
In einem in der Zeitschrift »Domus« veröffentlichten Artikel mit dem Titel »Schlußpunkt und da capo für die Architektur« brandmarkt Edoardo Persico scharf die mißverständliche programmatische Stellung der rationalistischen Bewegung: »Die Zweideutigkeit des ›Mediterranismus‹ hat den italienischen Rationalismus in seiner ganzen Entwicklung begleitet... Es ist natürlich eine falsche Kritik, die sich anmaßt, die Kunst des Gedankens eines Künstlers zu beurteilen; aber hier soll festgestellt werden, daß die Bevorzugung der am wenigsten kostspieligen Einfälle neben der Haltlosigkeit der Polemik einer der Gründe für die mittelmäßigen ästhetischen Ergebnisse ist, die der italienische Rationalismus gezeigt hat...«
Unter den Erneuerern ragen wegen ihrer Originalität und des Wertes ihres Beitrags Giuseppe Terragni und Giuseppe Pagano heraus.
Giuseppe Terragni kann als der Meister der italienischen rationalistischen Bewegung angesehen werden; seine Werke sind die einzigen, die denen der großen Architekten jener Epoche gleichkommen. Das Haus des Faschismus in Como (Bild 31), 1936 fertiggestellt und zweifellos das bedeutendste in der Zeit zwischen den beiden Kriegen in Italien entstandene Bauwerk, der Kindergarten »Sant'Elia« (Bild 32), ebenfalls in Como und 1937 errichtet, und das Wohnhaus am Corso Sempione, 1935, sind nicht nur Lehrbeispiele, sondern — zu jener Zeit — zugleich auch ein Ausgangspunkt für die jungen Avantgardisten Italiens.

33

34

35

Architecture", Edoardo Persico sharply attacks the ambiguous programmatic position of the Rationalist Movement: "The ambiguity of Mediterraneanism has accompanied Italian Rationalism throughout its development . . . It is of course a false criticism which pretends to judge the artistic thought of an artist. But is must be declared that, apart from the untenability of the arguments, the predilection for the least costly ideas is one of the reasons for the mediocre aesthetic results brought forth by Italian Rationalism . . .".

Among the reformers, Giuseppe Terragni and Giuseppe Pagano stand out because of their originality and because of the quality of their contributions.

Giuseppe Terragni can be regarded as the past master of the Italian Rationalist Movement. His works are the only ones comparable with those of the great foreign architects of that epoch. The House of Fascism at Como (Fig. 31), completed in 1936 and undoubtedly the most important inter-war building in Italy, the Sant'Elia Kindergarten likewise erected at Como in 1937 (Fig. 32), and the apartment house at the Corso Sempione (1935) not only represent outstanding examples but also become a point of departure for Italy's young avant-garde.

The programmatic rationalistic "classicism" of Terragni's buildings reveals an essentially intellectual quality. The House of Fascism at Como, distinguished by the logical strictness of a building modulated without any polemic publicity and with exemplary lucidity of expression, represents the perfection of an architectural idea and the final recognition of a new mode of expression.

After Terragni, Giuseppe Pagano is the second great personality of Italian Rationalism. The contribution to the renewal of culture made by Pagano is of fundamental significance. Supported by Edoardo Persico, he played a decisive part as the theoretician of Rationalism by his contributions to the review "Casabella" in the time from 1930 to 1943.

The Institute of Physics (Fig. 33), built by Pagano in 1932 as part of the University Precinct in Rome designed by Piacentini, and the Bocconi University in Milan (1938—1941) designed in collaboration with Predaval (Fig. 34), are his best works.

The year 1933 is important because of two extraordinary events: one was the contest for the railway station in Florence, the other the contest for the Palazzo del Littorio at the Exhibition of the Fascist Revolution in Rome. The First Prize in the contest for Florence Station (Fig. 39), awarded to Baroni, Berardi, Gamberini, Guarnieri, Lusanna and Michelucci, gave rise to heated discussion. Exception was taken to the expressiveness of the design and to the interposition of the new station into the urban fabric of Florence, which is dominated by the apse of Santa Maria Novella. It was due to this contest, whose assessors (and this is a very significant fact) also included Marinetti, that Florence came to possess the finest station in Europe. At the same time, modern architecture had its "official" debut in Italy.

The contest for the Palazzo del Littorio and the Exhibition of the Fascist Revolution at the Via dell'Impero in Rome brought forth more than a hundred designs and offered, to the young Italian architecture, a great opportunity of proving its worth.

The significance of this contest is described by Piacentini in the foreword to "Il Nuovo Stile Littorio". ". . . This contest took place at a season particulary favourable to our architecture, in the spring when the stems shed their old branches, when the sap is rising, and when the buds come forth. It took place after the dull and lifeless shapes of the imitative styles had been removed by a wholesome and creative movement, and at a time when architects approached their new tasks with fresh ideas, adhering to the timeless fundamentals of proportion and harmony, but tempering them with rational criteria and with designs in keeping with contemporary life . . .".

The most important among the designs submitted for the contest were two which were admitted to the second stage of the contest, viz. those by Carminati, Lingeri, Saliva, Terragni, Vietti (Fig. 35), and by Luigi Moretti (Fig. 36), and three which were not admitted, viz. those by Banfi, Belgiojoso, Danusso, Figini, Rogers (Fig. 37), by Cosenza, and by Ponti (Fig. 38).

Among the protagonists of Rationalist Architecture, Pier Luigi Nervi occupies an extremely important position, authentic in its avant-garde approach. His buildings

36

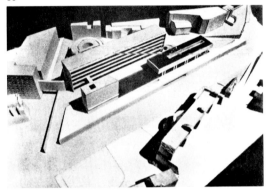

37

38

In dem programmatischen rationalistischen »Klassizismus« der Bauten Terragnis offenbart sich ein im wesentlichen geistiger Wert. Das Haus des Faschismus in Como mit der logischen Strenge einer Anlage, ohne polemisches Aufsehen und mit musterhafter Klarheit moduliert, repräsentiert die Vollkommenheit eines architektonischen Vortrags und die endgültige Anerkennung der neuen Ausdrucksform.

Giuseppe Pagano ist, nach Terragni, die zweite Persönlichkeit des italienischen Rationalismus. Der von Pagano zu Erneuerung der Baukunst geleistete Beitrag hat grundlegende Bedeutung. Unterstützt von Edoardo Persico spielte er durch seine von 1930 bis 1943 in der Zeitschrift »Casabella« veröffentlichten Schriften eine maßgebende Rolle als Theoretiker des Rationalismus. Das Institut für Physik (Bild 33) in dem von Piacentini errichteten Gebäudekomplex des römischen Universitätsviertels und die Bocconi-Universität in Mailand (1938–1941), die unter Mitarbeit von Predaval entworfen wurde (Bild 34), sind seine besten Arbeiten.

Das Jahr 1933 ist wegen zweier außerordentlicher Ereignisse wichtig: wegen des Wettbewerbs für den Bahnhof von Florenz und wegen des Wettbewerbs für den Palazzo del Littorio auf der Ausstellung der faschistischen Revolution in Rom. Der erste Preis im Wettbewerb für den Florentiner Bahnhof (Bild 39) von den Architekten Baroni, Borardi, Gamberini, Guarnieri, Lusanna und Michelucci löst eine heftige Diskussion aus. Man beanstandet die Expressivität des Entwurfs, und man verurteilt die Einfügung des neuen Bahnhofs in das städtebauliche Gewebe von Florenz, das von der Apsis von Santa Maria Novella beherrscht wird. Durch diesen Wettbewerb, dessen Preisgericht (und dies ist eine sehr bedeutsame Tatsache) auch Marinetti angehörte, kam Florenz zum schönsten Bahnhof Europas, und gleichzeitig hielt die moderne Architektur ihren »offiziellen« Einzug in Italien.

Über hundert Entwürfe wurden zum nationalen Wettbewerb für den Bau des Palazzo del Littorio und die Ausstellung der faschistischen Revolution in der Via dell'Impero in Rom eingereicht, und für die junge italienische Architektur bot sich hier eine große Gelegenheit, sich zu beweisen.

Über die Bedeutung des Wettbewerbs schreibt Piacentini im Vorwort zu »Il Nuovo Stile Littorio«: ». . . Dieser Wettbewerb fand zu einem für unsere Architektur besonders günstigen Zeitpunkt statt, der der Jahreszeit entspricht, in der sich in den von den alten Zweigen befreiten Stämmen die Säfte und Knospen erneuern. Er fand statt, nachdem eine heilsame, schöpferische Bewegung die matten und leblosen Formen der nachahmenden Stile entfernt hatte und sich die Architekten mit neuen Einsichten an neue Werke begaben, indem sie von den unverrückbaren Grundlagen der Proportion und der Harmonie ausgingen, aber mit Kriterien der Vernunft und der Formen, die dem zeitgenössischen Leben entsprechen . . .«

Unter den eingereichten Wettbewerbsentwürfen waren die von Carminati – Lingeri – Saliva – Terragni – Vietti (Bild 35) und Luigi Moretti (Bild 36) – beide zum Wettbewerb zweiten Grades zugelassen – sowie die von Banfi – Belgiojoso – Danusso – Figini – Rogers (Bild 37), von Cosenza und von Ponti (Bild 38) – alle drei vom Wettbewerb zweiten Grades ausgeschlossen – die gewichtigsten Arbeiten.

Unter den Protagonisten der rationalistischen Architektur nimmt Pier Luigi Nervi eine außerordentlich bedeutende und in ihrem Avantgardismus authentische Stel-

39

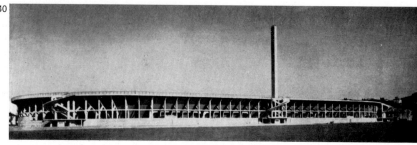

are characterised by strict formulation, based on calculation as well as on a profound technological knowledge of the materials used.

The Stadium in Florence (Fig. 40), built between 1930 and 1932, and the hangars at Orvieto and Orbetello (Fig. 41) built in 1936 and 1939, respectively, are among the most typical examples of Italian Rationalism.

In the introduction to his autobiography, Nervi writes as follows: "In examining the designs . . . or in selecting and adopting the technically best conception, I have never allowed my objectivity and clarity of judgement to be clouded by any preconceived aesthetic or cultural thesis or by the recollection of the solution of similar problems found by others or by myself. But I must confess that I was in danger of losing this clarity on the day on which, flattered by comments on the Municipal Stadium in Florence, I attempted for a time to allow my appraisal of a structural problem also to be influenced by the aesthetic factor in the form of theoretical or formal preconceptions."

"Within a short time, however, I convinced myself that the art of architectural expression is the more elusive the more one tries to achieve it deliberately . . ."

Nervi's polemic position in relation to the theoreticians of rationalistic architecture is just as determined as it is characteristic: he firmly believes in the architect as an individual. Together with Nervi, Luigi Figini and Gino Pollini, who first became known at the 5th Triennale in Milan, 1934, with their design for an artist's studio Fig. 42) and who, at intervals from 1957 onwards, built the Olivetti industrial estate at Ivrea (Fig. 43) which represents a milestone in modern Italian architecture. may be regarded as the leading interpreters of contemporary Italian architecture. Even in post-war architecture, Figini and Pollini occupy a special position as it is they who, after the death of Pagano and Terragni, represent the continuity of rationalistic tradition.

The generation of Rationalists was, however, completely unprepared for the gigantic problem of reconstruction. The building world was confronted with the urgent problems of standardisation and prefabrication which, because of the unsuitable structure of industry and the shortage of skilled labour, could not be overcome. In consequence, reconstruction proceeded by conventional means and without any clear programme. Whole districts of historic cities which had suffered war damage are being stylistically "remodelled".

The reconstruction of Por Santa Maria, Florence, is a clear indication how the results can be affected by a profound lack of cultural preparation. Highly significant in this connection is the judgement pronounced by Michelucci: ". . . The reconstruction of the town centre of Florence shows what can be achieved in practice with the different adaptation theories; it is the quintessence of a scholarly conception of architecture and town planning. Whether one likes it or not, it represents a petrified compromise, reflecting a situation which had already taken root in the spirit before it did so in architecture . . ." The folksy flavour and the questionable features of retailored regional architecture led to an academic conformism. The "Casa alle zattere" in Venice (Fig. 44) by Gardella and the Pirovano Home in Cervinia (Fig. 45) by Albini are the best-known examples of the resigned attitude adopted by many of the best Italian architects.

The following documentation of buildings erected during the last ten years marks the state of development reached by contemporary Italian architecture.

lung ein. Seine Bauten sind durch eine strenge Formulierung gekennzeichnet, die sowohl auf Berechnungen als auch auf profunden technologischen Kenntnissen beruhen.

Das Stadion von Florenz (Bild 40), das zwischen 1930 und 1932 errichtet wurde, und die Flughallen von Orvieto und Orbetello (Bild 41) aus dem Jahr 1936 beziehungsweise 1939 gehören zu den typischsten Beispielen des italienischen Rationalismus.

Im Vorwort zu seiner eigenen Monographie schreibt Nervi: ». . . Weder durch irgendeine vorgefaßte ästhetische oder kulturelle These noch durch die Erinnerung an die Lösungen gleichartiger Probleme, die von anderen oder von mir gefunden wurden, habe ich mir jemals bei der Untersuchung der Entwürfe . . . oder bei der Auswahl und Ausführung der technisch besten Konzeption die Objektivität und Klarheit des Urteils trüben lassen. Ich muß jedoch auch sagen, daß ich Gefahr lief, diese Klarheit an dem Tag zu verlieren, an dem ich in Anbetracht der schmeichelhaften Kommentare zum städtischen Stadion von Florenz eine Zeitlang versuchte, bei der Bewertung eines Bauproblems auch den ästhetischen Faktor in Form von theoretischen Voraussetzungen oder formalen Vorurteilen mit ins Spiel zu bringen. In kurzer Zeit überzeugte ich mich davon, daß die architektonische Ausdrucksfähigkeit etwas ist, was sich desto schwerer erreichen läßt, je vorsätzlicher man sich darum bemüht . . .«

Die polemische Stellung Nervis gegenüber den Theoretikern des Rationalismus ist bezeichnend; er glaubt fest an den als Individuum verstandenen Architekten.

Luigi Figini und Gino Pollini, die auf der 5. Triennale in Mailand 1934 mit dem Atelierhaus für einen Künstler (Bild 42) erstmals in Erscheinung traten und die 1957 mit dem Industriekomplex Olivetti in Ivrea begannen (Bild 43), können zusammen mit Nervi als die wichtigsten Interpreten der zeitgenössischen italienischen Architektur angesehen werden. Auch in der Nachkriegsarchitektur nehmen Figini und Pollini eine besondere Stellung ein, da sie seit dem Tode von Pagano und Terragni die Kontinuität der rationalistischen Tradition vertreten.

Dem riesigen Problem des Wiederaufbaues allerdings steht die Generation der Rationalisten völlig unvorbereitet gegenüber. Das Bauwesen sieht sich mit den drängenden Schwierigkeiten der Standardisierung und der Vorfertigung konfrontiert, die wegen der ungeeigneten Struktur der Industrie und wegen des Mangels an ausgebildeten Leuten nicht gelöst werden können. So geht der Wiederaufbau mit traditionellen Mitteln und ohne klares Programm vor sich; ganzen Vierteln historischer Städte wird eine stilistische »Umarbeitung« zuteil.

Sehr bezeichnend ist in dieser Hinsicht das Urteil Micheluccis: ». . . Der Wiederaufbau des Stadtzentrums von Florenz ist der Ausdruck dessen, was man mit den verschiedenen Anpassungstheorien praktisch erreichen kann; er ist der Extrakt einer schulmäßigen Auffassung der Architektur und des Städtebaues. Er ist, ob man will oder nicht, der zu Stein gewordene Kompromiß, der eine Situation widerspiegelt, die im Geist früher vorhanden war als im Bauwesen . . .« Der folkloristische Geschmack und die Fragwürdigkeiten der umgeschneiderten Regionalarchitektur münden in einen akademischen Konformismus. Die »Casa alle zattere« in Venedig (Bild 44) von Gardella und das Pirovano-Heim in Cervinia (Bild 45) von Albini sind die bekanntesten Beispiele, die die zum Verzicht neigende Haltung eines guten Teiles der besten italienischen Architekten aufzeigen.

Die nun folgende Dokumentation von Bauten, die in den letzten zehn Jahren errichtet wurden, kennzeichnet den Stand der italienischen Architektur der Gegenwart.

1. Living room wing. The steel bearing structure is extended in pergola fashion over balcony and outdoor sitting place, thus loosening up the facade.

1. Blick auf den Wohntrakt. Die Tragkonstruktion aus Stahl greift pergolaartig über Balkon und Freisitzplatz aus und lockert die Fassade auf.

This house, designed for a family of five people, stands in rural surroundings at the outskirts of Gallarate. With its obvious structural pattern and firm outlines, the house is in clear contrast to its surroundings with which it is linked by balconies and broad flights of stairs. Each of the four bedrooms as well as the guest room have a bathroom of their own. The residential zone is diversified by arranging it on several different levels. Family life is centred on the partly split-level living room with its gallery.

Das für eine fünfköpfige Familie entworfene Haus steht in ländlicher Umgebung am Rande von Gallarate. Balkons und breite Treppen verbinden das Gebäude mit der Umgebung, von der sich der konstruktiv klare, fest umrissene Baukörper deutlich abhebt. Die vier Schlafräume und das Gästezimmer sind jeweils mit einem eigenen Bad ausgestattet. Der Wohnbereich wird durch verschiedene, gegeneinander versetzte Ebenen gegliedert. Den Mittelpunkt des Familienlebens bildet der teilweise zweigeschossige Wohnraum mit dem Galeriegeschoß.

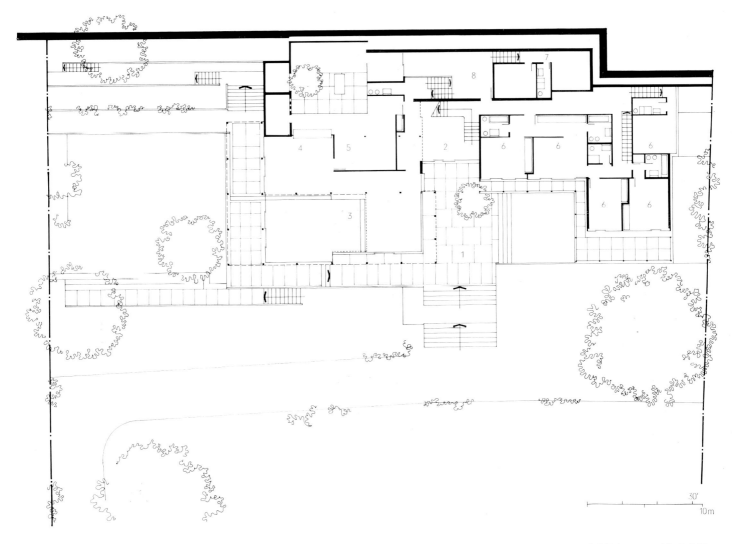

2. Plan. Key: 1 Entrance yard, 2 Entrance and hall, 3 Living room, 4 Dining area, 5 Kitchen, 6 Bedroom, 7 Staff, 8 Cloakroom.
3. Longitudinal section.

2. Grundriß. Legende: 1 Eingangshof, 2 Eingang und Diele, 3 Wohnraum, 4 Eßplatz, 5 Küche, 6 Schlafraum, 7 Personal, 8 Garderobe.
3. Längsschnitt.

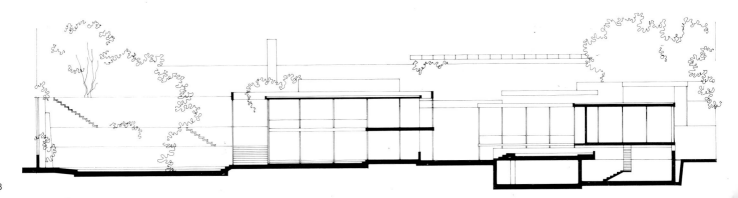

24

4. The steep escarpment behind the house is protected by several concrete retaining walls. This has permitted the creation of attractively planted terraces reached by flights of steps.
5. View from the garden side. On the left is the road.
6. Interior of the split-level living room with the gallery.
7. Bedroom wing, seen from the living room. By retracting the facade between the two wings, a courtyard, surrounded on three sides, has been created for the main entrance.

4. Der steile Hang hinter dem Haus wird durch mehrere Betonmauern gestützt. Es entstehen reizvoll bepflanzte Terrassen, zu denen verschiedene Treppen hinaufführen.
5. Gesamtansicht vom Garten. Links der Zugangsweg.
6. Blick in den zweigeschossigen Wohnraum mit dem Galeriegeschoß.
7. Blick aus dem Wohnraum auf den Schlafteil. Durch das Zurücknehmen der Fassade zwischen Wohn- und Schlaftrakt entsteht ein dreiseitig umschlossener Hof, an dem der Haupteingang liegt.

House at Santa Marinella at the Tyrrhenian Sea (1956—57)
Architect: Luigi Moretti

Einfamilienhaus in Santa Marinella am Tyrrhenischen Meer (1956—57)
Architekt: Luigi Moretti

1. The house as seen from the road.
2. Through the narrow slits in the coarse-textured walls, daylight can enter the house in a soft and diffused form.
3. The flight of steps leading down from the entrance hall to the garage forecourt is reminiscent of old Mediterranean architecture.

1. Ansicht des Hauses von der Straße.
2. Lichtschlitze in den grobkörnig strukturierten Wandflächen lassen ein sanftes Streulicht ins Innere dringen.
3. Blick auf die von der Eingangshalle zum tiefer liegenden Garagenvorhof führende Treppe, die an alte mediterrane Vorbilder erinnert.

Highly sculptural in appearance, this house, situated between road and sea-shore, provides an interesting solution to a difficult problem. The architect's basic idea was to create a refuge for the residents and to ensure the privacy of their family life. This idea is most evident from the almost wholly enclosed walls on the land side; but it is also discernible in the walled entrance patio. On entering, the visitor is immediately included in the peace and privacy of the house. The bedrooms, placed on a higher level, have access from the entrance hall. Dining and living room are placed parallel to the garden, jutting out towards beach and sea.

Zwischen der Straße und dem Meer gelegen, zeigt dieses Haus in der stark plastischen Modellierung eine interessante Lösung. Die Grundidee des Architekten war es, ein Refugium für die Hausbewohner zu schaffen und das Familienleben vor den Blicken Außenstehender zu schützen. Dieser Gedanke ist am deutlichsten an den zur Landseite hin fast völlig geschlossenen Außenwänden abzulesen, er klingt aber auch in dem von Mauern umgebenen Eingangshof an. Der Besucher wird beim Eintritt sofort in die Ruhe und die Intimität des Hauses einbezogen. Der Zugang zu den höher gelegenen Schlafzimmern erfolgt von der Eingangshalle aus. Speise- und Wohnzimmer sind parallel zum Garten geführt und greifen weit gegen Badestrand und Meer aus.

4. With its expressive and plastic interplay of great shapes, the building forms a clear contrast with its surroundings.

5,7. Ground floor and upper floor plans. Key: 1 Terrace, 2 Living room, 3 Dining area with adjacent kitchen, 4 Garden, 5 Guest room, 6 Lobby, 7 Bedroom, 8 Staff, 9 Entrance hall, 10 Entrance court, 11 Garage drive, 12 Garage forecourt, 13 Garage, 14 Roof terrace, 15 Pergola.

6. Main entrance, seen from the entrance yard.

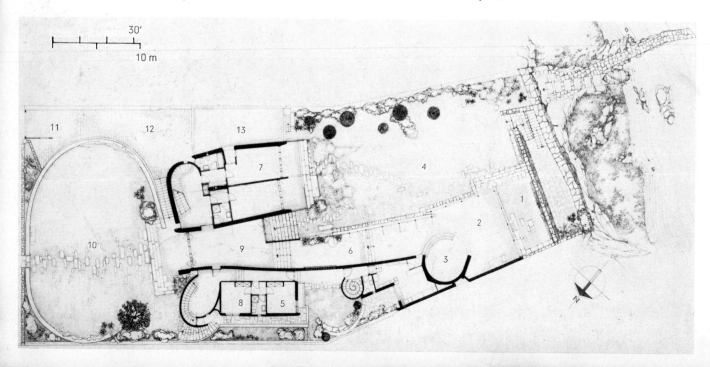

4. Das Gebäude hebt sich mit dem ausdrucksvollen und plastischen Spiel seiner Formen klar von der Umgebung ab.

5,7. Grundrisse von Erd- und Obergeschoß. Legende: 1 Terrasse, 2 Wohnraum, 3 Eßplatz mit anschließender Küche, 4 Garten, 5 Gastzimmer, 6 Verbindungshalle, 7 Schlafraum, 8 Personal, 9 Eingangshalle, 10 Eingangshof, 11 Garagenzufahrt, 12 Garagenhof, 13 Garage, 14 Dachterrasse, 15 Pergola.

6. Blick aus dem Eingangshof auf den Haupteingang.

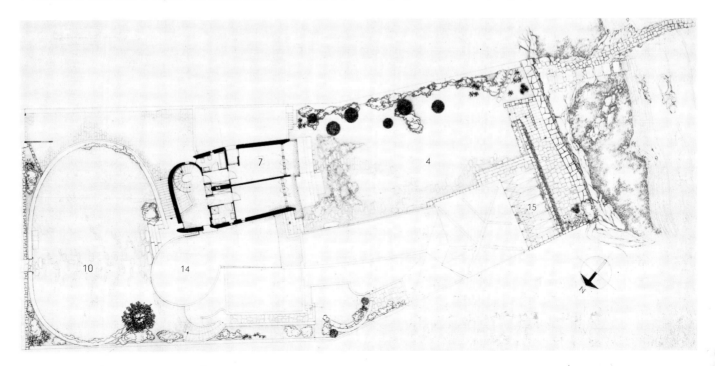

"La Scala" House at Portese, Lake Garda (1958—60)
Architect: Vittoriano Viganò. Civil Engineers: Leo Finzi and Edoardo Nova

Haus »La Scala« in Portese am Gardasee (1958—60)
Architekt: Vittoriano Viganò. Statik: Leo Finzi und Edoardo Nova

1. View from the west. The curtain wall has been retracted to provide a spacious roofed terrace.
2. View from the east. The house stands about 150 ft. above the lake which is reached via a reinforced concrete flight of stairs supported by a single pier.

1. Ansicht von Westen. Die Glasfassade ist so weit zurückgenommen, daß eine geräumige, überdachte Terrasse entsteht.
2. Gesamtansicht von Osten. Die fünfundvierzig Meter Höhenunterschied zum See werden durch eine freitragende, auf einem einzigen Pfeiler ruhende Treppe überwunden.

This single-storey holiday house is of the open-plan type. Living room, dining room and bedroom are merged together. The only isolated rooms are kitchen, bathroom and guest room. The structure is reduced to essentials. A trapezoidal floor slab of reinforced concrete supports the I-Steel columns which, in their turn, support the trapezoidal reinforced concrete slab of the roof. Because of the sloping ground, about one-half of the floor slab, facing the lake, is clear of the ground, providing just enough room for a study associated with a spacious, partly covered terrace. The lake is reached from the house via a freely supported flight of stairs.

Das eingeschossige Ferienhaus wurde als Einraumhaus entworfen. Wohn-, Eß- und Schlafbereich gehen ineinander über. Die einzigen isolierten Räume sind Küche, Bad und Gästezimmer. Die Konstruktion ist auf die wesentlichen Elemente reduziert. Auf einer trapezförmigen Bodenplatte aus Stahlbeton ruhen Doppel-T-Träger, die die gleichfalls trapezförmige Dachplatte aus Stahlbeton tragen. Das vom Boden abgehobene Gebäude kragt etwa zur Hälfte über eine Geländestufe zum See hin aus. Unter dieser Auskragung fand ein Studio Platz, vor dem eine geräumige, teilüberdachte Terrasse liegt. Die Verbindung zum See stellt eine freitragende Treppe her.

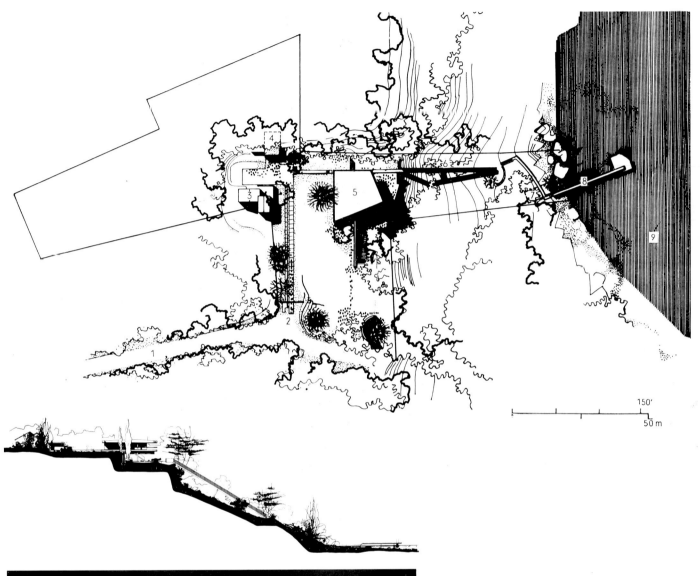

3. Site plan. Key: 1 Access road, 2 Entrance, 3 Gateway and gardener's house, 4 Garage, 5 Residence, 6 Freely supported flight of stairs, 7 Yacht harbour, 8 Jetty, 9 Baia del Vento.
4. Cross-section of the lake-side escarpment.
5. View from the living room across the terrace onto the lake. Most of the glass walls are designed as sliding doors.

3. Lageplan. Legende: 1 Zufahrtstraße, 2 Eingang, 3 Pforte und Haus des Gärtners, 4 Garage, 5 Wohnhaus, 6 Freitragende Treppe, 7 Hafen, 8 Mole, 9 Baia del Vento.
4. Geländequerschnitt.
5. Blick aus dem Wohnraum über die vorgelagerte Terrasse auf den See. Die Glaswände sind zum größten Teil als Schiebetüren ausgebildet.

Holiday house at Termini di Sorrento (1962—63)
Architect: Bruno Morassutti

Ferienhaus in Termini di Sorrento (1962—63)
Architekt: Bruno Morassutti

The appearance of this house is governed by the two flat roofs, each supported by four concrete columns. In their radiant whiteness, the roofs are reminiscent of sails, in keeping with the seaside situation of the house. The large windows do not constitute an optical restriction; they mainly serve to protect the interiors against the weather. The two roof shells, projecting on all sides, cover two self-contained parts of the house of different size and height, one set back in relation to the other and separated by a flight of stairs leading down to the sea. One part is reserved for guests, the other contains the living room, kitchen, bedroom and ancillary rooms. The rooms, characterized by gallery floor and open plan, merge with each other. Columns and roofs are of raw concrete, window frames of wood. The steeply stepped garden terraces are retained by rubble walling.

1. The house appears to float above the robust terrace walls. On the left is the larger one of the two parts of the house, with living room and gallery, surrounded by rubble walls on three sides. The roof "sail" is separated from the solid walls by a strip of ventilating windows. On the right is the guest house.

Das äußere Bild dieses Gebäudes wird durch die beiden flachen Dächer bestimmt, die auf je vier Betonsäulen ruhen. Sie sind in blendendem Weiß gehalten und erinnern, der Lage des Hauses am Meer entsprechend, an aufgespannte Segel. Die großen Fenster geben optisch keine Raumbegrenzung. Sie dienen in erster Linie zum Schutz der Innenräume gegen die Witterung. Die beiden ringsum vorgezogenen Dachschalen überdecken zwei gegeneinander versetzte, verschieden große und hohe Baukörper, die durch eine zum Meer hinabführende Treppe voneinander getrennt sind. Der eine dieser Baukörper ist den Gästen vorbehalten, im anderen befinden sich Wohnraum, Küche und Schlafräume mit den dazugehörigen Nebenräumen. Galeriegeschoß und offener Grundriß lassen die Räume ineinander übergehen. Für Stützen und Dächer wurde Sichtbeton, für die Fensterrahmen Holz und für die Stützmauern der Terrassen Naturstein verwendet.

1. Das Haus scheint über den kräftigen Terrassenmauern zu schweben. Links der größere der beiden Baukörper mit Wohnraum und Galerie, die auf drei Seiten von Natursteinmauern umgeben sind. Ein Glasstreifen setzt die Dachsegel von den massiven Wänden ab. Rechts das Gästehaus.

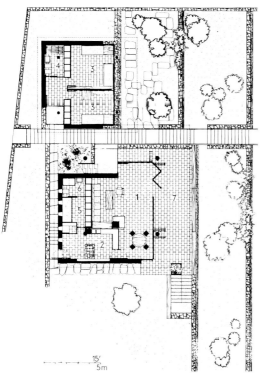

2. Plan. Key: 1 Living room, 2 Kitchen, 3 Guest room, 4 Bathroom and W.C., 5 Bedroom, 6 Shower bath and W.C., 7 Roofed terrace.

3. Interior of the large bedroom on the gallery floor. The raw rubble wall is similar to the retaining walls of the garden terraces.

4. The bedroom on the gallery floor merges with a small study. Daylight can enter through the fully glazed main front which extends over two storeys, and through toplight ribbons.

5. The front part of the living room extends through two storeys and can be opened up by glass doors to the terrace. Interior and exterior are integrated by using the same ceramic floor tiling.

2. Grundriß. Legende: 1 Wohnraum, 2 Küche, 3 Gästezimmer, 4 Bad und Toilette, 5 Schlafraum, 6 Dusche und Toilette, 7 Überdachte Terrasse.

3. Blick in den großen Schlafraum auf dem Galeriegeschoß. Die unverputzte Seitenwand besteht aus Bruchsteinen wie die Stützmauern der Terrassen.

4. Der Schlafraum auf dem Galeriegeschoß geht in ein kleines Studio über. Die Belichtung erfolgt von der zweigeschossigen, vollverglasten Hauptfront her und über Oberlichtbänder.

5. Der im vorderen Teil zweigeschossige Wohnraum läßt sich durch Glastüren zur Terrasse öffnen. Innen und außen sind durch den gleichen Fußbodenbelag aus Keramikfliesen zu einer Einheit verbunden.

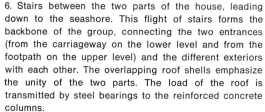

6. Stairs between the two parts of the house, leading down to the seashore. This flight of stairs forms the backbone of the group, connecting the two entrances (from the carriageway on the lower level and from the footpath on the upper level) and the different exteriors with each other. The overlapping roof shells emphasize the unity of the two parts. The load of the roof is transmitted by steel bearings to the reinforced concrete columns.

7,8. Views of the Gulf of Sorrent, framed by the two roof "sails", with the Isle of Capri in the background.

6. Blick auf die zum Meer führende Treppe zwischen den beiden Gebäuden. Die Steintreppe bildet das Rückgrat der Anlage, indem sie die beiden Zugänge (von der bergabgelegenen Fahrstraße und vom Fußpfad oberhalb des Hauses) sowie die verschiedenen Außenräume miteinander verbindet. Die übereinandergreifenden Dachschalen binden die beiden Baukörper aneinander. Die Dachlast wird über Metallauflager auf die Stahlbetonstützen übertragen.

7,8. Blick vom Haus auf das Meer. Im Hintergrund, zwischen beiden Segeln, Capri.

Apartment house in Milan (1959—60)
Architects: Angelo Mangiarotti and Bruno Morassutti

Mehrfamilienhaus in Mailand (1959—60)
Architekten: Angelo Mangiarotti und Bruno Morassutti

1. View from the road. The central part of the building with the projecting staircase and lift shaft contains the floor landings.
2. Typical floor plan. Key: 1 Landing, 2 Entrance and hall, 3 Living room, 4 Nursery, 5 Master bedroom, 6 Bathroom, 7 W.C., 8 Kitchen, 9 Dining room.
3. Ground level plan. Key: 1 Access path, 2 Entrance hall, 3 Children's playground, 4 Caretaker's flat, 5 Garage drive, 6 Terrace.

1. Gesamtansicht von der Straße. Der verbindende Bauteil mit dem vorgezogenen Treppenhaus und Liftschacht enthält die öffentlichen Verkehrsflächen.
2. Normalgeschoßgrundriß. Legende: 1 Vorplatz, 2 Eingang und Diele, 3 Wohnraum, 4 Kinderzimmer, 5 Elternschlafraum, 6 Bad, 7 WC, 8 Küche, 9 Eßzimmer.
3. Erdgeschoßgrundriß. Legende: 1 Zugang, 2 Eingangshalle, 3 Spielfläche für Kinder, 4 Wohnung des Hausmeisters, 5 Garagenzufahrt, 6 Terrasse.

This "Three-Cylinders House" at San Siro contains nine apartments. It is composed of three separate units of circular plan, linked by a joint core with lift and staircase. Each of the cylinders is supported by a central column which carries the bearing structure of the first floor in mushroom fashion, leaving the ground level open. The facades are enlivened by the alternation of glass and wall panels, different on each floor. The circular shape offers optimum sunshine and daylight conditions and leaves a high degree of freedom in the design and arrangement of the rooms.

Das »Drei-Zylinder-Haus« in San Siro hat neun Wohnungen. Es setzt sich aus drei Baukörpern mit kreisrundem Grundriß zusammen, die durch einen gemeinsamen Verkehrskern miteinander verbunden sind. Jeden dieser Zylinder trägt eine zentrale Stütze, auf der wie ein Strahlenkranz die Tragkonstruktion für die Geschoßplatte des ersten Obergeschosses ruht. Das Erdgeschoß ist nicht umbaut. Die Fassaden werden durch die in den einzelnen Geschossen wechselnde Abfolge von Glas und Wandelementen belebt. Die Kreisform gibt optimale Besonnungs- und Belichtungsmöglichkeiten und läßt große Freiheit in der Grundrißgestaltung und in der Anordnung der Räume.

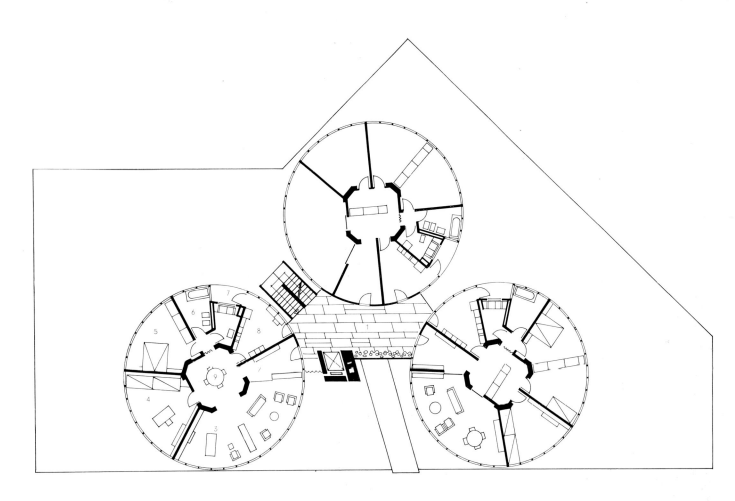

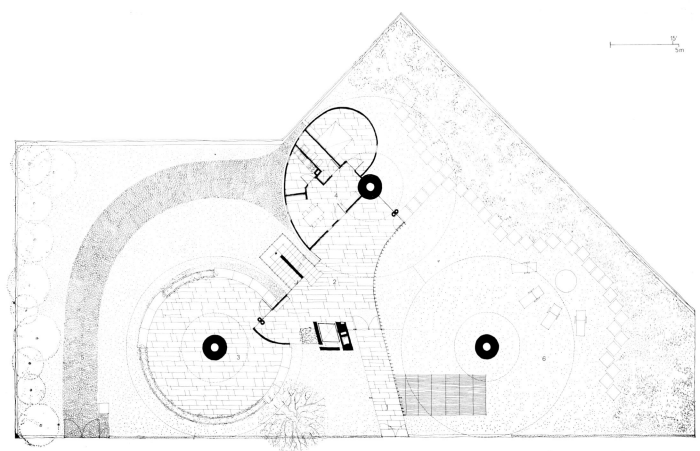

Apartment house at the Viale Quattro Venti in Rome (1962—63)
Architects: Ennio Borzi, Giovanni Bruno and Franco Tamburini

Wohnhaus an der Viale Quattro Venti in Rom (1962—63)
Architekten: Ennio Borzi, Giovanni Bruno und Franco Tamburini

This apartment house at the Viale Quattro Venti is distinguished from other modern residential buildings in Rome by its clearly conceived three-dimensional treatment. The edges of the structural floor slabs, left in exposed concrete, interrupt the texture of the brick facade and serve to emphasize the serrated pattern of the main front. Owing to this staggered frontage, all the living rooms have the benefit of corner windows facing west and south so that the residents have the best possible view. Moreover, there is room for a small balcony in front of each corner window. The near-triangular plan of the building is conditioned by the site.

Das Wohnhaus in der Viale Quattro Venti unterscheidet sich von den sonstigen in Rom üblichen Neubauten durch die Klarheit seiner plastischen Gestaltung. Die Stirnseiten der Geschoßdecken aus Sichtbeton unterbrechen die Struktur der Fassadenverkleidung aus Backstein und unterstreichen die sägezahnartige Bewegung der Hauptfront. Durch die Staffelung des Grundrisses können alle Wohnräume von zwei Seiten, von Westen und Süden, über Eckfenster belichtet werden; die Bewohner genießen dadurch eine optimale Aussicht. Zugleich ergibt sich vor jedem Eckfenster ein Freiraum in Form eines kleinen Balkons. Die Grundrißform des Gebäudes ist durch seine Lage auf einem Eckgrundstück bedingt.

1. General view from the west. The floor slab edges, left exposed, emphasize the horizontal stratification of the building.
2,3. The kitchen balconies, protected by fixed sun blinds, and the interplay of light and shade contribute to the plastic featuring of the facade.
4. Plan of second and third floor. Key: 1 Living-cum-dining room, 2 Study, 3 Kitchen, 4 Bedroom.

1. Gesamtansicht von Westen. Die sichtbar belassenen Vorderkanten der Geschoßdecken betonen die horizontale Schichtung des Gebäudes.
2,3. Die mit feststehenden Sonnenblenden versehenen Küchenbalkons und das Spiel von Licht und Schatten tragen zur plastischen Auflockerung der Fassade bei.
4. Grundriß des zweiten und dritten Obergeschosses. Legende: 1 Wohn-Eßraum, 2 Arbeitszimmer, 3 Küche, 4 Schlafraum.

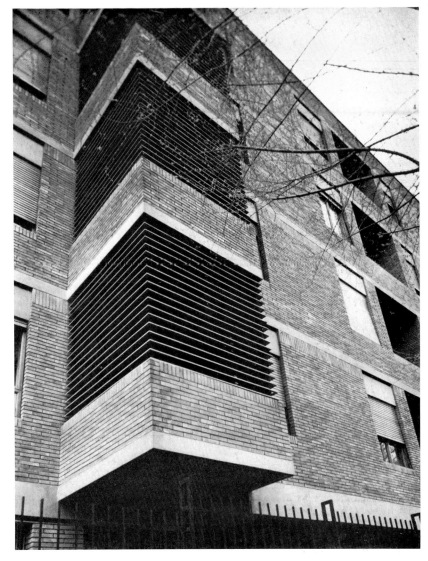

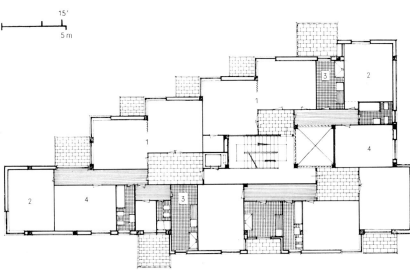

Apartment house at the Piazzale Aquileia, Milan (1964—65)
Architect: Vico Magistretti

Mehrfamilienhaus am Piazzale Aquileia in Mailand (1964—65)
Architekt: Vico Magistretti

1. The block is set back from the road and stands in a garden at the intersection of Via Lipari and Piazzale Aquileia. Its obvious features are the formal strictness of its design and the strong emphasis on the individual elements. Even from outside, the different sizes of the apartments, including those with a living room extending over two storeys, can be clearly discerned.

1. Das Haus ist von der Straße zurückgenommen und steht in einem Garten an der Einmündung der Via Lipari auf den Piazzale Aquileia. Die ins Auge fallenden Merkmale sind die formale Strenge im Aufbau und die klare Hervorhebung der einzelnen Elemente. Schon in der Außenansicht läßt sich die unterschiedliche Größe der Wohnungen, von denen einige einen zweigeschossigen Wohnraum haben, erkennen.

This nine-storey tower block is horizontally divided into three groups of three storeys each. Each of these groups can be subdivided into three apartments taking up an entire floor, six apartments occupying half a storey each, or two duplex apartments taking up one-and-a-half storey each. The bearing structure is formed by L-shaped reinforced concrete supports which stand side-by-side or are interlacing so that they permit a flexible subdivision of the floor areas. Access to the apartments is from the lift or the spiral staircase.

Das turmartige, neunstöckige Gebäude ist vertikal in drei Gruppen von je drei Geschossen gegliedert. Jede dieser Gruppen kann aufgeteilt werden: in drei Wohnungen, die jeweils ein ganzes Geschoß einnehmen, in sechs Wohnungen, von denen jede ein halbes Geschoß belegt, oder in zwei Duplex-Wohnungen, die je eineinhalb Geschosse in Anspruch nehmen. L-förmige Stahlbetonwände bilden die tragende Struktur und schließen sich zu Raumsäulen zusammen, die nebeneinander stehen oder ineinandergreifen und so die flexible Aufteilung der Geschoßflächen erlauben. Der Zugang zu den Wohnungen erfolgt über den Aufzug oder das zylindrische Treppenhaus.

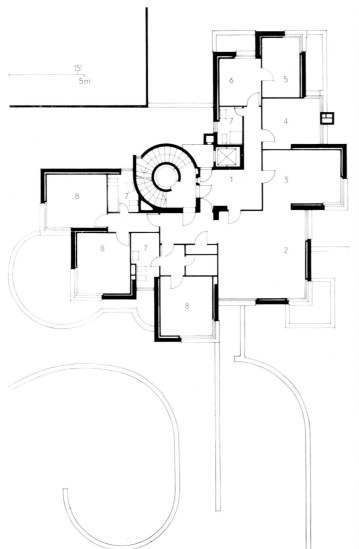

2. Plan of an apartment taking up the whole of one storey. Key: 1 Entrance and hall, 2 Living room, 3 Dining room, 4 Kitchen, 5 Maid's room, 6 Utility room, 7 W.C., shower bath and bathroom, 8 Bedroom.
3. The L-shaped supports are clearly discernible from outside. Notches in the exposed concrete of the smooth walls, which are interrupted by the widely overhung balconies, indicate the different floor levels.

2. Grundriß einer Wohnung, die ein ganzes Geschoß einnimmt. Legende: 1 Eingang und Diele, 2 Wohnraum, 3 Eßzimmer, 4 Küche, 5 Mädchenzimmer, 6 Hauswirtschaftsraum, 7 WC, Dusche, Bad, 8 Schlafraum.
3. Deutlich sind von außen die Raumsäulen zu erkennen. Einkerbungen im Sichtbeton der glatten Wandflächen, die von den weit auskragenden Balkons unterbrochen werden, deuten die einzelnen Geschosse an.

Block of flats at Ivrea (1956—57)
Architects: Marcello Nizzoli and Mario Oliveri

Wohnblock in Ivrea (1956—57)
Architekten: Marcello Nizzoli und Mario Oliveri

1. Entrance side. Large balconies permit close contact with the surroundings.
2,3. Top floor plan and ground floor plan (bottom). Key: 1 Master bedroom, 2 Children's room, 3 Kitchen, 4 Living room with dining area, 5 Study, 6 Bed-sitting room.
4. General view. The vertical lines of the staggered block on the left are in contrast with the horizontal lines of the block on the right where the ground floor has been kept open.

1. Blick auf die Eingangsseite.
2,3. Grundrisse von Obergeschoß und Erdgeschoß (unten). Legende: 1 Elternschlafraum, 2 Kinderzimmer, 3 Küche, 4 Wohnraum mit Eßplatz, 5 Arbeitszimmer, 6 Schlaf- und Arbeitsraum.
4. Gesamtansicht. Die vertikalen Linien des gestaffelten linken Flügels kontrastieren zu den betont horizontalen des rechten Flügels, dessen Erdgeschoß offen blieb.

This block of flats, erected for employees of the Olivetti company, stands on slightly sloping ground not far from the works. In order to meet diverse housing requirements, the 18 flats are of five different types, with 3, 4 or 5 rooms. From outside, the different size of the flats can be recognized from the division of the group into three blocks of unequal height and different architectural treatment. Part of the ground floor is kept open and serves, together with the adjacent open space, as a playground for children.

Das für Angestellte der Firma Olivetti errichtete Wohnhaus steht auf einem schwach fallenden Gelände nicht weit von den Fabrikbauten entfernt. Um vielfältige Wohnansprüche befriedigen zu können, gibt es unter den insgesamt achtzehn Wohnungen fünf verschiedene Typen mit drei, vier und fünf Zimmern. Die unterschiedliche Größe der Wohnungen läßt sich von außen an der Aufgliederung des Gesamtkomplexes in drei ungleich hohe und formal gegeneinander abgesetzte Flügel ablesen. Das Erdgeschoß bleibt teilweise offen und dient, ebenso wie die angrenzende Grünfläche, als Kinderspielplatz.

Block of flats at the Via Millo, Chiavari (1965—66)
Architect: Franco Enrico Delmonte. Civil Engineer: Arnoldo Boggiano

Appartementhaus in der Via Millo in Chiavari (1965—66)
Architekt: Franco Enrico Delmonte. Statik: Arnoldo Boggiano

1. View from the road.

1. Ansicht von der Straße.

This unconventionally designed building is situated at the seaside resort of Chiavari on the Riviera di Levante. It might be described as a block of holiday flats. Its twenty flats are spread over six storeys, accessible from the centrally placed staircase and lift. The facade design is dominated by the front edges of the structural floors which have been left visible and form an integral part of the breast walls of the large balconies surrounding the entire block. The building materials include raw concrete and white cement for the facade treatment, asbestos cement for the roofing, and timber for the balustrades.

Dieses eigenwillig gestaltete Haus steht in dem Touristen- und Badestädtchen Chiavari an der Riviera di Levante. Man kann es als Ferienappartementhaus bezeichnen. Seine zwanzig Wohnungen sind auf sechs Geschosse verteilt und über die zentral angelegte Treppe und einen Aufzug zu erreichen. Die Fassadengliederung wird durch die sichtbar belassenen Vorderkanten der Geschoßdecken bestimmt, die mit den rings um das Gebäude geführten Brüstungen der großen Balkons zu einer Einheit verbunden sind. Als Baustoffe wurden verwendet: Sichtbeton, weißer Zement für den Verputz der Fassaden, Eternit für die Dächer und Holz für die Geländer.

2. The gap between the balcony parapets and the projecting structural floors emphasizes the effect on the concrete girdle. The parapet units, which are difficult to produce, were cast in specially manufactured timber moulds.

3. General view. Colour scheme: the walls are kept in white whilst the concrete parapets, the edges of the structural floors and the asbestos cement roofing are in different shades of grey.

4. Standard floor plan. Key: 1 Hall, 2 Living room, 3 Bedroom, 4 Kitchen.

2. Die Balkonbrüstungen sind gegen die vorgezogenen Decken durch eine Einkerbung abgesetzt, die den Eindruck des Betongürtels verstärkt. Die schwierig herzustellenden Brüstungen wurden in eigens angefertigten Schalformen aus Holz gegossen.

3. Gesamtansicht. Farbgebung: Wandflächen weiß, Betonbrüstungen und Kanten der Geschoßdecken sowie Eternitdach in verschiedenen Graustufen.

4. Normalgeschoßgrundriß. Legende: 1 Diele, 2 Wohnraum, 3 Schlafraum, 4 Küche.

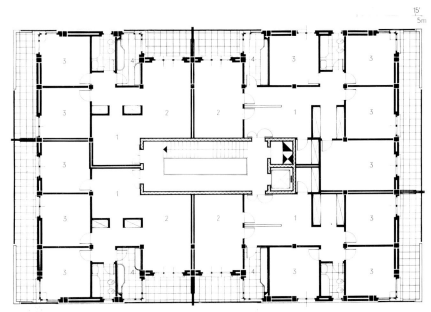

15'
5m

Apartment house at the Giardino d'Arcadia in Milan (1957—59)
Architects: Giulio Minoletti and Giuseppe Chiodi

Wohnhaus am Giardino d'Arcadia in Mailand (1957—59)
Architekten: Giulio Minoletti und Giuseppe Chiodi

1. A park-side situation is particularly attractive for a town house.
2. Plan. Key: 1 Entrance and hall, 2 Living room, 3 Dining area, 4 Study, 5 Kitchen, 6 Maid's room, 7 Cupboard room, 8 Master bedroom, 9 Spare room, 10 Nursery.
3. General view. By means of sun protection louvers which can be shifted sideways, shaded zones can be created at will.
4. The balcony flora, converting the loggias into miniature gardens, ensures an even closer association between the apartments and the park.

1. Die Lage am Rande eines Parks ist für ein Haus im Stadtzentrum besonders günstig.
2. Grundriß. Legende: 1 Eingang und Diele, 2 Wohnraum, 3 Eßplatz, 4 Arbeitszimmer, 5 Küche, 6 Mädchenzimmer, 7 Schrankraum, 8 Elternschlafraum, 9 Gastzimmer, 10 Kinderzimmer.
3. Gesamtansicht. Mittels horizontal verschiebbarer Lamellenblenden lassen sich an jeder gewünschten Stelle Schattenbereiche schaffen.
4. Das Grün der Loggien, die wie kleine Gärten wirken, verbindet das Haus und die Wohnungen noch unmittelbarer mit dem Park.

This apartment house, situated in a Milan district dating back to the 17th century, faces one of the few remaining old parks in the town centre. A characteristic feature of the building is the variety of types of dwellings contained in it. There are no two apartments with identical plan. The architect was thus able to take the individual wishes of the tenants into account. This variety of the interior is externally reflected in the markedly irregular facade. The deeply recessed loggias are integral parts of the flats, providing a link with the park.

Dieses Mietshaus steht in einem Mailänder Stadtteil aus dem 17. Jahrhundert und wendet sich mit seiner Hauptfront zu einem der wenigen erhaltenen alten Parks der Innenstadt. Das Charakteristikum des Gebäudes ist seine Vielzahl von Wohnungstypen. Es gibt keine zwei Wohnungen mit dem gleichen Grundriß. Damit konnte der Architekt den differenzierten Wohnwünschen der Mieter Rechnung tragen. Diese Vielfalt im Inneren findet auch im Äußeren ihren Ausdruck und führt zu einer stark aufgelockerten Fassade. Die sehr tief eingeschnittenen Loggien sind echte Wohnräume, die die Verbindung zum Park herstellen.

Apartment house at Coronata, Genoa (1957—59)
Architect: Robaldo Morozzo della Rocca

Mehrfamilienhaus in Coronata, Genua (1957—59)
Architekt: Robaldo Morozzo della Rocca

This apartment house, erected for employees of the Ansaldo Company, stands on a hill-side slope. The sharply outlined building has forty flats, spread over ten storeys and served by two staircases. All the living and dining rooms face the sea and are provided with loggias. The bedrooms and bathrooms are concentrated in the rear of the building, facing the hill. A characteristic feature is the serration of the facade, prompted by the utility requirements of the plan. The triangular loggias cut into the facade in saw-tooth fashion provide an interesting diversification and an attractive pattern of light and shade.

Dieses für die Mitarbeiter der Firma Ansaldo errichtete Mehrfamilienhaus steht am Abhang eines Hügels. Das scharf abgegrenzte Volumen des Gebäudes setzt sich aus vierzig Wohnungen zusammen, die auf zehn Geschosse verteilt und über zwei Treppenhäuser zugänglich gemacht sind. Alle Wohnräume und Eßzimmer liegen auf der dem Meer zugewandten Seite und haben Loggien. Die Schlaf- und Sanitärräume dagegen sind in der dem Hang zugekehrten Längshälfte des Hauses zusammengefaßt. Charakteristisch für das Gebäude ist die Fassadenfaltung, die sich aus der funktionell bedingten Grundrißgliederung ergibt. Es entstehen sägezahnartig eingeschnittene Loggien mit dreieckigem Grundriß, die die Fassade auflockern und mit einem reizvollen Licht- und Schattenmuster überziehen.

48

1,2. Distant and close views of the sea-side façade. The loggias, staggered on alternate floors, dissolve the façade into a reticular texture, contained in a frame. A light touch is provided by the loggia balustrades which are in the same bright colour as the ''frame'' of the building.
3. Typical floor plan. The broken line indicates the stagger of the loggias on alternate floors. Key: 1 Entrance, 2 Kitchen with dining area, 3 Living room, 4 Master bedroom, 5 Children's room.

1,2. Gesamtansicht und Fassadenausschnitt aus der dem Meer zugekehrten Hausfront. Die vertikal gegeneinander versetzten Loggien lösen die Außenhaut in eine Netzstruktur auf, die in einen Rahmen gefaßt ist. Eine Auflockerung ergibt sich durch in der Farbe des »Rahmens« gehaltene Brüstungselemente an den Loggien.
3. Normalgeschoßgrundriß. Die gestrichelte Linie deutet die Versetzung der Loggien im darüberliegenden Geschoß an. Legende: 1 Eingang, 2 Küche mit Eßplatz, 3 Wohnraum, 4 Elternschlafraum, 5 Kinderzimmer.

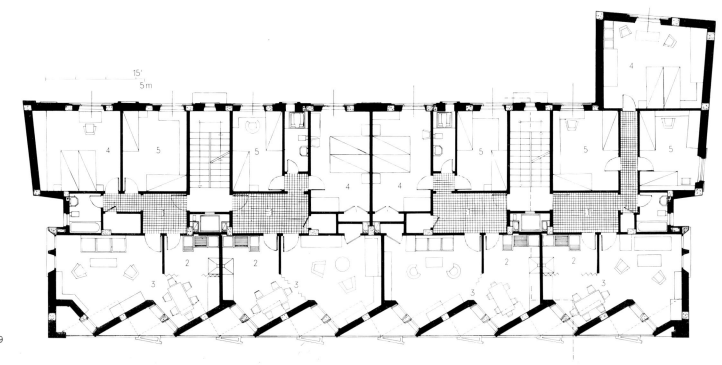

Group of apartment houses at the Cassia Antica in Rome (1958—60)
Architects: Mario Paniconi and Giulio Pediconi

Wohnhausgruppe an der Cassia Antica in Rom (1958—60)
Architekten: Mario Paniconi und Giulio Pediconi

1. View from the west. The facade is diversified and enlivened by loggias, balconies and recesses.
2. Site plan.

1. Ansicht der Hausgruppe von Westen. Loggien, Balkons und die Staffelung des Grundrisses schaffen eine bewegte Fassade.
2. Lageplan.

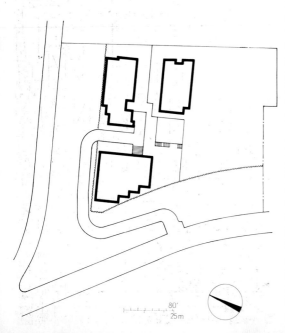

The three constituent blocks of this group surround a patio with gardens and small piazzas. This patio is the centre for all the 62 flats in this housing scheme which must undoubtedly be counted among the most interesting projects of its kind recently realised in Rome. As the ground slopes gently, it was possible to place the garage, which can take 80 cars and contains a number of store rooms for the tenants, partly below ground. Access to each block is provided by an inside staircase and two lifts. There are three apartments on each floor. A special point was made of providing large windows, offering a wide view. Characteristic features are the marked three-dimensional treatment of the facades and the careful attention to all details. The brick cladding of the facades forms a clear contrast to the edges of the structural floors.

Die Hausgruppe ist in drei Blöcke aufgegliedert, die einen bepflanzten, durch kleine Plätze gestalteten Freiraum begrenzen. Dieser Freiraum ist das Zentrum für die insgesamt zweiundsechzig Wohnungen des Gesamtkomplexes, den man ohne Zweifel zu den interessantesten in den letzten Jahren in Rom erbauten Anlagen dieser Art zählen muß. Da das Gelände leicht abfällt, konnte die Garage mit Einstellplätzen für achtzig Autos und einer Anzahl von Abstellräumen für den Gebrauch der Mieter halb unterirdisch angelegt werden. Jedes Gebäude wird über eine innenliegende Treppe und zwei Aufzüge erschlossen. Alle Geschosse sind in jeweils drei Wohnungen aufgeteilt. Besonderer Wert wurde auf große Fensteröffnungen gelegt, durch die man einen weiten Ausblick hat. Charakteristisch für die Häuser ist die reiche Fassadengliederung und die sorgfältige Ausführung aller Details. Die Fassaden wurden mit Backsteinen verkleidet, von denen sich die Vorderkanten der Geschoßdecken deutlich abheben.

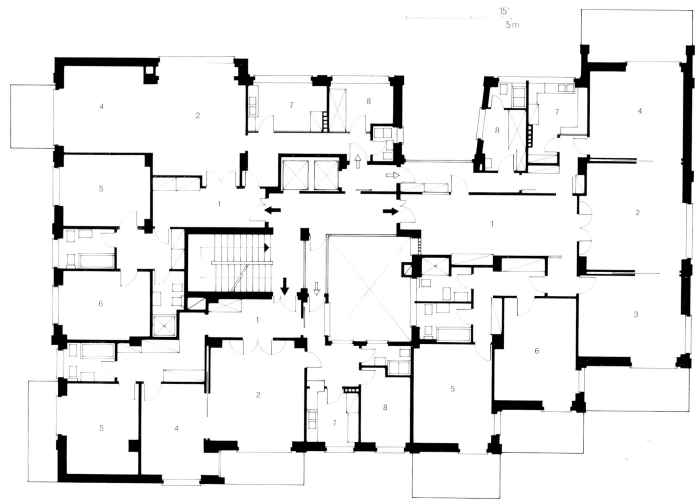

3. Typical floor plan. Key: 1 Entrance, 2 Living room,
3 Study, 4 Dining room, 5 Master bedroom, 6 Children's
room, 7 Kitchen, 8 Maid's room.
4. Part of the facade, seen from the west block. The
outline of the building is slurred by the filigree pattern
of the railings and the slender rodding of the facades.

3. Normalgeschoßgrundriß. Legende: 1 Eingang, 2 Wohnraum, 3 Arbeitszimmer, 4 Eßzimmer, 5 Elternschlafraum,
6 Kinderzimmer, 7 Küche, 8 Mädchenzimmer.
4. Fassadenausschnitt des nach Westen vorgeschobenen
Baus. Die zarten Balkongitter und das leichte Fassaden-
gestänge lösen die Konturen des Baukörpers auf.

"Marina Grande" group of apartment houses at Arenzano (1961—63)
Architect: Vico Magistretti

Wohnhausgruppe Marina Grande, Arenzano (1961—63)
Architekt: Vico Magistretti

1. General view. In the centre is the railway gallery which traverses the entire site.
2. Cross-section of the central building.

1. Gesamtansicht. In der Mitte die Galerie für die Eisenbahn, die den gesamten Komplex durchstößt.
2. Querschnitt durch das Mittelgebäude.

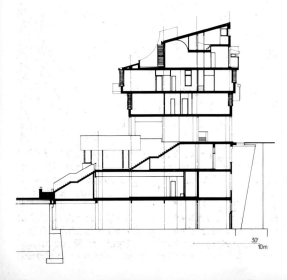

This group of apartment houses on the cliffs of Arenzano consists of several buildings which are placed parallel to the shore and separated by courtyards. A special problem arose from the presence of the railway which here crosses the site a few yards from the Ligurian Sea. In order to create an uninterrupted building site between sea and escarpment, the railway was covered in gallery fashion, thus seemingly becoming part of the development scheme. The roof of this gallery serves as a seaside promenade. Viewed from the sea, the buildings clearly show a horizontal stratification with two contrasting layers: a base with emphatically horizontal lines, interrupted and relieved by the outside flights of stairs, and an upper layer crowning all the buildings which, with its lively three-dimensional features, forms an attractive contrast. Apart from shops and restaurants, there are also a night club and an aquatics club.

Die Hausgruppe an der Steilküste von Arenzano besteht aus mehreren, durch Höfe voneinander getrennten Gebäuden, die parallel zum Ufer aneinandergereiht sind. Ein besonderes Problem ergab sich dadurch, daß an dieser Stelle der ligurischen Küste die Eisenbahn nur wenige Meter vom Meer entfernt über das Baugelände geführt ist. Um nun eine im Ganzen bebaubare, ununterbrochene Fläche zwischen dem Meer und dem Hang zu schaffen, wurde der Schienenstrang galerieartig überdacht und auf diese Weise optisch in den Gebäudekomplex einbezogen. Das Dach dieser Galerie dient als Promenade. Die Anlage ist, vom Meer aus gesehen, in der Horizontalen in zwei deutlich gegeneinander abgesetzte, gegensätzliche Schichten gestuft: eine untere mit betont waagrechten Linien, die durch die vor der Fassade liegenden Treppen unterbrochen und aufgelockert werden, und die obere, die in ihrer plastisch-lebendigen Gestaltung einen reizvollen Kontrast bildet und die ganze Anlage krönt. In dem Gebäudekomplex gibt es neben Läden und Restaurants auch eine Nachtbar und einen Wassersportclub.

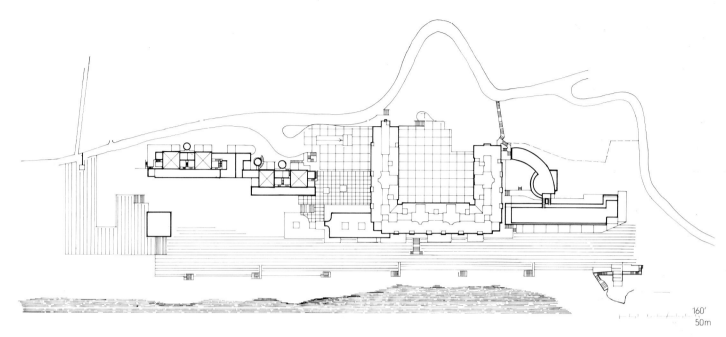

3. Site plan.
4. A view of the upper part of the central building, distinguished by intensive three-dimensional treatment.

3. Lageplan.
4. Blick auf den plastisch gestalteten oberen Teil des Mittelgebäudes.

1. View of the three house types. On the left the three-storey terrace houses for craftsmen, in the centre two six-storey blocks, and on the right part of the facade of a ten-storey tower block.

1. Ansicht der drei Haustypen. Links die dreigeschossigen Reihenhäuser für die Handwerker, in der Mitte zwei sechsgeschossige Blöcke und rechts ein Teil der Fassade eines zehngeschossigen Hauses.

The estate is situated in a new residential district in a north-eastern suburb of Milan. The scattered houses, embedded in green landscape, have ten, six or three storeys and a total population of some 2000. Of particular interest is the three-storey type of terrace house designed for craftsmen who have their workshop on the ground floor and a two-storey maisonette above it. The bearing structure for all these buildings is of reinforced concrete with brick fillings.

Die Siedlung liegt in einem Neubaugebiet im Nordosten Mailands. In den locker gruppierten, in Grün gebetteten zehn-, sechs- und dreigeschossigen Häusern wohnen etwa 2000 Menschen. Besonderes Interesse verdient der dreigeschossige Reihenhaustyp, in dem Handwerker untergebracht sind. Die über zwei Geschosse reichende Wohnung liegt über der Werkstatt im Erdgeschoß. Bei allen Gebäuden besteht das konstruktive Gerüst aus Stahlbeton. Die Wände wurden mit Backsteinen ausgefacht.

2. Open space between the informally grouped buildings which are linked by footpaths.

3. One of the ten-storey tower blocks, containing 40 two-room flats.

4. Site plan. Vehicular traffic is relegated to spur roads.

2. Blick auf die Grünfläche zwischen den locker gruppierten Baukörpern, die durch reine Fußgängerwege miteinander verbunden sind.

3. Ansicht eines zehngeschossigen Punkthauses mit vierzig Zweizimmerwohnungen.

4. Lageplan. Der Fahrverkehr wird von außen über Stichstraßen herangeführt.

Capo Nero tourist centre at the Ligurian Riviera (1957—66)
Architect: Luigi Carlo Daneri

Touristenzentrum Capo Nero an der ligurischen Riviera (1957—66)
Architekt: Luigi Carlo Daneri

Because of its size and successful adaptation to its environments, this group of buildings, situated between Ospedaletti and San Remo, is among the best-known post-war tourist centres in Liguria. Sub-division into a series of concatenated or staggered blocks, all facing the sea, has given rise to dramatic effects and lively setting. The always perspicuous bearing structure and the continuous lines of the balconies ensure uniformity of design throughout. The materials used — concrete and stone — are left exposed.

1. The continuous balconies extending over the entire facade form outdoor extensions of the hotel rooms and forcefully emphasize the horizontal stratification of the building.

1. Die über die ganze Fassadenbreite reichenden, durchlaufenden Balkons erweitern den Wohnraum nach draußen und bewirken eine kräftige horizontale Schichtung des Baukörpers.

Der Gebäudekomplex, der zwischen Ospedaletti und San Remo liegt, gehört aufgrund seiner Größe und der gelungenen Anpassung an das Gelände zu den bekanntesten nach dem Krieg in Ligurien errichteten Touristenzentren. Durch die Aufteilung in verschiedene Blöcke aus gereihten oder gestaffelten Volumina, die sich zum Meer wenden, werden dramatische Wirkungen erzielt und die Anlage lebendig gegliedert. Die stets klar erkennbare konstruktive Struktur und die durchlaufenden Linien der Balkons sorgen für eine einheitliche Gestaltung der gesamten Anlage. Die verwendeten Materialien, Beton und Stein, sind naturbelassen.

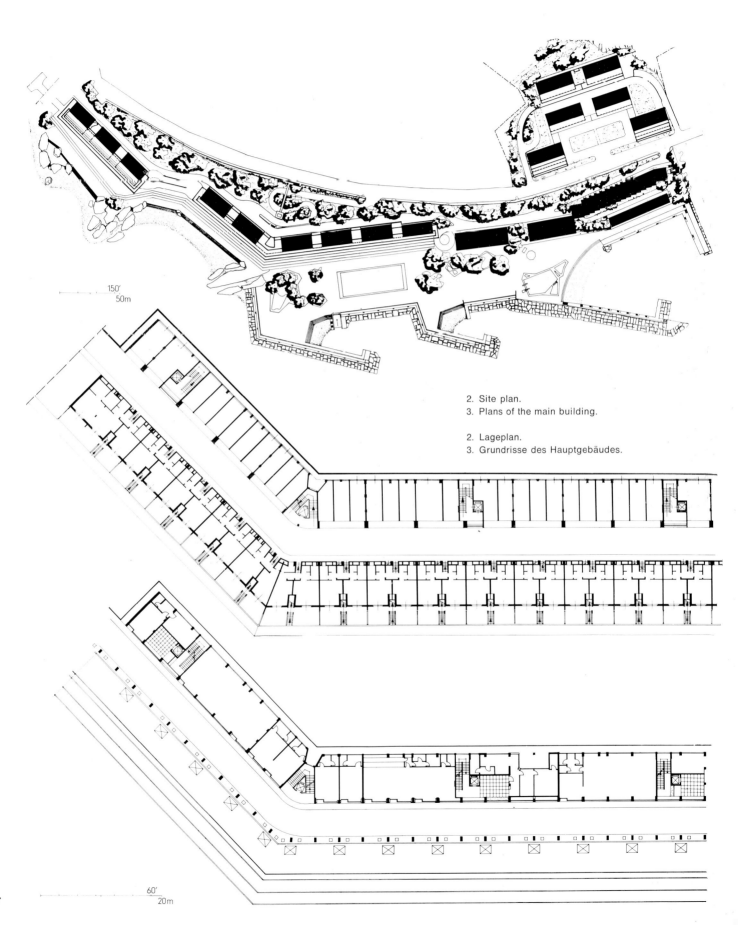

2. Site plan.
3. Plans of the main building.

2. Lageplan.
3. Grundrisse des Hauptgebäudes.

150'
50m

60'
20m

4. From the buildings, skilfully arranged on different levels, the view is across the swimming pool onto the sea.
5. Cross-sections.

4. Aus den geschickt gruppierten Gebäuden auf verschiedenem Niveau blickt man über das Schwimmbecken auf das Meer.
5. Querschnitte.

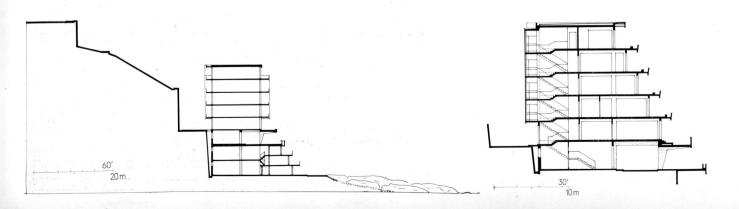

60'
20m

30'
10m

6. All the balconies can be sun-protected by awnings. The rough texture of the rubble walls is in attractive contrast to the exposed concrete faces.
7. From every point at the shore, there are new, surprising and ever-changing views on the different, strongly featured buildings.

6. Alle Balkone lassen sich durch Markisen gegen die Sonne schützen. Die grobe Struktur der Natursteinmauern kontrastiert reizvoll zu den schalungsrohen Betonflächen.
7. Von jeder Stelle am Ufer aus ergeben sich neue überraschende und stets wechselnde Ausblicke auf die verschiedenen Gebäude mit ihrer kräftigen Fassadengliederung.

Children's Village at Opicina, Trieste (1949—58)
Architect: Marcello D'Olivo

Kinderdorf in Triest-Opicina (1949—58)
Architekt: Marcello D'Olivo

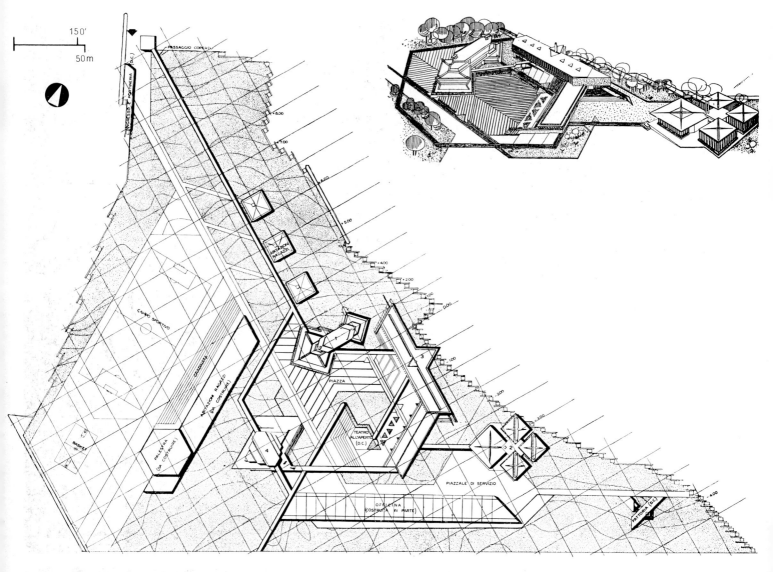

1. Site plan and isometric view.

1. Lageplan des Gesamtkomplexes und Isometrie.

The children's village, embedded in green landscape, is situated on a hill at Opicina at the outskirts of Trieste. The group of buildings comprises dormitories, refectory, school, a workshop building and a printing shop — all surrounding a central piazza. The diversity of the architectural designs of the individual buildings is somewhat at variance with the unity obviously aimed at in the project as a whole.

Das von Grün umgebene Kinderdorf liegt auf einem Hügel in Opicina, in der unmittelbaren Umgebung von Triest. Der Gesamtkomplex setzt sich aus Wohnbauten, einer Mensa, der Schule, einem Werkstattbau und einer Druckerei zusammen, die um einen zentralen Platz als gemeinsamem Mittelpunkt gruppiert sind. Die Vielfalt in der architektonischen Gestaltung der einzelnen Baukörper widerspricht etwas der offensichtlich in der Anlage des Ganzen gesuchten Einheitlichkeit.

2. A view of the school building and one of the dormitories, facing the central piazza with a facade broken up by loggias.
3. Part of the refectory.
4. Interior of the printing shop.

2. Blick auf die Schule und einen Wohnbau mit der in Loggien aufgelösten Front zum Zentralplatz hin.
3. Teilansicht der Mensa.
4. Blick in die Druckerei.

Montechiaro Holiday Home of Italsider Ltd. near Cesana Torinese (1959—60)
Architect: Renato Severino

Ferienheim Montechiaro der Italsider GmbH bei Cesana Torinese (1959—60)
Architekt: Renato Severino

1. The Montechiaro Holiday Home in its high-alpine setting, seen from south-east.

1. Gesamtansicht des Heimes von Südosten vor dem Hintergrund der Hochgebirgslandschaft.

The Montechiaro Holiday Home, situated in the Eastern Alps and accommodating 250 children, consists of a single three-storey block of great depth in relation to its height. At the request of the great Italian steel combine, the building is erected exclusively in steel. The Home is occupied by successive groups of children of the company's employees. Kitchen, infirmary, supervisors and administration are at ground level; so is the gymnastics hall which extends into the main floor. On the latter are the lounges, dining rooms, hobby and play rooms. The dormitories are on the top floor.

Das Montechiaro-Ferienheim für 250 Kinder, das in den Ostalpen liegt, besteht aus einem einzigen, niedrigen und breit hingelagerten dreigeschossigen Baukörper. Es wurde im Auftrag des großen italienischen Stahlkonzerns als reine Stahlkonstruktion errichtet. Hier können die Kinder der Angestellten umschichtig ihre Ferien verbringen. Küche, Krankenstation, Direktions- und Verwaltungsräume und auch die durch zwei Geschosse reichende Turnhalle sind im Erdgeschoß untergebracht. Das Hauptgeschoß nimmt die Aufenthalts-, Speise- und Bastelräume und die Spielzimmer auf. Die Schlafräume befinden sich im Obergeschoß.

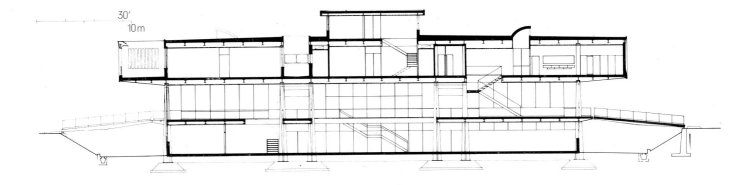

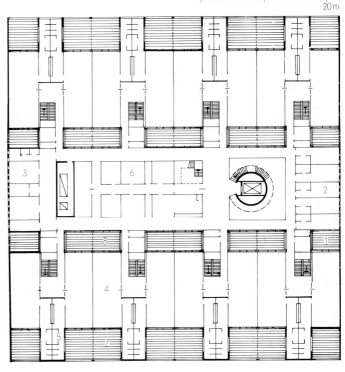

2. Section.
3. Top floor plan. Key: 1 Patios, 2 Staff and supervisors' rooms, 3 Infirmary, 4 Children's dormitories, 5 Bathrooms and W. C.s, 6 Service rooms, 7 Loggias, 8 Patios.
4. North side, by night. Lower floor and main floor are completely surrounded by glass curtains so that the building appears to float.

2. Schnitt.
3. Grundriß des Obergeschosses. Legende: 1 Innenhöfe, 2 Zimmer für Angestellte und Heimleiter, 3 Krankenstation, 4 Kinderschlafräume, 5 Bad und WC, 6 Hauswirtschaftsräume, 7 Loggien, 8 Innenhöfe.
4. Die Nordfassade bei Nacht. Untergeschoß und Hauptgeschoß sind ringsum verglast und geben dem Gebäude den Anschein der Schwerelosigkeit.

5. East side. In front of the top floor dormitories are roofless loggias. The roof of the penthouse, where the teaching staff are accommodated, can be glimpsed by the side of the staircase tower (cf. Fig. 1). Access is by bridges at main floor level.

6. One of the top floor corridors with the spiral stairs connecting all floors.

7. Interior of the two-storey vestibule. The bearing steel columns are concealed by cladding. Because of the relatively great depth of the building, the party walls are likewise of glass so as to improve daylight conditions.

5. Die Ostseite. Vor den Schlafräumen im Obergeschoß liegen nach oben offene Loggien. Neben dem Treppenturm ist die Dachkante des Penthauses zu erkennen, in dem die Lehrer untergebracht sind (vergleiche Bild 1). Der Zugang erfolgt ebenerdig über die Brücken ins Hauptgeschoß.

6. Blick in einen Flur des Obergeschosses und das zylindrische Treppenhaus mit der Wendeltreppe, die alle Geschosse miteinander verbindet.

7. Blick in die zweigeschossige Halle des Erdgeschosses. Die tragenden Stahlelemente des Gebäudes sind durch eine Verkleidung verdeckt. Aus belichtungstechnischen Erwägungen und aufgrund der großen Tiefe des Gebäudes wurden auch die Raumtrennwände in Glas ausgeführt.

Marchiondi Spagliardi Institute for difficult children at Baggio, Milan (1959)
Architect: Vittoriano Viganò

Marchiondi-Spagliardi-Institut für schwererziehbare Kinder in Baggio, Mailand (1959)
Architekt: Vittoriano Viganò

The different buildings of the Institute form a small, self-contained community for children difficult to educate. The group comprises a school unit and a dormitory unit, surrounded by open space affording plenty of opportunity for physical exercise and sports activities. All the buildings are reinforced concrete structures where the concrete has been left exposed both inside and outside. Because of the use of exposed concrete and the dogmatic juxtaposition of volumes, the character of the project is not fully in keeping with the paedagogic functions and objectives of an Institute designed for children.

Die verschiedenen Bauten des Instituts bilden zusammen ein kleines selbständiges Gemeinwesen, in dem schwererziehbare Kinder betreut werden. Der Gesamtkomplex besteht aus einer Schule und Wohnbauten. Sie sind von Grünflächen umgeben, auf denen sich die Kinder austoben und sportlich betätigen können. Alle Gebäude sind Stahlbetonkonstruktionen, die innen und außen schalungsroh belassen wurden. Die Verwendung von Sichtbeton und die gegeneinandergestellten Volumina verleihen der Anlage einen Charakter, der nicht unbedingt mit den pädagogischen Funktionen und Absichten des für Kinder errichteten Instituts harmoniert.

1. A view of the dormitory building. The bearing structure placed outside the facade, and the projecting, almost wholly enclosed concrete cubes create a highly diversified facade.
2. Staircase of the dormitory building.
3. Site plan.

1. Blick auf das Schlafsaalgebäude. Das vor die Hausfront gestellte tragende Gerüst und die vorgezogenen, fast völlig geschlossenen Betonwürfel schaffen eine bewegte, stark strukturierte Fassade.
2. Treppe im Schlaftrakt.
3. Lageplan.

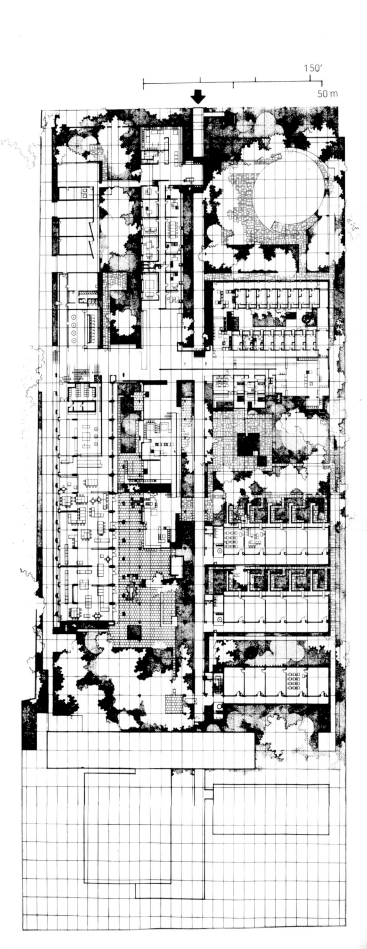

4. The main longitudinal passage is covered by a roof which is suspended from the cantilevered roof girders of the adjacent building and serves to emphasize the linking function of the passage.

5. The self-contained stairway tower at the end of the dormitory building provides a further plastic accent.

6. A view of the dormitory building. The exposed concrete structure in front of the facade is reminiscent of timber construction.

4. Das Dach über dem in der Längsrichtung verlaufenden Hauptweg, das unter die auskragenden Dachunterzüge des angrenzenden Gebäudes gehängt ist, betont die verbindende Funktion dieser Verkehrsachse.

5. Das vorgezogene, frei stehende Treppenhaus an der Stirnfront des Schlafsaalgebäudes setzt einen zusätzlichen plastischen Akzent.

6. Ansicht des Schlafsaalgebäudes. Die vor der Fassade liegende Sichtbetonstruktur erinnert an Holzkonstruktionen.

Olivetti Welfare Centre in Ivrea (1954—57)
Architects: Luigi Figini and Gino Pollini

Sozialgebäude der Firma Olivetti in Ivrea (1954—57)
Architekten: Luigi Figini und Gino Pollini

The Olivetti Welfare Centre, inscribed in an hexagonal module system, faces the factory buildings of the Olivetti Company, designed by the same architects in 1940. The contrast between the sober and straight lines of the factory buildings and the gay and light interplay of shapes in the new buildings results in an attractive confrontation which is further emphasized by the arcades covering part of the intermediate piazza. The two wings of the new building are placed at the same obtuse angle as the road. One of them contains, on the upper floor, the premises for cultural activities and social welfare; in the other wing is the health centre. The deep arcade at street level with its widely spaced, slender columns serves as a filter zone between interior and exterior; its roof forms the first-floor terrace. Parts of the reinforced concrete structure are left exposed or are covered by no-fines concrete panels. The arcade columns are of granite.

Das auf einem hexagonalen Grundrißschema aufgebaute Sozialgebäude steht den von den gleichen Architekten 1940 entworfenen Fabrikbauten der Firma Olivetti gegenüber. Aus dem Kontrast der Baukörper — auf der einen Seite die nüchternen, geraden Linien der Werkstattbauten und auf der anderen das heitere, leichte Spiel der Formen — ergibt sich eine spannungsreiche Wechselbeziehung, die durch das Ausgreifen des verbindenden Platzes bis in den Laubengang des Sozialgebäudes noch betont wird. Im einen seiner beiden Flügel, die im stumpfen Winkel dem Knick der Straße folgen, sind im ersten Obergeschoß die Räume für die kulturelle und soziale Betreuung untergebracht, der andere nimmt die Einrichtungen für die Gesundheitsfürsorge auf. Die Decke des breiten Laubenganges im Erdgeschoß mit den weit auseinanderstehenden, schlank dimensionierten Stützen bildet die Terrasse des ersten Obergeschosses. Er dient als Übergangszone zwischen innen und außen. Das Gebäude ist eine Stahlbetonkonstruktion, die zum Teil schalungsrauh belassen oder mit Waschbetonplatten abgedeckt wurde. Für die Stützen des Laubenganges ist Granit verwendet.

1. General view of the Welfare Centre, facing the factory buildings on the left. The step-like retraction of the upper floors has resulted in an interesting stagger effect.

1. Gesamtansicht, links die Fabrikbauten. Die Zurücknahme jedes Geschosses gegenüber dem darunterliegenden ergibt eine interessante Höhenstufung.

2–4. Plans of roof storey (top), first floor (centre) and ground floor.

The wings on the left, standing a few steps higher than the other, contains the health centre with waiting rooms and surgeries for various medical officers (gynaecologist, internal specialist, oculist, dentist, and ear, nose and throat specialist). On the top floor are a flat for the male nurse and a lounge for the medical officers. In the wing on the right, which is used for welfare and cultural purposes, are a lecture room, a credit bureau, the social welfare offices, the headquarters of the welfare assistants and, on the top floor, further community rooms and offices.

2 – 4. Grundrisse von Dachgeschoß (oben), erstem Obergeschoß (Mitte) und Erdgeschoß.

Im linken, einige Stufen höher stehenden Gebäudeteil das Gesundheitszentrum mit Warte- und Krankenzimmern und Behandlungs- und Untersuchungsräumen für verschiedene Ärzte (Gynäkologe, Internist, Augen-, Zahn- und Hals-Nasen-Ohren-Arzt); im Dachgeschoß die Wohnung des Krankenpflegers und ein Ärzteaufenthaltsraum. Im rechten Gebäudeteil, der der sozialen und kulturellen Betreuung dient, Vortragssaal, Kreditbüro, Büros der Sozialfürsorge, Büros für Sozialhelfer und im Dachgeschoß weitere Gemeinschaftseinrichtungen und Verwaltungsräume.

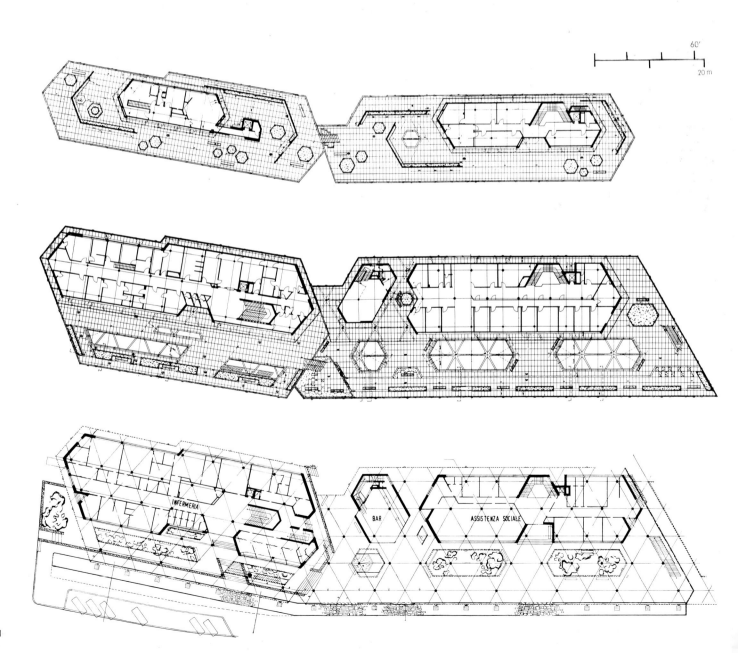

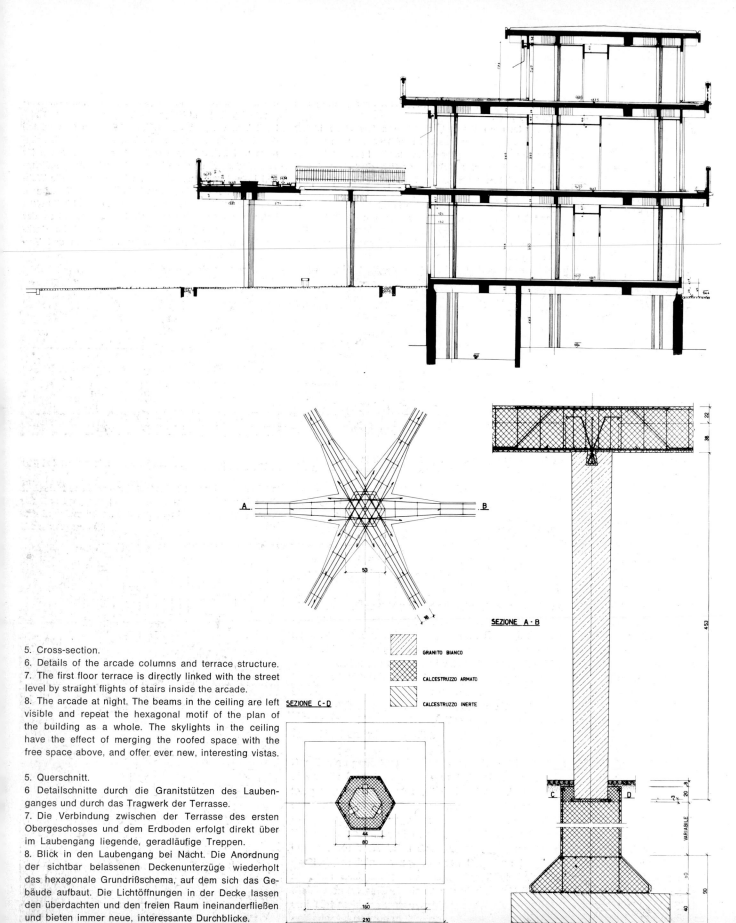

5. Cross-section.
6. Details of the arcade columns and terrace structure.
7. The first floor terrace is directly linked with the street level by straight flights of stairs inside the arcade.
8. The arcade at night. The beams in the ceiling are left visible and repeat the hexagonal motif of the plan of the building as a whole. The skylights in the ceiling have the effect of merging the roofed space with the free space above, and offer ever new, interesting vistas.

5. Querschnitt.
6 Detailschnitte durch die Granitstützen des Laubenganges und durch das Tragwerk der Terrasse.
7. Die Verbindung zwischen der Terrasse des ersten Obergeschosses und dem Erdboden erfolgt direkt über im Laubengang liegende, geradläufige Treppen.
8. Blick in den Laubengang bei Nacht. Die Anordnung der sichtbar belassenen Deckenunterzüge wiederholt das hexagonale Grundrißschema, auf dem sich das Gebäude aufbaut. Die Lichtöffnungen in der Decke lassen den überdachten und den freien Raum ineinanderfließen und bieten immer neue, interessante Durchblicke.

SEZIONE C-D

SEZIONE A-B

GRANITO BIANCO

CALCESTRUZZO ARMATO

CALCESTRUZZO INERTE

Mess Building of the Olivetti Works in Ivrea (1957—59)
Architect: Ignazio Gardella. Civil Engineer: Antonio Migliasso

Casino der Olivetti-Werke in Ivrea (1957—59)
Architekt: Ignazio Gardella. Statik: Antonio Migliasso

1. West side. The building lies in the centre of a tree-studded lawn, and the emphasis on horizontal lines is well in keeping with the environment.

1. Ansicht von Westen. Das Gebäude liegt inmitten einer mit Baumgruppen bestandenen Rasenfläche und paßt sich in seiner betont horizontalen Linienführung gut der Umgebung an.

The Mess Building is part of an extensive recreation and leisure-time centre which Olivetti have created for their staff. The large polygon-shaped building is situated in a park at the foot of Montenavale Hill. Through deliberate adaptation to the contour lines, it has been completely merged with its setting. Each floor is surrounded by terraces which are connected with the ground level by footbridges or stairs closely integrated with the footpaths in the park. Apart from a canteen for 200 people, the building also contains rest rooms and a library. The bearing structure is of reinforced concrete; some of the walls are faced with clinkers. Window and door fittings are of varnished iron. The surrounding terraces are guarded and accentuated by iron railings of filigree lightness.

Das Casino gehört zu dem umfangreichen Erholungs- und Freizeitzentrum, das die Firma für ihre Angestellten und Arbeiter geschaffen hat. Das große Gebäude mit polygonalem Grundriß liegt in einem Park am Fuße des Hügels von Montenavale. Um seine völlige Verschmelzung mit der Umgebung zu erreichen, wurde es weitgehend der Bewegung des Geländes angepaßt. Rings um jedes Geschoß sind Terrassen geführt und durch Brückenstege oder Treppen mit dem Terrain verbunden. Sie verknüpfen das Gebäude eng mit dem Wegesystem des Parkes. In der Kantine können zweitausend Personen beköstigt werden. Sie enthält unter anderem auch Ruheräume und eine Bibliothek. Das konstruktive Gerüst ist in Stahlbeton ausgeführt, die Wände sind zum Teil mit Klinker verkleidet. Für Fenster- und Türbeschläge wurde lackiertes Eisen verwendet. Filigranartig wirkende Eisengeländer begrenzen und betonen die umlaufenden Terrassen.

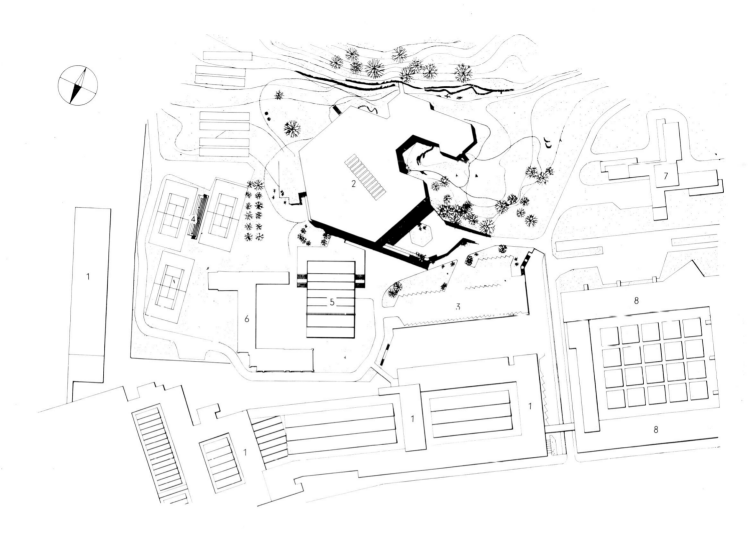

2. Interior of one of the staircases, distinguished by the rhythmic alternation of white marble and black slate in the balustrade.

3. Site plan. Key: 1 Factory buildings, 2 Mess building, 3 Car parks, 4 Tennis courts, 5 Theatre, 6 Sports and recreation centre, 7 Research centre, 8 Factory buildings.

4. Plan of lower floor. Key: 1, 3, 4 Stairs, 2 Escalator, 5 Side entrance, 6 Tea room with dance floor, 7 Espresso bar, 8 Dining room, 9 Writing room, 10 Library, 11 Rest room, 12 Television room, 13,14 Lavatories, 15 Cloak room, 16 Food stores, 17 Meals elevator, 18 Office, 19 Entrance to guests' dining room, 20 Workers' canteen.

2. Blick in ein Treppenhaus, dessen Charakter durch die rhythmische Abfolge weißer Marmor- und schwarzer Schieferflächen in der Balustrade bestimmt wird.

3. Lageplan. Legende: 1 Fabrikgebäude, 2 Casino, 3 Parkplätze, 4 Tennisplätze, 5 Theater, 6 Sport- und Erholungszentrum, 7 Forschungszentrum, 8 Fabrikgebäude.

4. Grundriß des Untergeschosses. Legende: 1, 3, 4 Treppe, 2 Rolltreppe, 5 Nebeneingang, 6 Tanzkaffee, 7 Espressobar, 8 Speisesaal, 9 Schreibraum, 10 Bibliothek, 11 Ruheraum, 12 Fernsehraum, 13, 14 Toiletten, 15 Garderobe, 16 Lebensmittellager, 17 Speisenaufzug, 18 Büro, 19 Eingang Gästespeiseraum, 20 Arbeiterkantine.

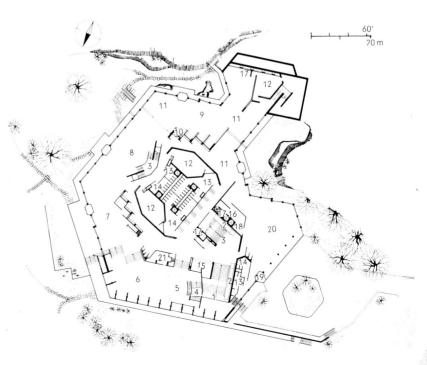

5. The perfect adaptation of the building to its surroundings is particulary evident from this view from southwest.

6. Hexagonal courtyard, seen from the south. On the ground floor of the projecting part of the building is the workers' canteen.

7. Large windows, nearly reaching from floor to ceiling, contribute to the close association of interiors and exteriors. The slender columns are matched by the filigree pattern of the balustrade.

5. Diese Ansicht von Südwesten zeigt besonders deutlich, wie vollkommen das Gebäude in seine Umgebung eingebunden ist.

6. Blick von Süden in den hexagonalen Innenhof. Im Untergeschoß des vorspringenden Bauteils der Arbeiterspeisesaal.

7. Große, fast raumhohe Fenster tragen zur engen Verbindung von innen und außen bei. Den schlank dimensionierten Gebäudestützen entspricht das zartgliedrige Brüstungsgitter.

Primary school at Bolladello (1963—64)
Architect: Carlo Moretti

Grundschule in Bolladello (1963—64)
Architekt: Carlo Moretti

1. Entrance side.

1. Ansicht der Eingangsseite.

This little school with five class rooms, standing in an isolated position at the outskirts of the town, is distinguished from the great number of similar buildings by the lucidity of its plan and the integrity of its design. The class rooms are accessible from an oblong, centrally placed common room which receives daylight through the window ribbons at the ends and an additional shed-type skylight. The long side opposite the class rooms is taken up by cloakrooms, toilets, masters' rooms and headmaster's study. At the corner, a recess has been created for an open porch which is used as a concourse during breaks. Throughout, the concrete of the structure has been left exposed. The concrete platform carrying the building is slightly raised above ground and curved up at the edges so as to form a trough. The balustrade thus created surrounds the entire building and is merely interrupted by the stairs leading to the entrance hall. Its height is the same as that of the fascia of the flat roof which projects far enough to provide effective sun and weather protection for the recessed windows.

Klarheit der Grundrißdisposition und formale Geschlossenheit heben diese kleine, fünfklassige Schule aus der Masse ähnlicher Bauten heraus. Die Klassenzimmer sind über den langgestreckten, zentralen Gemeinschaftsraum zugänglich. Er wird über die Fensterbänder an den Stirnseiten und durch ein zusätzliches, shedähnliches Oberlicht belichtet. An der dem Klassentrakt gegenüberliegenden Längsseite sind Garderoben, Toiletten, Lehrerzimmer und Rektorat aufgereiht. An der Ecke wurde eine offene Vorhalle ausgespart, die als Pausenhalle dient. Das frei am Ortsrand stehende Gebäude wurde ganz in schalungsrauh belassenem Sichtbeton ausgeführt. An den Rändern ist die etwas vom Baugrund abgehobene Bodenplatte wannenförmig aufgewölbt. Die Brüstung, die auf diese Weise entsteht, läuft um den ganzen Baukörper. Ihre Höhe korrespondiert mit dem Rand des Flachdachs, das weit auskragt, um den zurückgesetzten Fenstern Sonnen- und Wetterschutz zu geben.

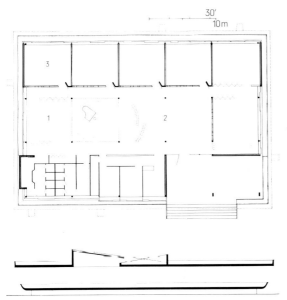

2,3. Plan and section. Key: 1 Special class room, divisible by partitions, 2 Common room, 3 Class rooms.
4. Corner of the building with the open entrance porch which serves as a concourse during breaks.
5. Entrance porch with the entrance to the common room.

2,3. Grundriß und Schnitt. Legende: 1 Durch Zwischenwände abteilbarer Sonderklassenraum, 2 Gemeinschaftsraum, 3 Klassenzimmer.
4. Detailansicht mit offener Eingangshalle.
5. Blick durch die Pausenhalle auf den Eingang zum Gemeinschaftsraum.

1. Corner of the building with entrance and common rooms. The delicate concrete structure is emphasized by the large windows.

1. Teilansicht mit dem Eingang und den Gemeinschafts-räumen. Die zarte Betonstruktur wird durch die großen Fenster unterstrichen.

Placed in an old park, the school building has been kept as transparent as possible so that it should blend well with its setting. Large windows permit an almost unimpeded view on the trees of the park. For the same reason, the space below the partly raised lower floor has been kept open and the building placed on cross walls so as to permit free passage. The materials used — concrete for the structural frame, brick and glass for the walls, asbestos cement for the roof — also help to merge the school with its surroundings.

Damit sich die Schule möglichst gut in ihre Umgebung, einen alten Park, einfügt, ist der Baukörper weitgehend transparent gehalten. Große Glasflächen gestatten den nahezu ungehinderten Ausblick auf die Bäume des Parkes. Auch das teilweise über Niveau liegende Untergeschoß wurde im Hinblick auf die angestrebte Verschmelzung des Gebäudes mit der Umgebung gestaltet: Senkrecht zur Längsachse angeordnete Wandscheiben unter dem Klassenzimmertrakt vermeiden die Unterbrechung des Geländeflusses, man kann ungehindert unter dem Gebäude durchgehen. Die verwendeten Materialien, Beton für das konstruktive Gerüst, Backstein und Glas für die Wände und Eternit für das Dach, tragen ebenfalls dazu bei, die Schule in ihre Umgebung einzupassen.

2. Lower floor plan. Key: 1 Entrance hall, 2 Headmaster,
3 Common room, 4 Class rooms.
3. Basement plan. Key: 1 Workroom, 2 Heating, 3 Teaching aids, 4 Covered space used as concourse during
breaks, 5 Rear entrance, 6 Main entrance.
4. East facade. The school is distinguished from other
buildings by this architect by a greater strictness of
composition.

2. Grundriß des Erdgeschosses. Legende: 1 Eingangshalle, 2 Direktor, 3 Gemeinschaftsraum, 4 Klassenzimmer.
3. Grundriß des Untergeschosses. Legende: 1 Werkraum,
2 Heizung, 3 Lehrmittel, 4 Überdachter Pausenraum,
5 Nebeneingang, 6 Hauptzugang.
4. Blick auf die Ostfassade. Die Schule unterscheidet
sich von den anderen Bauten des Architekten durch die
größere Strenge der Linienführung.

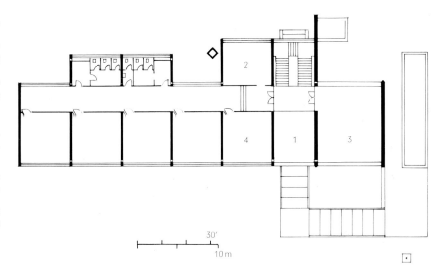

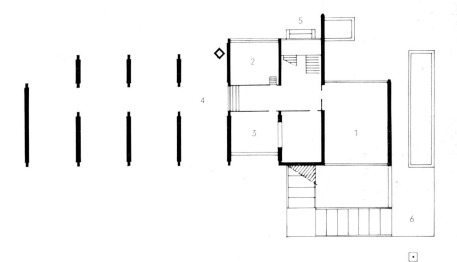

Primary school in Milan (1959)
Architect: Vittorio Gandolfi

Grundschule in Mailand (1959)
Architekt: Vittorio Gandolfi

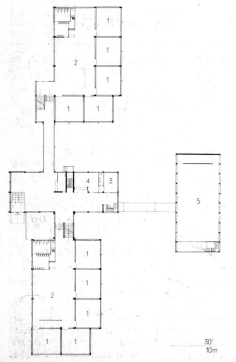

1. Covered way connecting one of the class room wings with the central building.
2. Ground floor plan. Key: 1 Class room, 2 Common room, 3 Headmaster, 4 Administration, 5 Gymnastics hall.

1. Blick auf die geschlossene Galerie zwischen Unterrichtsflügel und Mittelbau.
2. Erdgeschoßgrundriß. Legende: 1 Klassenzimmer, 2 Gemeinschaftsraum, 3 Direktor, 4 Verwaltung, 5 Turnhalle.

This school in the "Ca' Granda Nord" district consists of four buildings interlinked by two covered ways and one staircase. The classrooms in each of the two main wings are grouped around a common room. The gymnastics hall forms the outer boundary of the school site and, together with the covered way leading to it, divides the grounds into two large garden areas. The school has accommodation for 600 children. The bearing structure is of reinforced concrete with brick panelling.

Der Schulkomplex im Stadtviertel »Ca' Granda Nord« ist in vier Gebäude gegliedert, die durch zwei geschlossene Galerien und durch ein Treppenhaus miteinander verbunden sind. In den beiden Unterrichtsflügeln befinden sich die zwei Gemeinschaftsräumen zugeordneten Klassenzimmer. Die Turnhalle schließt den Schulbereich nach außen ab und gliedert ihn zugleich in zwei Grünräume. In der Schule werden 600 Kinder unterrichtet. Die konstruktiven Elemente bestehen aus Stahlbeton, die Wände wurden mit Ziegeln ausgefacht.

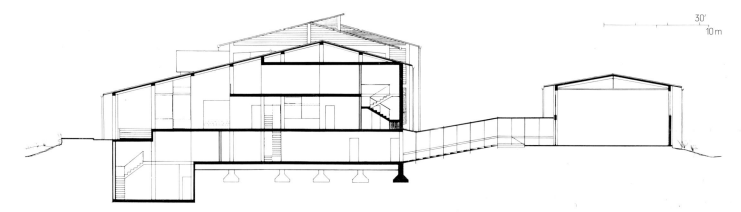

3. Cross-section of central building and gymnastics hall.
4. Interior of the fully glazed covered way between the central building and one of the class room wings.
5. Common room in one of the two class room wings.

3. Querschnitt durch Mittelbau und Turnhalle.
4. Blick in den voll verglasten Verbindungsgang vom Unterrichtsflügel zum Mittelbau.
5. Einer der beiden Gemeinschaftsräume in einem Klassenzimmertrakt.

The peculiar shaping of this school building, erected in the outskirts of Busto Arsizio in a rather unattractive environment in the new Sempione district, is due to structural considerations. The ten classrooms for a total of 300 children are divided into three groups with three, three and four rooms, respectively. Each of these groups forms a separate unit with a common room for collective teaching as a centre of gravity. In addition, there are the masters' room, a gymnastics hall, a caretaker's flat, and the usual sanitary installations. A covered way serves as link with the outside world. The large open space in the centre, almost wholly surrounded by buildings, serves as a venue during breaks and as a playground. The structural units of exposed reinforced concrete are not in discord with the large windows and the rubble masonry.

Diese Schule, deren eigenwillige plastische Gestaltung aus der Konstruktion erwächst, steht am Rande von Busto Arsizio in einer wenig ansprechenden Umgebung im neuen Stadtteil Sempione. Die zehn Klassenzimmer für 300 Schüler sind in drei Gruppen von zweimal drei und einmal vier Räumen aufgeteilt. Vor jeder dieser Gruppen liegt als Schwerpunkt ein Gemeinschaftsraum für den Gruppenunterricht. Zum Schulkomplex gehören außerdem das Lehrerzimmer, eine Turnhalle, eine Hausmeisterwohnung und die üblichen sanitären Anlagen. Ein überdachter Gang verbindet den Schulbereich mit dem Außenraum. Die zentrale Grünfläche dient als Pausenhof und Spielplatz. Die konstruktiven Elemente aus Sichtbeton schließen sich ohne Bruch an die großen Glasflächen und das Natursteinmauerwerk an.

1. View from one of the common rooms on the open space in the centre. The serrated window front is protected against the high-rising sun by a honeycomb-shaped combination of concrete blinds.

1. Blick aus einem Gemeinschaftsraum auf die zentrale Grünfläche. Die aufgefaltete Fensterwand erhält durch eine vorgelagerte wabenförmige Kombination aus Betonblenden Schutz gegen steil einfallende Sonne.

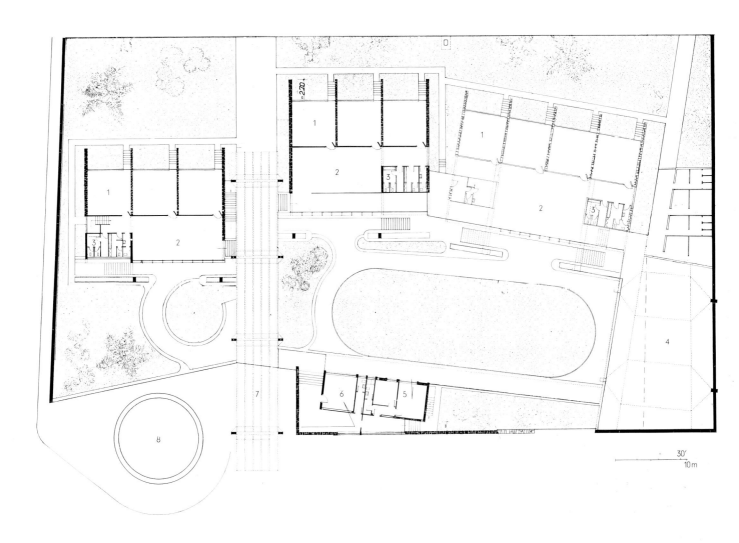

2. Plan. Key: 1 Class room, 2 Common room, 3 Lavatories, 4 Gymnastics hall, 5 Caretaker's flat, 6 Masters' room, 7 Covered way, 8 Water basin.

3. Frontal view of one of the common rooms. On the large window front, the plastic treatment of the ceiling is projected onto the vertical. But the design of the sun protection grille appears to have resulted not so much from utilitarian considerations but from the desire to enliven and diversify the facade.

2. Grundriß. Legende: 1 Klassenzimmer, 2 Gemeinschaftsraum, 3 Schülertoilette, 4 Turnhalle, 5 Wohnung des Hausmeisters, 6 Lehrerzimmer, 7 Überdachter Gang, 8 Wasserbecken.

3. Außenansicht eines Gemeinschaftsraumes. Die große Glasfront wiederholt die plastische Durchbildung der Decke in der Vertikalen. Die Gestaltung des Sonnenschutzrasters dürfte jedoch mehr aus formalen Erwägungen einer Auflockerung und Belebung der Außenfront als aus solchen der Zweckmäßigkeit resultieren.

Technical College at Busto Arsizio (1963—64)
Architects: Enrico Castiglioni and Carlo Fontana

Berufsschule in Busto Arsizio (1963—64)
Architekten: Enrico Castiglioni und Carlo Fontana

The two colleges accommodated in this group of buildings, viz. the "Iinstitute for Industrial Technology" and the "State Institute for Industry and Crafts", offer training facilities for up to a thousand students. The group consists of two symmetrically arranged wings which form an obtuse angle with each other and are connected by a lower building, containing the vestibule from which each of the colleges can be reached through separate entrances. All the class rooms are on the upper floors. The ground floor contains the apprentice shops. The architectural design of the group is governed by the characteristically curved bearing structure which is projecting from the facade — a design which has obviously been governed by aesthetic considerations. As a result, the building conveys a strong impression of unity and compactness while fully complying with functional requirements.

In den beiden in diesem Schulkomplex untergebrachten Instituten (Institut für industrielle Technik und staatliches Institut für Industrie und Handwerk) können bis zu tausend Schüler unterrichtet werden. Die Anlage besteht aus zwei symmetrisch angeordneten, im stumpfen Winkel zueinandergestellten Gebäudeflügeln, die durch ein niedrigeres Zwischenglied, die Eingangshalle, miteinander verbunden sind. Beide Institute erreicht man von dieser Halle aus über getrennte Eingänge. Alle Unterrichtsräume befinden sich in den oberen Stockwerken. Das Erdgeschoß enthält die Lehrwerkstätten. Die architektonische Gestaltung des Komplexes wird durch das vor die Fassade gezogene, in schwungvollen Kurven geführte konstruktive Gerüst bestimmt, wobei offensichtlich formale Überlegungen im Vordergrund standen.

1. View of the north end of the building. The slight curvature of the facade is in keeping with that of the crosswalls which flatten out above the apprentice shops.

1. Blick auf die Stirnfront des nördlichen Gebäudeflügels. Die leichte Krümmung der Fassade korrespondiert mit der Kurve der querliegenden Wandscheiben, die über den Lehrwerkstätten ausläuft.

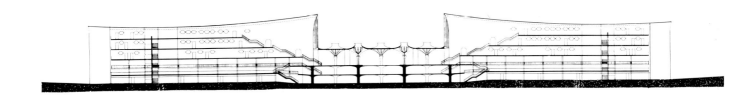

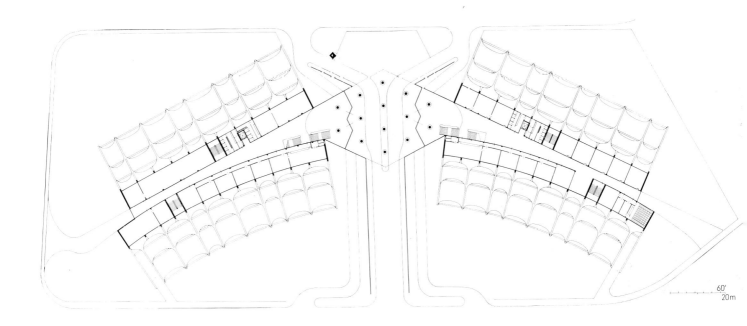

2. Longitudinal section.
3. First floor plan with class rooms. The corridors become narrower towards the ends of the building.
4. Facade detail. The extraneous parts of the supports also serve as sun blinds. The curvature motif is taken up by the roofs above the apprentice shops and the breast panels of the class rooms.

2. Längsschnitt.
3. Grundriß des ersten Obergeschosses mit Klassenräumen. Die Erschließungsflure werden zu den Gebäudeenden hin schmäler.
4. Fassadendetail. Die außenliegenden Stützenelemente dienen gleichzeitig als Sonnenblenden. Die Dächer über den Lehrwerkstätten und die Brüstungen der Unterrichtsräume nehmen das Kurvenmotiv auf.

1. Interior of the church, as seen from the main entrance towards the altar. Because of the transparent walls, the daylight is evenly dispersed. The bearing structure remains visible.

1. Innenansicht. Blick vom Haupteingang auf den Altar. Das Schiff wird durch die durchscheinenden Wände gleichmäßig belichtet. Das konstruktive Skelett bleibt sichtbar.

This parish church of an industrial suburb north-west of Milan stands on completely level ground in the centre of a large open space. The church precinct proper is surrounded by a rubble wall. The church has two entrances, viz. a main entrance which is reached via a ramp of steps and is mainly used on solemn occasions, and a subsidiary entrance at a lower level leading to chapel, confessionals and sacristy. Four reinforced concrete columns, tapered towards the top, support the precast concrete structure of the roof which consists of six beams of X-shaped cross-section carrying a roofing of rhombic concrete units. The walls are composed of a 1/4″ thick plastic foil inserted between glass panes.

Diese Pfarrkirche eines Industrievororts nordwestlich von Mailand steht auf völlig ebenem Gelände inmitten einer großen Grünfläche. Eine Feldsteinmauer umgibt den engeren Kirchenbezirk. Der Zugang erfolgt entweder über eine Treppenrampe zu dem Haupteingang, der vorzugsweise bei feierlichen Gelegenheiten benutzt wird, oder über einen etwas tiefer gelegenen Weg zum Nebeneingang in das Untergeschoß mit Kapelle, Beichtstühlen und der Sakristei. Vier Stahlbetonstützen, die sich nach oben verjüngen, tragen die Dachkonstruktion aus Beton-Fertigteilen. Sie setzt sich aus 6 x-förmigen Balken zusammen, auf denen die Dachhaut aus rhombischen Betonelementen aufliegt. Die Wände bestehen aus einer 2,5 mm dicken Plastikfolie zwischen Glasscheiben, die von leichten Metallrahmen gehalten werden.

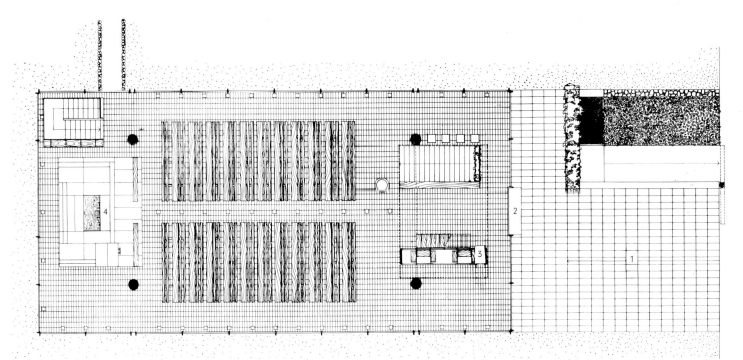

2. Plan at church floor level. Key: 1 Ramp of steps,
2 Main entrance, 3 Choir and organ gallery, 4 Altar.
3. Interior of the chapel at lower floor level.
4. General view. To the left of the crucifix is the sliding
door of the main entrance, extending over the full width
of one wall panel. On the right, the subsidiary entrance
leading to the lower floor from which an inside flight of
stairs leads up to the church proper.

2. Grundriß des Kirchengeschosses. Legende: 1 Treppenrampe, 2 Haupteingang, 3 Chor- und Orgelempore,
4 Altar.
3. Blick in die Kapelle des Untergeschosses.
4. Gesamtansicht. Links vom Kreuz die Schiebetür des
Haupteingangs in der Breite eines Wandfeldes, rechts
der tiefer gelegene Nebeneingang zum Untergeschoß,
von dem aus man über eine interne Treppe in die Kirche
hinaufsteigt.

"Sacra Famiglia" Parish Church in Genoa (1956—58)
Architects: Adolfo De Carlo, Andrea Mor, Ludovico Quaroni and Angelo Sibilla

Pfarrkirche Sacra Famiglia in Genua (1956—58)
Architekten: Adolfo De Carlo, Andrea Mor, Ludovico Quaroni und Angelo Sibilla

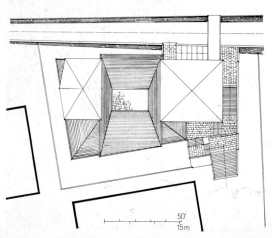

The church, situated in a suburb flanking the river Bisagno, is erected on older foundation walls. Because of the steeply sloping ground, the entire group of buildings, consisting of church, rectory and parish office, has access from several levels. The lowest level is taken up by parish hall and offices. On the level above are church and sacristy, on the highest level the priest's manse and a day nursery. Distinguished by a strict and sober design, by the absence of any obtrusive accents in the interior, and by its quasi-crenellated belfry, this house of worship is reminiscent of Genoa's medieval churches.

Die Kirche steht in der Vorstadt, die sich am Fluß Bisagno entlangzieht. Sie wurde auf alten Grundmauern errichtet. Der gesamte Komplex, bestehend aus Kirche, Pfarrhaus und Pfarramt, hat wegen des stark fallenden Geländes mehrere Zugänge auf verschiedenen Ebenen. Der Gemeindesaal und die sich anschließenden Pfarramtsräume liegen auf tiefstem Niveau. Darüber befinden sich Kirche und Sakristei und noch ein Geschoß höher die Wohnung des Pfarrers und ein Kindertagesheim. Die Strenge und Nüchternheit des Gotteshauses, sein von jeglichen kräftigen Akzenten freier Innenraum und die zinnenartigen Dachstützen des Glockenturms erinnern an die mittelalterlichen Kirchen Genuas.

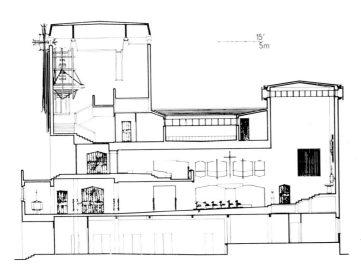

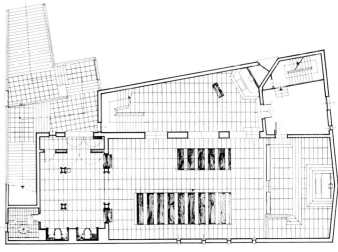

1. The large, ten metres high iron crucifix in the open corner of the belfry.
2. Site plan.
3. Longitudinal section.
4. Plan at church floor level.
5. General view of the church at the foot of the hill. The broad flight of stairs leads to the main portal of the church at the foot of the belfry. On the left, part of the aisle.

1. Das große, zehn Meter hohe Eisenkreuz in der offenen Ecke des Glockenturmes.
2. Lageplan.
3. Längsschnitt.
4. Grundriß des Kirchengeschosses.
5. Gesamtansicht der Kirche am Fuße des Steilhanges. Die breite Freitreppe führt zum Hauptportal der Kirche am Fuß des Turmes. Links der Ansatz des Seitenschiffes.

Church of the Madonna of the Poor at Baggio near Milan (1952—54)
Architects: Luigi Figini and Gino Pollini

Madonna der Armen, Kirche in Baggio bei Mailand (1952—54)
Architekten: Luigi Figini und Gino Pollini

The church is situated at the centre of the Ina-Casa housing estate at Baggio, near Milan. In their design, the architects have reduced their objectives to bare essentials: The building is conceived solely as a wrapping for the interior, and is therefore reminiscent of the mysticism of early Christian basilicas. Precisely calculated volumes of light of different intensities enter the room from above, submerging the altar zone in a flood of light, but letting the nave recede into subdued brightness. The reinforced concrete structure, free from any superfluous embellishments, bears witness to an architectural attitude which is far removed from the general conformity of official ecclesiastic architecture.

Die Kirche wurde im Zentrum der Ina-Casa-Siedlung in Baggio bei Mailand errichtet. In ihrem Entwurf reduzierten die Architekten die Bauaufgabe auf das Wesentliche: Die Kirche ist als reine Ausprägung des Innenraumes aufgefaßt und erinnert dadurch stark an die Mystik frühchristlicher Kirchen. Genau berechnete Lichtmengen verschiedener Intensität strömen von oben in den Raum, tauchen den Altarbezirk in eine Flut von Licht und lassen das Hauptschiff in seiner gedämpften Helligkeit zurücktreten. Die von allen überflüssigen Details freie Stahlbetonkonstruktion ist das Abbild einer Architekturauffassung, die sich weit vom allgemeinen Konformismus der offiziellen Kirchenarchitektur entfernt.

1. Pulpit and altar seen from the nave. The roof is raised above the altar.

1. Blick aus dem Hauptschiff auf Kanzel und Altar, über dem die Raumhöhe zunimmt.

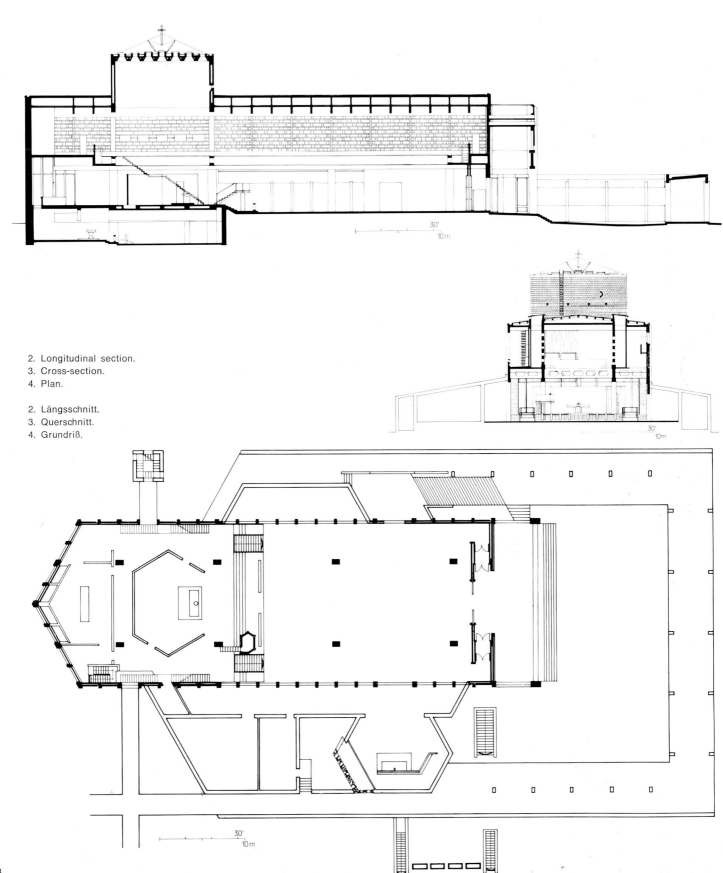

2. Longitudinal section.
3. Cross-section.
4. Plan.

2. Längsschnitt.
3. Querschnitt.
4. Grundriß.

5. Church interior at night.
6. Crypt.
7. The volume of light entering through the raised roof above the altar is skilfully distributed so that clearly marked zones of different brightness are formed. The nave receives daylight through the apertures between the precast concrete blocks of the upper storey. The subdivision of the interior into zones of different brightness is further emphasized by the open-web concrete beam across the front of the altar zone.

5. Nachtaufnahme.
6. Blick in die Krypta.
7. Die aus der kuppelähnlichen Erhöhung über dem Altarbereich einfallende Lichtmenge wird geschickt so verteilt, daß sich fest umrissene Raumbezirke verschiedener Helligkeit bilden. Das Hauptschiff erhält Tageslicht über die Öffnungen zwischen den Betonblocksteinen des Obergadens. Die lichttechnische Teilung des Kirchenraums wird verstärkt durch die Anordnung des Betonträgers quer über dem Altarbereich.

San Giovanni Church near Florence (1961)
Architect: Giovanni Michelucci

Kirche San Giovanni bei Florenz (1961)
Architekt: Giovanni Michelucci

The church, dedicated to the memory of the workers who lost their lives during the construction of the Autostrada del Sole, stands against the picturesque background of the Tuscan landscape in the vicinity of Florence. With its consistent design, the church must no doubt be counted among Michelucci's most integrated and interesting works. The characteristic dynamic design of the interior is mainly intended to give the worshippers a sense of protection, an impression which has been achieved despite the seemingly contrasting materials. The heavy rubble masonry, reminiscent of medieval buildings, is in harmony with the fantastic concrete structures supporting the roof. The integrity of the building is also emphasized by the partial downward extension of the copper roof.

1. The church seen from north-east. In the centre, the side entrance near the main altar. The coarse rubble walls are in contrast with the ribbed copper roofing which, with its vertical texture, mitigates the apparent weightiness of the stone walls.

1. Ansicht der Kirche von Nordosten. In der Bildmitte der Nebeneingang beim Hauptaltar. Die groben Natursteinmauern kontrastieren zu der gerippten Kupferhaut des Daches, dessen vertikale Strukturierung der lastenden Schwere der Steinwände entgegenwirkt.

Die Kirche, die dem Andenken der beim Bau der Autostrada del Sole ums Leben gekommenen Arbeiter gewidmet ist, steht in der Nähe von Florenz vor dem malerischen Hintergrund der toskanischen Landschaft. Sie ist wegen ihrer einheitlichen Gestaltung ohne Zweifel zu den geschlossensten und interessantesten Werken Micheluccis zu zählen. Der dynamische, eigenwillig gestaltete Kirchenraum soll dem Gläubigen vor allem das Gefühl der Geborgenheit vermitteln, ein Eindruck, der trotz scheinbar gegensätzlicher Materialien erreicht wird. Das schwere Mauerwerk aus Natursteinen geht ohne Bruch mit den phantastischen Betonkonstruktionen zusammen, die die Decken stützen. Auch das teilweise weit heruntergezogene Kupferdach unterstreicht die Geschlossenheit des Bauwerks.

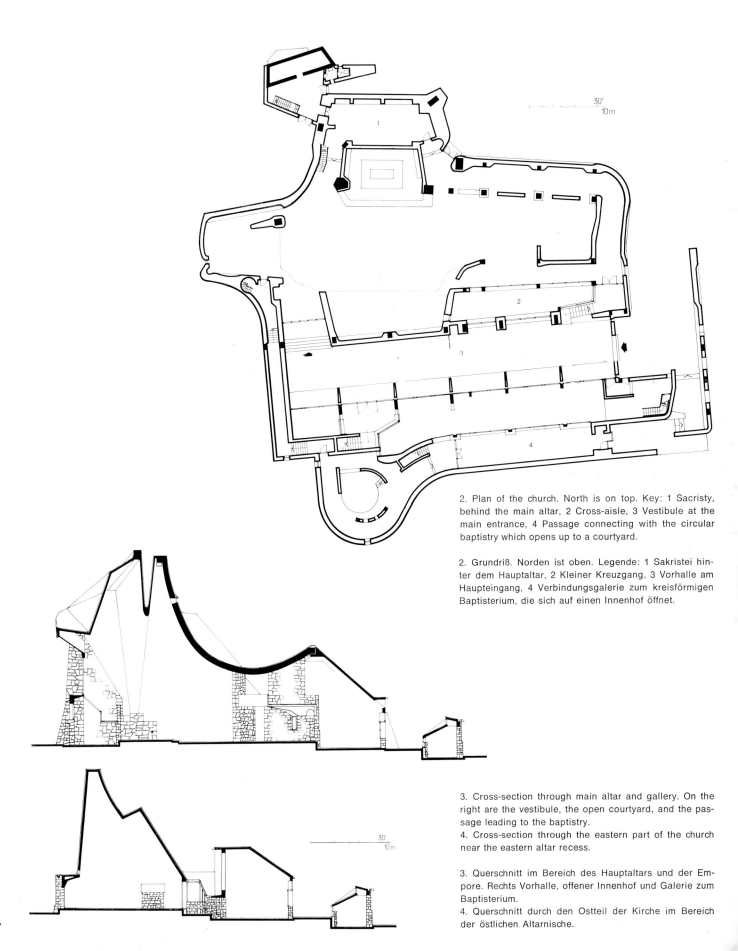

2. Plan of the church. North is on top. Key: 1 Sacristy, behind the main altar, 2 Cross-aisle, 3 Vestibule at the main entrance, 4 Passage connecting with the circular baptistry which opens up to a courtyard.

2. Grundriß. Norden ist oben. Legende: 1 Sakristei hinter dem Hauptaltar, 2 Kleiner Kreuzgang, 3 Vorhalle am Haupteingang, 4 Verbindungsgalerie zum kreisförmigen Baptisterium, die sich auf einen Innenhof öffnet.

3. Cross-section through main altar and gallery. On the right are the vestibule, the open courtyard, and the passage leading to the baptistry.
4. Cross-section through the eastern part of the church near the eastern altar recess.

3. Querschnitt im Bereich des Hauptaltars und der Empore. Rechts Vorhalle, offener Innenhof und Galerie zum Baptisterium.
4. Querschnitt durch den Ostteil der Kirche im Bereich der östlichen Altarnische.

5. Interior of the nave with the west altar. On the right are the steps leading to the main altar. The sagging roof is reminiscent of a tent. Daylight enters through a number of apertures, most of them not visible, high-lighting certain zones and leaving others to recede into semi-darkness.

6. High altar, with the glass window above the sacristy. The supports looking like petrified trees play an important part in the sculptural treatment of the interior.

7. Interior of cross-aisle.

5. Blick in das Kirchenschiff und auf den Westaltar. Rechts die Stufen zum Hauptaltar. Die durchhängende Decke erinnert an ein Zelt. Durch verschieden gestaltete, zu einem Großteil nicht sichtbare Öffnungen fällt Licht ins Innere, hebt Raumbereiche hervor und läßt andere in ein unbestimmtes Halbdunkel zurücktreten.

6. Der Hochaltar mit dem Glasfenster über der Sakristei. Die Stützen, die wie steinerne Bäume wirken, spielen bei der plastischen Modellierung des Raumes eine wichtige Rolle.

7. Blick in den kleinen Kreuzgang.

Museum for Modern Art in Turin (1954—59)
Architects: Carlo Bassi and Goffredo Boschetti

Museum für Moderne Kunst in Turin (1954—59)
Architekten: Carlo Bassi und Goffredo Boschetti

1. Aerial photograph.
2. Cross-section of the central building.

1. Luftaufnahme des Gesamtkomplexes.
2. Querschnitt durch den Zentralbau.

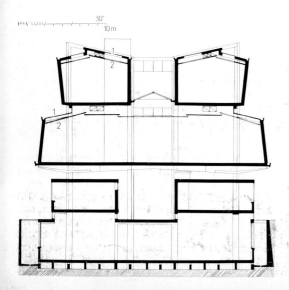

The museum is situated at the Corso Galileo Ferraris, occupying an island site surrounded by streets. The group consists of three buildings of Z-shaped plan, so arranged that the axis of the central building connecting the two wings is taken diagonally across the rectangular site. The central building is reserved for permanent displays. The smaller west wing is used for temporary exhibitions whilst the third wing contains a lecture room and library. All the exhibition rooms have top lighting. As the section of the central building shows, this has been achieved by cantilevering the first floor, splaying the outer walls at different angles, and placing a light-well in the centre of the building.

Das Museum liegt am Corso Galileo Ferraris auf einem rings von Straßen umgebenen inselartigen Grundstück. Der Komplex besteht aus drei Bauten. Sie sind in Form eines Z so angeordnet, daß die Längsachse des die beiden Flügel verbindenden Zentralbaues diagonal über das Rechteck des Grundstücks geführt ist. Der Zentralbau dient Dauerausstellungen, im kleineren Westflügel finden Wechselausstellungen statt, und der dritte Trakt enthält einen Vortragssaal und die Bibliothek. Alle Ausstellungsräume haben Oberlicht. Wie der Schnitt zeigt, wurde dies beim Zentralbau durch das Auskragen des ersten Obergeschosses, durch die unterschiedlichen Neigungswinkel der Außenwände und den Lichtschacht in der Mitte des Gebäudes erreicht.

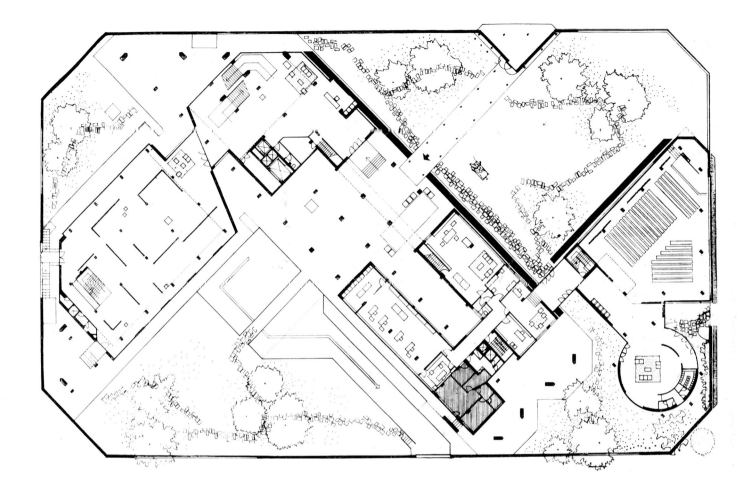

3. Ground floor plan.
4. Detail of the end wall of the central building, distinguished by its three-dimensional treatment.
5. Entrance side of the central building with the covered way leading from the street to the main entrance.

3. Erdgeschoßgrundriß der Gesamtanlage.
4. Detail der stark plastisch durchgeformten Stirnfront des Zentralbaues.
5. Die Zugangsseite des Zentralbaues mit dem überdachten Weg von der Straße zum Haupteingang.

6. Interior of one of the exhibition rooms on the first floor. The paintings are hung on freely placed display screens.

7. The main stairs have separate flights for up and down traffic.

8. Garden area, seen from the main entrance, with a fountain in the foreground on the right. The verge of gardens surrounding the buildings is meant to form a transition and buffer zone between the latter and the outer world.

6. Blick in einen Ausstellungsraum des ersten Obergeschosses. Die Bilder hängen an frei stehenden Stellwänden.

7. Die Haupttreppe setzt sich aus zwei Treppenläufen zusammen, von denen der eine zum Hinaufsteigen und der andere zum Hinabgehen dient.

8. Blick vom Haupteingang auf die Grünzone. Rechts im Vordergrund ein Springbrunnen. Der die Gebäude umgebende Grünstreifen soll als Übergangs- und Pufferzone zwischen dem Innen und Außen wirken.

1. Part of the lakeside facade, dominated by the interplay of the penetrating and intersecting horizontal, vertical and curved lines.

1. Teilansicht der seeseitigen Fassade, mit dem Spiel der sich durchdringenden und überschneidenden horizontalen, vertikalen und gekrümmten Linien.

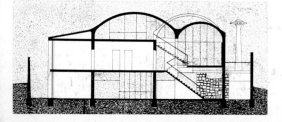

The design for this restaurant dates back to the "fanciful" period of this architect's activities. Its attraction is mainly due to the plastic treatment and the simplicity of the structure. The large arches, integrated with the column-borne terraces which project towards the lake, convey an impression of lightness as if the structure were floating above the ground. The restaurant zone is mainly confined to the terraces and the glass-curtained rooms facing the lake.

Das Restaurant gehört zu den Bauten aus der »phantastischen« Periode des Architekten. Es besticht vor allem durch seine Plastizität und die Einfachheit der angewendeten konstruktiven Mittel. Große Bögen erwecken zusammen mit den auf Stützen gestellten Terrassen, die sich zum See vorschieben, den Eindruck der Schwerelosigkeit und lösen den Bau vom Boden. Der Restaurationsbereich beschränkt sich in der Hauptsache auf die Terrassen und die seeseitigen, voll verglasten Räume.

2. Cross-section of the building just behind the facades. An interesting feature is the staggering of the floor levels in the partly two-storeyed, partly three-storeyed building.
3. Restaurant room on the upper floor. The stairs in the foreground lead to the upper gallery under the higher arch.
4. The restaurant, seen from the lake.

2. Schnitt durch das Gebäude hinter der Fassadenebene. Interessant die Versetzung der Geschoßebenen in dem zwei- und dreigeschossigen Gebäude.
3. Blick in den Restaurationsraum des Obergeschosses. Die im Vordergrund sichtbare Treppe führt auf die vom größeren Bogen umschlossene Empore.
4. Gesamtansicht des Restaurants vom See aus.

Riding Hall of the Turin Riding Club (1960–61)
Architects: Roberto Gabetti, Aimaro Oreglia D'Isola and Giuseppe Raineri

Reithalle des Turiner Reitclubs (1960–61)
Architekten: Roberto Gabetti, Aimaro Oreglia D'Isola und Giuseppe Raineri

1. Bird's eye view. The riding hall receives daylight through high-level ribbons of windows.

1. Gesamtansicht aus der Vogelschau. Die Reithalle erhält über hochliegende Fensterbänder Tageslicht.

The Riding Hall of the Turin Riding Club is situated between Turin and Stupinigi. The characteristically shaped building, conceived as a monoblock and dominated by the large, clearly discernible, prismatic roof structure, is in stark contrast to its surroundings. The riding hall proper is placed in the centre and flanked by stables, fodder rooms, changing rooms, offices and club premises. The grandeur of the roof is enhanced by the arcade which surrounds the entire building.

Die Reithalle des Turiner Reitclubs steht zwischen Turin und Stupinigi. Der Komplex, der als ein einheitlicher geschlossener Block konzipiert wurde, hebt sich von seiner Umgebung durch seine eigenwillige Gestaltung ab, die durch das gewaltige, klar gegliederte prismatische Volumen des Daches bestimmt wird. Um die in der Mitte liegende Reithalle gruppieren sich Stallungen, Futterkammern, Umkleideräume, Büros und Clubräume. Ein um das ganze Gebäude geführter Laubengang unterstreicht die großflächige Wirkung des Daches.

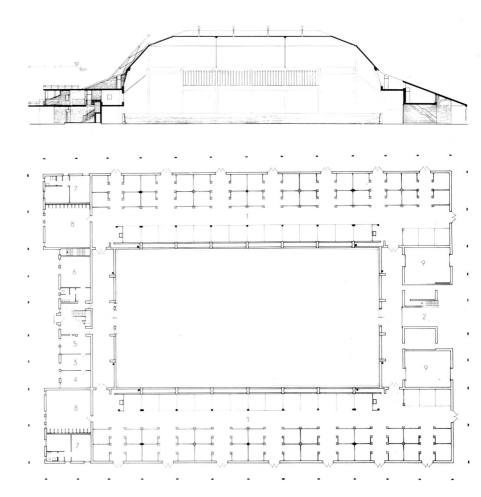

2. Longitudinal section.
3. Ground floor plan. Key: 1 Stables, 2 Entrance, 3 Administration, 4 Chairman, 5 Secretary, 6 Office, 7 Dwelling, 8 Harness room, 9 Fodder room.
4. Front view. The vast, integral roof is interrupted by a balcony which extends over the full width of the entrance hall.

2. Längsschnitt.
3. Grundriß des Erdgeschosses. Legende: 1 Stallungen, 2 Eingang, 3 Verwaltung, 4 Vorsitzender, 5 Sekretariat, 6 Büro, 7 Wohnung, 8 Sattelkammer, 9 Futterkammer.
4. Frontalansicht. Die geschlossene Dachfläche wird über dem Eingang durch einen Balkon unterbrochen, dessen Breite der der Eingangshalle entspricht.

Olympic Ice Rink at Cortina d'Ampezzo (1952—55)
Architects: Mario Ghedina, Riccardo Nalli and Francesco Uras

Olympisches Eislaufstadion in Cortina d'Ampezzo (1952—55)
Architekten: Mario Ghedina, Riccardo Nalli und Francesco Uras

The Ice Rink, situated in the heart of the Dolomites, was built for the skating events of the Olympic Winter Games in 1956. The stands, surrounding the Ice Rink on three sides, have three tiers of seat rows, one above the other. The space behind the rows of seats is used for cloak rooms and changing rooms. The architects were obviously inspired by Alpine styles. This is apparent from the type of roofing, reminiscent of Alpine cottages, and also from the extensive use of wood for the cladding of the reinforced concrete structure.

Das Eislaufstadion im Herzen der Dolomiten wurde für die Olympischen Winterspiele 1956 gebaut. Die Eisfläche wird auf drei Seiten von dem Tribünengebäude mit den drei übereinander angeordneten Zuschauerrängen umschlossen. In dem hinter den Sitzreihen verbleibenden Raum sind Toiletten und Umkleideräume untergebracht. Offensichtlich verwendeten die Architekten alpenländische Stilelemente. Dies läßt sich einerseits an der Art der Dacheindeckung erkennen, die an Bauernhäuser erinnert, und andererseits an der reichlichen Verwendung von Holz, mit dem die Stahlbetonkonstruktion verkleidet ist.

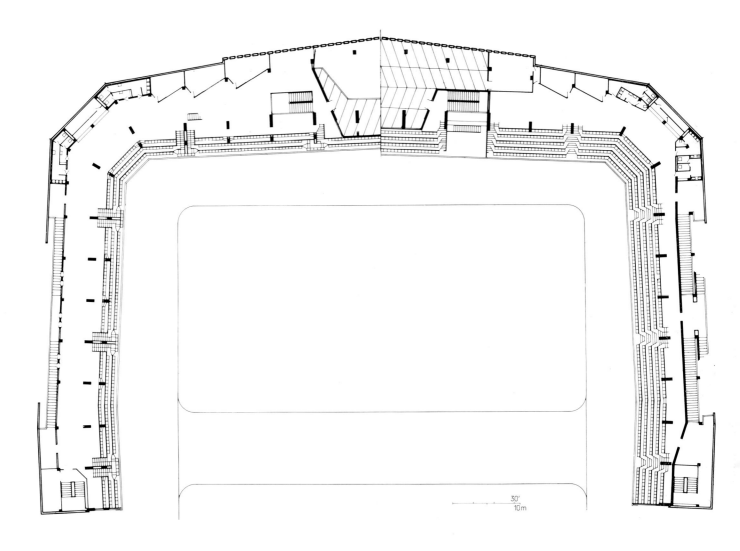

1. General view of the Ice Rink with two of the three stands which conform to a U-shaped plan.
2. The tiers are arranged almost vertically one above the other and the rows of seats rise so steeply that each spectator has an unimpeded view.
3. Plan of upper tiers (left) and lower tiers (right).
4. Section of a stand.

1. Blick über die Eisfläche auf zwei Schenkel der Tribünenanlage, die U-förmig angelegt ist.
2. Ausschnitt. Die Ränge liegen fast vertikal übereinander und sind sehr steil gestuft, so daß jeder Besucher gute Sicht hat.
3. Grundriß. Links die höher gelegenen Ränge, rechts die untersten Ränge.
4. Querschnitt durch das Tribünengebäude.

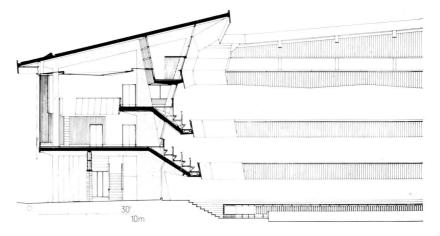

Stadium in Naples (1955—57)

Architects: Carlo Cocchia, Sergio Bonamico, Dagoberto Ortensi, Claudio Dall'Olio, Luigi De Simoni, Mario Ghedina, Mario Procesi and Francesco Uras. Civil Engineer: Attilio Linari

1. A view of the two tiers. The upper tier serves as a roof for part of the lower tier.

1. Blick auf die beiden Ränge, von denen der obere als Dach für einen Teil der unteren Sitzreihen dient.

The stadium, designed for 60 000 spectators, has two tiers, with the upper tier serving as a roof for part of the lower tier. The latter is placed directly on the ground. In contrast, the upper tier seats, which consist of step-shaped beams, are carried by 56 supports of exposed reinforced concrete and by widely cantilevered beams. As any superfluous trimmings have been omitted, the stadium — and particulary its interior — demonstrates the beauty of the purely functional design — an effect which is further enhanced by the apparent weightlessness of the seemingly floating upper tier.

2. Exterior of one of the stairways leading to the upper tier which are force-locked between the disc-shaped concrete supports.

2. Außenansicht einer der Treppen zum oberen Rang, die zwischen die tragenden Betonscheiben eingespannt sind.

Pages / Seiten 112, 113.

3. Plan of the lower tier.
4. A view of the upper tier which is accessible from a closely spaced system of stairways from the bottom as well as from the top.
5. Part of the exterior of the stadium. Only the upper tier is visible, as the lower tier is below ground level.

3. Grundriß des unteren Ranges.
4. Blick auf den oberen Rang, der über ein dichtes System von Treppen sowohl von unten als auch von oben erschlossen wird.
5. Teilansicht des Stadions von außen. Nur der obere Rang ist sichtbar, der untere liegt unter Niveau.

Das 60 000 Zuschauer fassende Stadion hat zwei übereinanderliegende Ränge, von denen der obere den unteren zum Teil überdeckt. Der tiefer gelegene Rang ruht unmittelbar auf dem Erdboden. Die oberen Sitzreihen dagegen, die sich aus gestuften, balkenförmigen Elementen zusammensetzen, werden von 56 schalungsroh belassenen Stahlbetonstützen und weit ausladenden Kragbalken getragen. Durch den Verzicht auf jedes überflüssige Beiwerk zeigt das Stadion, vor allem in der Innenansicht, die Schönheit der rein zweckgebundenen Form, deren Wirkung noch durch die Leichtigkeit des scheinbar schwebenden oberen Ranges gesteigert wird.

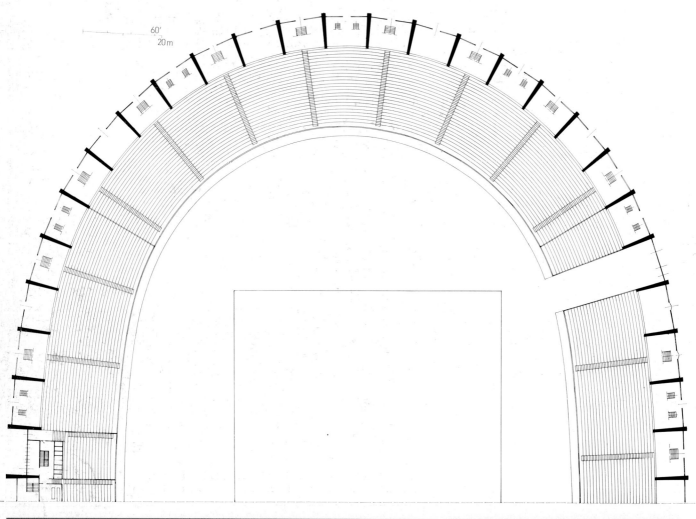

1. The Cycle Track, seen from one of the short sides.
2. Plan. Key: 1 Cycle track, 2 Grandstand, 3 Opposite stand, 4 Grandstand building with ancillary rooms for reporters, officials, etc., 5 Box offices, 6 Entrance, 7 Cyclists' camp with changing rooms, offices and lounges, 8 Bar and toilets, 9 Entrance ramps to the track, 10 Ball games.
3. Section of grandstand and mound.

1. Gesamtansicht in Richtung der kürzeren Achse.
2. Grundriß. Legende: 1 Rennbahn, 2 Haupttribüne, 3 Gegentribüne, 4 Tribünengebäude mit Nebenräumen für Reporter, Wettkampfleitung usw., 5 Kasse, 6 Eingang, 7 Fahrerlager mit Umkleide-, Büro- und Aufenthaltsräumen, 8 Bar und Toiletten, 9 Zufahrten zur Rennbahn, 10 Spielfeld.
3. Schnitt durch Haupttribüne und Wall.

The Cycle Track built for the Olympic Summer Games in 1960 is part of a larger sports centre. At sports venues of more conventional type, it was usually impossible to offer all the spectators an equally good view of the track. This problem has here been solved by the novel and ingenious arrangement of the tiers. The seats are staggered not only amphitheatrically but also within each row, i.e., the seats of each row, combined in pairs, are slightly staggered in height. This arrangement has the incidental advantage of preventing overcrowding. This original solution has given excellent results. With the exception of the concrete-built grandstand, the circumference of the Cycle Track consists of earth mounds.

Die aus Anlaß der Olympischen Sommerspiele des Jahres 1960 errichtete Radrennbahn gehört zu einem größeren Sportzentrum. In den herkömmlichen Bauten dieser Art war es nicht möglich, allen Zuschauern eine gleich gute Sicht auf die Rennbahn zu bieten. Dieses Problem wurde hier durch die wohlüberlegte Anordnung der Ränge gelöst. Neu ist, daß die Sitze nicht nur vertikal in Form einer Treppe gestuft angelegt sind. Jede Sitzreihe wird außerdem noch in der Horizontalen abgetreppt. Das heißt, die Bankreihen sind in — in der Höhe gegeneinander versetzte — Doppelsitze aufgelöst. Damit wird zugleich eine Überbesetzung unmöglich gemacht. Mit dieser originellen Lösung wurden ausgezeichnete Resultate erzielt. Die Wälle der Radrennbahn sind aus Erde aufgeschüttet, mit Ausnahme der in Beton errichteten Haupttribüne.

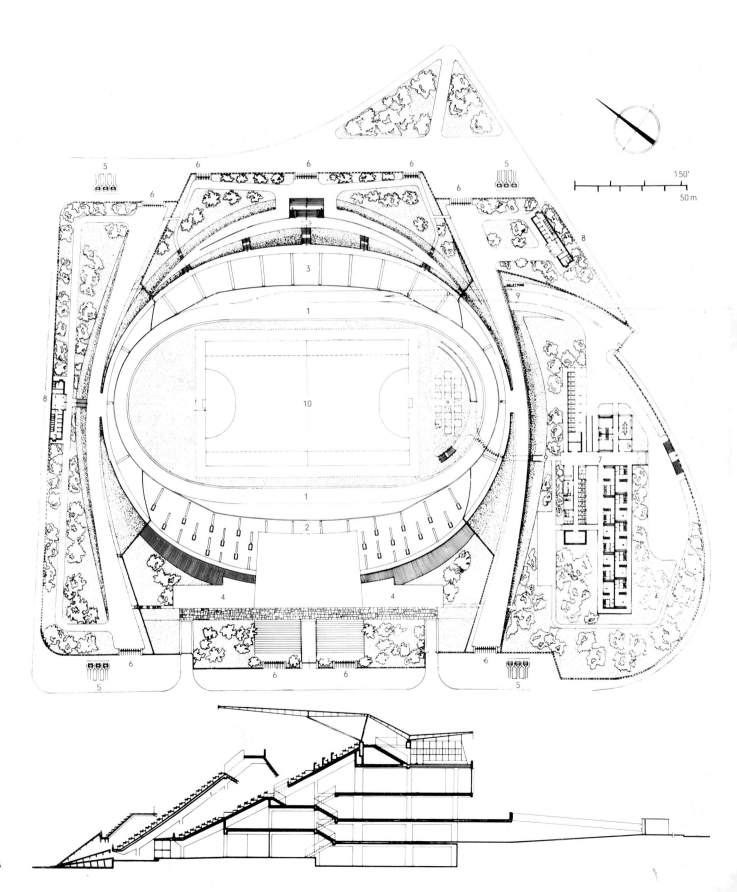

4. A view of the grandstand. The slight vertical stagger of adjacent pairs of seats is clearly visible.
5. This view in the longitudinal direction reveals the contours of the stands which are concentrated on the long sides of the stadium.
6. Aerial view from south-east.

4. Blick auf die Zuschauerränge. Man erkennt deutlich die in der Höhe gegeneinander versetzten Doppelsitze.
5. Der Blick in der Längsachse zeigt den Höhenabfall der Zuschauerränge, die sich so auf die Längsseiten der Anlage konzentrieren.
6. Luftaufnahme von Südosten.

Bathing establishment at the Viale Zara in Milan (1956—58)
Architects: Egizio Nichelli and Gino Bozzetti

Schwimmsportzentrum am Viale Zara in Mailand (1956—58)
Architekten: Egizio Nichelli und Gino Bozzetti

This bathing establishment with three swimming pools is among the most interesting modern sports venues in Italy. It is distinguished by its consistent sculptural treatment and aesthetic integrity. The zone reserved for bathing is strictly separated from that for spectators. People using the swimming pools pass from the main entrance of the central building through the changing rooms and shower baths whilst spectators and other visitors use a second entrance leading directly to the restaurant and the adjacent gardens. Bathers and non-bathers are also separated in the three-level restaurant where the former use the ground floor and the latter the upper floor. The basement is taken up by staff and catering premises. Changing cabins and shower baths are in the main building which is placed parallel to the swimming pools. Its basement contains technical installations and further cloakrooms.

Dieses Schwimmsportzentrum mit drei Becken gehört zu den interessantesten italienischen Sportanlagen aus jüngerer Zeit. Es zeichnet sich durch die einheitliche plastische Durchbildung und formale Ausgewogenheit aus. Die Zone für Badegäste ist streng vom Bereich für Nichtbadende getrennt. Badegäste benützen den Weg vom Haupteingang zum Hauptgebäude mit den Umkleideräumen und Duschen; Zuschauer und andere Besucher gelangen über einen zweiten Zugang direkt zum Restaurant mit der anschließenden Gartenanlage. Auch in dem dreigeschossigen Restaurant werden unter den Gästen Badende und Nichtbadende unterschieden: erstere nehmen im Erdgeschoß Platz, letzteren ist das Obergeschoß vorbehalten. Im Untergeschoß liegen Personal- und Wirtschaftsräume. Umkleideräume und Duschen sind in dem großen Hauptgebäude untergebracht, das parallel zu den Becken verläuft. Im Untergeschoß befinden sich technische Einrichtungen und weitere Garderoben.

1. General view. In the foreground are the two larger swimming pools, in the background the diving tower at the third pool. On the right is the main building with the changing cabins and shower baths. The restaurant is in the building at the far end.

1. Gesamtansicht. Im Vordergrund die beiden größeren Becken, im Hintergrund der Sprungturm mit dem dritten Becken. Rechts davon das Hauptgebäude mit den Umkleidekabinen und Duschen. Im Quertrakt das Restaurant.

118

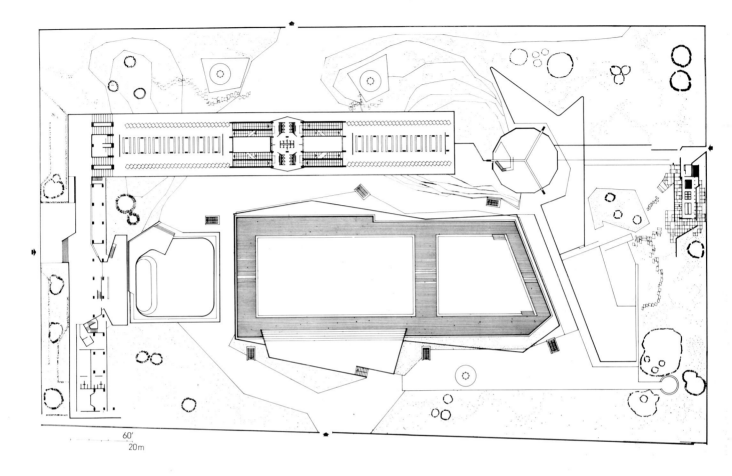

2. Site plan.
3. Typical floor plan of the main building. Key: 1 Cloak rooms, 2 Changing cabins, 3 Showers.
4. Longitudinal section of the main building.

2. Lageplan.
3. Normalgeschoßgrundriß des Hauptgebäudes. Legende: 1 Kleiderablage, 2 Umkleidekabinen, 3 Duschen.
4. Längsschnitt durch das Hauptgebäude.

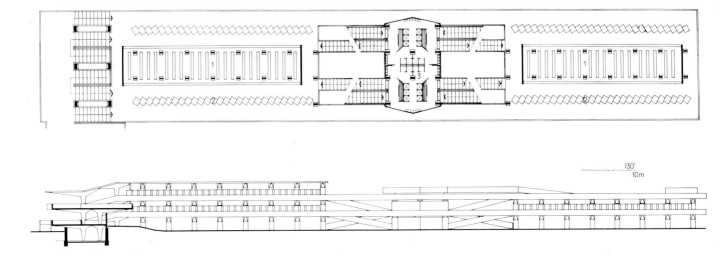

5. Main building and deep swimming pool, seen from the passage below the bridge at the small diving pool.
6. In the background the diving tower, in the foreground the deep swimming pool.

5. Blick aus der Passage unter der Verbindungsbrücke am Sprungbecken auf Hauptgebäude und Schwimmbekken.
6. Blick auf den Sprungturm. Im Vordergrund das Freischwimmbecken.

7. The flight of stairs visible on the right leads to the
main building with the changing cabins.
8. Bathing zone seen from the surrounding roof terrace.

7. Die vorne rechts sichtbare Treppe führt zum Hauptgebäude mit den Umkleidekabinen.
8. Ansicht der Badezone von der oberen umlaufenden
Terrasse aus.

1. General view. The centre of the shell is formed by a circular lantern.
2. Section.
3. Ground floor plan. The ancillary premises are situated below the upper rows of seats.

1. Gesamtansicht. Im Zentrum der Kuppel eine kreisförmige Dachlaterne.
2. Schnitt.
3. Grundriß des Erdgeschosses. Die Nebenräume liegen unter den oberen Sitzreihen.

The Minor Palace was built for the Olympic Games in 1960 and is situated in the Sports Ground of the City at the Viale Tiziano. Designed for 4000 to 5000 spectators, the hall is covered by a hemispherical shell roof of 60 metres (197 ft.) diameter, consisting of precast reinforced concrete units. The load is transmitted by 36 Y-shaped reinforced concrete supports to the 2,5 metres (8'2") wide prestressed concrete ring serving as foundation. Toilets, store rooms and caretaker's flat are accommodated in the ring zone below the seats. Lucidity of interior and exterior design is the outstanding feature of this building which can be regarded as a prototype of structural harmony.

Der Kleine Sportpalast wurde im Hinblick auf die Olympischen Spiele 1960 erbaut und liegt im Sportgelände der Stadt am Viale Tiziano. Die Halle für 4000–5000 Zuschauer ist mit einer kugelschalenförmigen Kuppel von 60 m Durchmesser aus vorgefertigten Stahlbetonelementen überdacht, deren Last durch 36 Y-förmige Stahlbetonstützen auf den 2,5 m breiten, vorgespannten Stahlbetonring des Fundamentes übertragen wird. Die Toiletten, Lagerräume und die Wohnung des Hausmeisters wurden in der unter den Sitzreihen liegenden Ringzone untergebracht. Konstruktive Klarheit im Innen- und Außenbau sind die wesentlichen Merkmale dieses Bauwerks, das ein Musterbeispiel baulicher Harmonie darstellt.

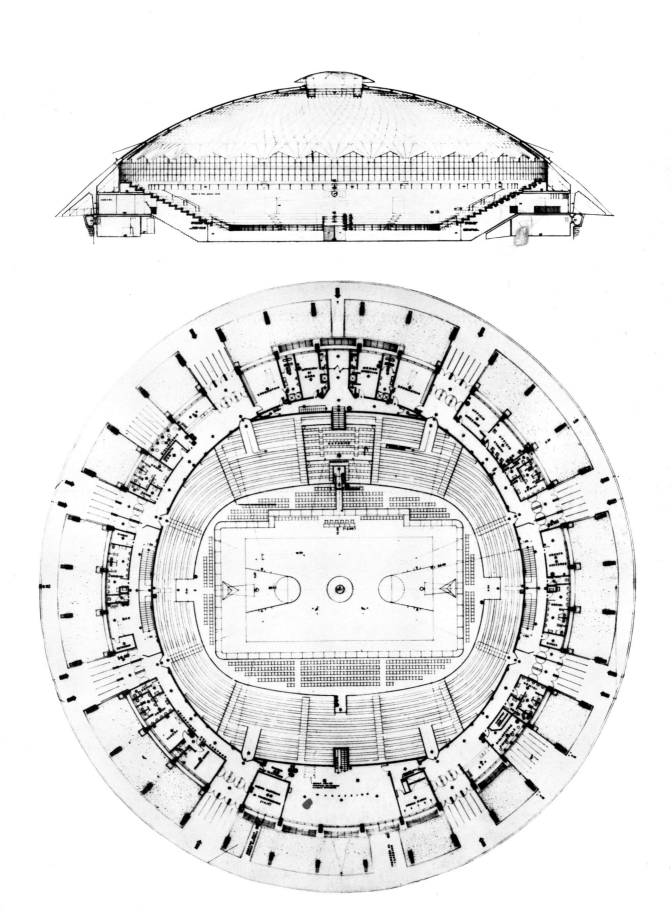

4. The plan shows the arrangement of the seats and the Y-shaped supports. At the top of the latter, the roof shell has a diameter of 60 metres (197 ft).
5. Interior of the roof shell with the network of interpenetrating ribs, consisting of 1620 precast reinforced concrete units.

4. Der Grundriß zeigt die Anordnung der Sitzreihen und der Y-förmigen Stützen. Die Kuppel hat am oberen Ende der Stützen einen Durchmeser von 60 m.
5. Detailaufnahme der Kuppel von innen mit den sich netzförmig durchdringenden Rippen aus 1620 Stahlbeton-Fertigteilen.

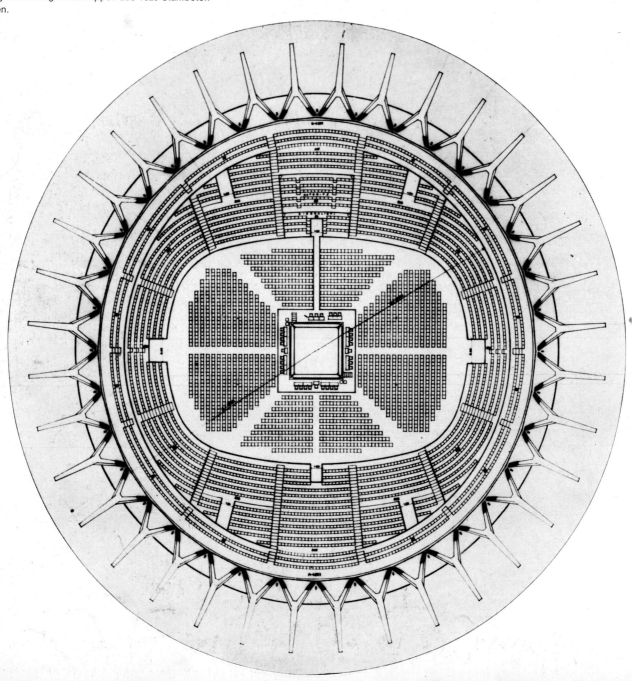

6. A close-up of the transition between roof shell and support.
7. One of the eight entrances for spectators.
8. Interior of the hall, seen from the lower gallery.

6. Blick auf die Nahtstelle zwischen Kuppel und Stützen.
7. Einer der acht Zuschauereingänge.
8. Blick von der unten umlaufenden Galerie in die Halle.

Sports Palace in Rome (1958—60)
Civil engineering design: P. L. Nervi. Planning: P. L. Nervi and M. Piacentini
Sportpalast in Rom (1958—60)
Entwurf: P. L. Nervi. Planung: P. L. Nervi und M. Piacentini

1. Interior of the cupola which is composed of a series of precast reinforced concrete ribs.
2. Section. The cupola has a diameter of 100 metres (328 ft) and is carried by inclined supports which transmit the vault thrust to the foundations.
3. Plan at gallery level.

1. Detailansicht der Kuppel, die sich aus einer Reihe von vorgefertigten Stahlbetonrippen zusammensetzt.
2. Schnitt. Die Kuppel hat einen Durchmesser von 100 m und wird von geneigten Stützen getragen, die den Gewölbeschub auf die Fundamente ableiten.
3. Grundriß in Höhe der umlaufenden Galerie.

The Sports Palace, built for the Olympic Games in 1960, is designed for 16 000 spectators and can be used for a great variety of sports or artistic events. Twelve stairways lead to the three tiers of amphitheatrically arranged seats. The hall is roofed by a hemispherical shell of 100 metres (328 ft.) diameter with ribs of precast reinforced concrete units. The vault thrust is transmitted to the foundations through inclined supports. The circular outer wall of the hall is completely glazed.

Der für die Olympischen Spiele 1960 erbaute Sportpalast hat 16 000 Plätze und kann für die verschiedensten Massenveranstaltungen sportlicher oder künstlerischer Art verwendet werden. Über zwölf Treppenaufgänge gelangt das Publikum zu den drei Rängen mit ihren stufenartig ansteigenden Sitzreihen. Das Gebäude ist mit einer halbkugelförmigen Kuppel von 100 m Durchmesser überdacht, deren Rippen aus vorgefertigten Stahlbetonelementen bestehen. Der Gewölbeschub wird über schräggestellte Stützen auf die Fundamente übertragen. Das Ringstück, das die Außenfront der Halle abschließt, ist voll verglast.

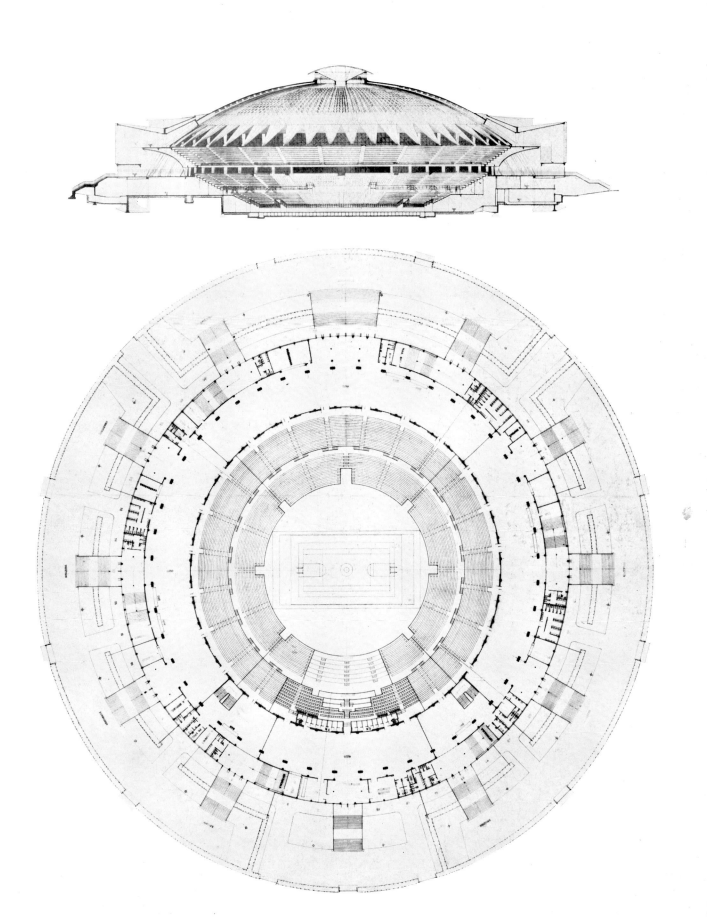

130

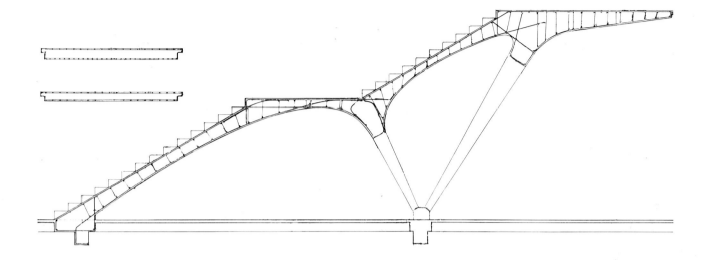

4. The Sports Palace at night.
5. Interior. The floodlights are mounted in the lantern of the cupola.
6. Steel reinforcement of the internal flights of stairs.
7. One of the internal flights of stairs with its inclined supports.

4. Ansicht der Sporthalle bei Nacht.
5. Innenansicht. Die Scheinwerfer sind in der Dachlaterne angebracht.
6. Bewehrungsplan der inneren Treppen.
7. Blick auf eine der inneren, auf Stützen ruhenden Treppen.

Flower Market at Pescia (1951)
Architects: Emilio Brizzi, Enzo and Giuseppe Gori, L. Ricci and L. Savioli

Blumenmarkthalle in Pescia (1951)
Architekten: Emilio Brizzi, Enzo und Giuseppe Gori, L. Ricci und L. Savioli

The design of the market hall is based on one that was awarded a prize in a competition held in 1948. The market area is covered by a shell roof which is supported by triangular concrete piers and is otherwise open on all four sides. The weight of the roof is transferred to the supporting piers by means of segmental arches. The space between these piers, which absorb the vault thrust in the diagonal direction, remains open so that cross-ventilation is available all the time. The roof merely serves as a protection against rain and sun. Goods are delivered at the short sides of the hall whilst the long sides are taken up by store rooms. The building also contains a bank, a bar, and a shop selling pest control agents.

Die Markthalle entstand auf der Grundlage eines preisgekrönten Wettbewerbsentwurfs aus dem Jahre 1948. Ihre Verkaufsfläche wird von einer nach allen vier Seiten offenen, gewölbten Dachschale überspannt, die auf dreieckförmigen Betonscheiben ruht. Die Dachlast wird durch Segmentbögen auf die Stützscheiben übertragen. Der Raum zwischen diesen Scheiben, die den Gewölbeschub in der Diagonalen ableiten, bleibt offen, so daß eine ständige Querlüftung möglich ist. Die Dachschale dient lediglich als Schutz gegen Regen und Sonne. Die Warenanlieferung erfolgt über die Stirnseiten der Halle. An den Längsfronten liegen Lagerräume. Eine Bank, eine Bar und ein Geschäft für Schädlingsbekämpfungsmittel ergänzen das Bauprogramm.

1. The large area covered by the roof shell is bordered, on either side, by five forecourts formed by the space between the store rooms and the concrete piers.
2. Cross-section.

1. Die große von der Dachschale überdeckte Fläche wird nach den Seiten durch fünf Höfe begrenzt, die zwischen den Lagerräumen und den Stützscheiben entstehen.
2. Querschnitt.

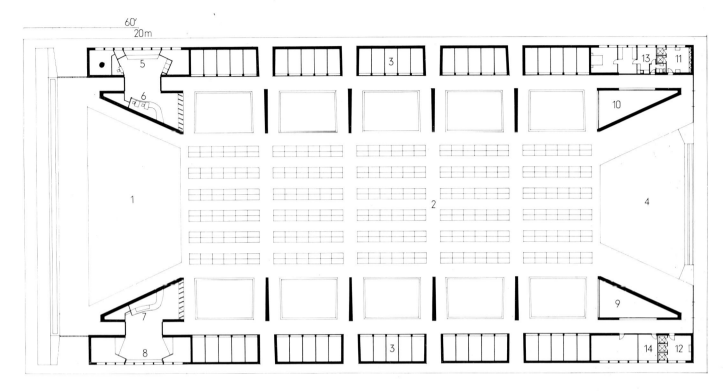

3. Plan. Key: 1 Entrance, 2 Market area, 3 Store rooms, 4 Auctions, 5 Administration, 6 Bank, 7 Bar, 8 Shop for pest control agents, 9,10, Bicycle parking, 11,12 Lavatories, 13 Supervisor, 14 First-aid post.

3. Grundriß. Legende: 1 Eingang, 2 Verkaufsfläche, 3 Lagerräume, 4 Versteigerungen, 5 Verwaltung, 6 Bank, 7 Bar, 8 Geschäft für Schädlingsbekämpfungsmittel, 9,10 Abstellplatz für Fahrräder, 11, 12 Toiletten, 13 Aufsicht, 14 Erste Hilfe.

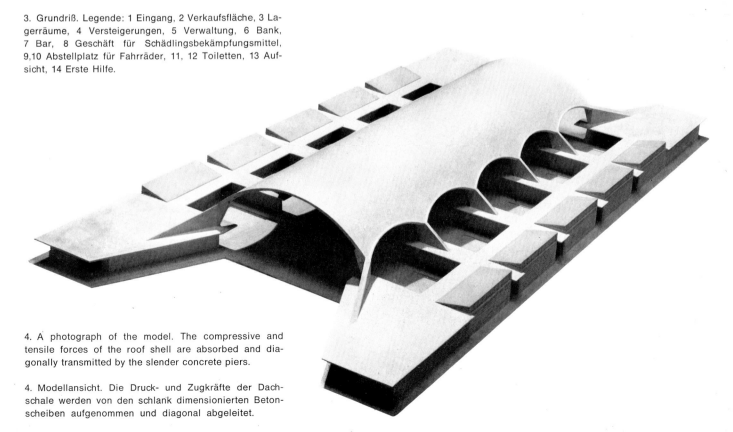

4. A photograph of the model. The compressive and tensile forces of the roof shell are absorbed and diagonally transmitted by the slender concrete piers.

4. Modellansicht. Die Druck- und Zugkräfte der Dachschale werden von den schlank dimensionierten Betonscheiben aufgenommen und diagonal abgeleitet.

Exhibition Hall for the Turin Motor Show (1958—60)
Architect: Riccardo Morandi

Ausstellungshalle des Autosalons Turin (1958—60)
Architekt: Riccardo Morandi

1. Transverse view of interior. The floor area exceeds 100 000 sq.ft.
2. Site plan. Road connection is provided by depressed driveways leading to one end of the hall.
3. Cross-section.
4. Partial longitudinal section.
5. Detail of bearing structure in the vicinity of a stanchion.

1. Blick in Richtung der Querachse. Die Halle hat eine Grundfläche von mehr als 10 000 Quadratmetern.
2. Lageplan: Der Anschluß an das Straßennetz erfolgt über vertieft angelegte, zur Stirnseite der Halle geführte Zugänge.
3. Querschnitt.
4. Längsschnitt (Ausschnitt).
5. Detailschnitt im Bereich einer Stütze.

The new pavilion occupies part of the Turin exhibition ground at the Valentino and is erected on the site of an old racecourse. It has been placed underground so as to minimize encroachment on the park and to enable the regained ground level area above the hall to be used as a children's playground. The task of creating a covered exhibition hall, providing a floor area of 69×151 metres (226×495 ft.) with a minimum number of stanchions, was solved by adopting a reinforced concrete structure where the loads are transmitted to the foundations through a reticular pattern of inter-penetrating roof beams and inclined twin stanchions.

Die neue Ausstellungshalle gehört zum Turiner Messegelände am Valentino. Sie wurde auf dem Grundstück einer alten Galopprennbahn errichtet, und zwar unter der Erde, da damit die geringste Einbuße an Parkgelände verbunden war und sich die — den Maßen der Halle entsprechende — wiedergewonnene Fläche als Kinderspielplatz verwenden ließ. Der Architekt löste die Aufgabe, einen möglichst stützenfreien überdachten Ausstellungsraum von 69×151 Metern zu schaffen, durch eine Stahlbetonkonstruktion, deren Lasten über sich netzförmig durchdringende Deckenunterzüge und schräggestellte Stützenpaare auf das Fundament übertragen werden.

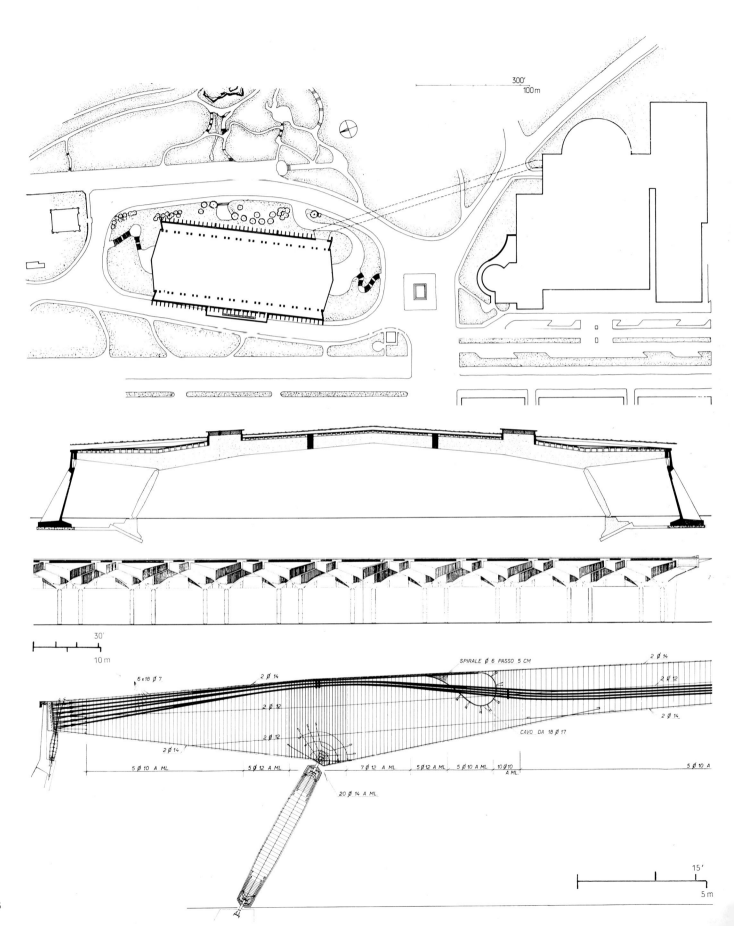

300'
100 m

30'
10 m

6 x 18 Ø 7   2 Ø 14   SPIRALE Ø 6 PASSO 5 CM   2 Ø 14

2 Ø 12   2 Ø 12

2 Ø 12   2 Ø 14

2 Ø 12   CAVO DA 18 Ø 17

2 Ø 14

5 Ø 10 A ML   5 Ø 12 A ML   7 Ø 12 A ML   5 Ø 12 A ML   5 Ø 10 A ML   10 Ø 10   5 Ø 10 A
                                                                                        A ML

20 Ø 14 A ML

15'

5 m

6. Longitudinal view of interior.
7,8. The stanchions supporting the reticular system of roof beams are arranged in pairs, with centre-to-centre distances of 3.20 metres (10¹/₂ft.) between the two stanchions of each pair, and 11 metres (approx. 36 ft.) between adjacent pairs. The reticulation of the support structure, clearly revealing its load-bearing function, gives the hall an appearance of power blended with elegance. Daylight can enter through the wholly glazed end walls and through top lights.

6. Blick in Richtung der Längsachse der Halle.
7,8. Die Stützenpaare mit einem Zwischenraum von 3,20 Metern, auf denen die netzartig verflochtenen Deckenunterzüge ruhen, stehen in Abständen von elf Metern. Der Schwung der konstruktiven Elemente, deren tragende Funktion klar zu erkennen ist, gibt dem Raum eine kraftvolle Eleganz. Die Belichtung erfolgt über die ganz verglasten Stirnseiten der Halle und über Oberlichter.

Palace of Labour at Turin (1960—61)
Architects: Pier Liugi Nervi and Antonio Nervi

Palast der Arbeit in Turin (1960—61)
Architekten: Pier Luigi Nervi und Antonio Nervi

1. Interior of the hall during the "Italia 61" exhibition.
2. Section. A mezzanine is sketched in at intermediate height.
3. Plan.

1. Blick in die Halle während der Ausstellung »Italia 61«.
2. Schnitt. In halber Höhe ist eine Zwischendecke angedeutet.
3. Grundriß.

The hall was built for a great national exhibition celebrating the centenary of the unification of Italy, but was designed for subsequent conversion into a Technical College. The area, amounting to some 25 000 sq.ft., is roofed by sixteen self-contained, square-shaped, mushroom-type roofs. This solution not only provided the desired flexibility for the conversion but also enabled the hall to be erected within the short time allowed. The entire building was erected within a period of no more than 11 months. The fully glazed facades are wind-braced by steel ribs and connected with the main structure by means of hinges and swing links.

Die Halle wurde anläßlich der Hundertjahrfeier der Einigung Italiens für eine große Nationalausstellung erbaut. Sechzehn quadratische, voneinander unabhängige Deckenfelder, von denen jedes auf einem Pilzpfeiler ruht, überdachen die 25 000 m² große Grundfläche des Gebäudes. Diese Lösung bot nicht nur die gewünschte Flexibilität in der Nutzung — im Hinblick auf die vorgesehene Umgestaltung des Gebäudes zu einem Berufsausbildungszentrum —, sondern ermöglichte auch die geforderte kurze Bauzeit: Der ganze Komplex wurde in nur 11 Monaten erstellt. Die voll verglasten Fassaden wurden mit Stahlrippen gegen Winddruck ausgesteift und über Gelenke und Pleuelstangen mit der Hauptstruktur verbunden.

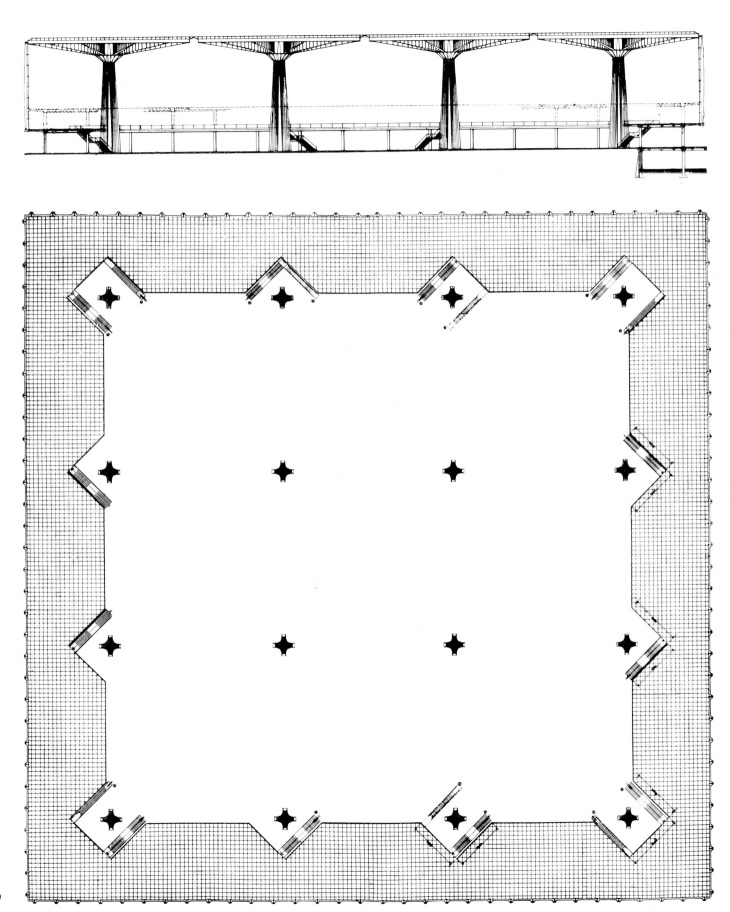

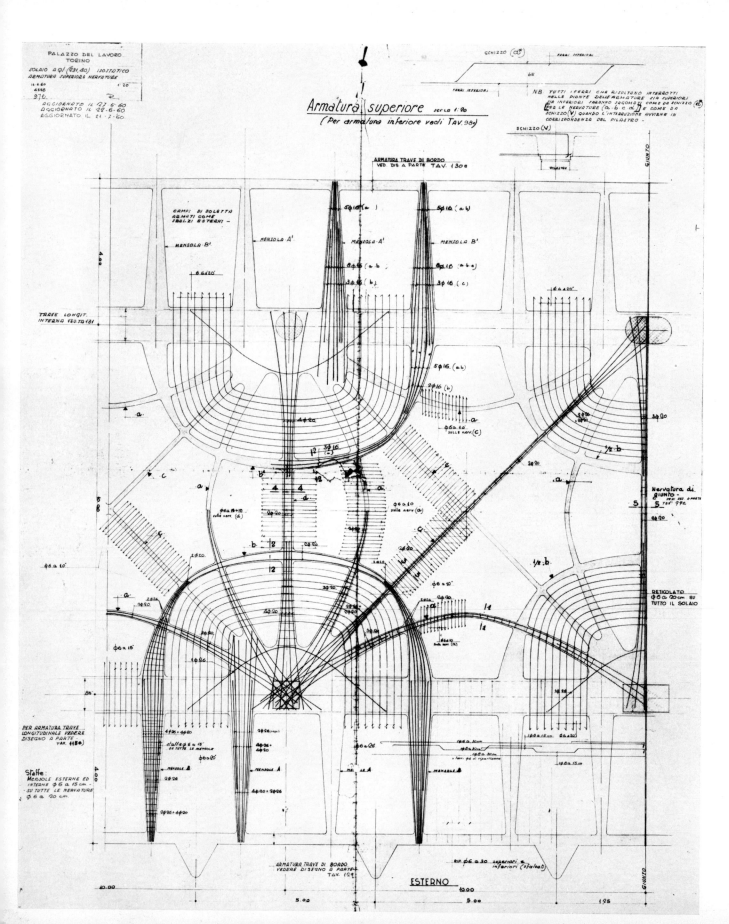

4. Steel reinforcement of the ribbed roof.

5. Arrangement of the roof units. Each of the sixteen square-shaped, mushroom-type steel roofs, which have a side length of 40 m (131 ft), is supported by a central reinforced concrete pillar of 20 metres (66 ft) height.

4. Bewehrungsplan der Rippendecke.

5. Deckenplan. Jede der sechzehn quadratischen Pilzplatten in Stahlstruktur mit einer Seitenlänge von 40 m wird von einem 20 m hohen, zentralen Stahlbetonpfeiler getragen.

6. General view of the hall.
7. One of the reinforced concrete pillars with cruciform cross-section.
8. Geometrical representation of one of the pillars.
9. Steel reinforcement of a pillar. The top ends of the reinforcing bars are welded to the steel beams of the roof.

6. Gesamtansicht der Halle.
7. Einer der Pfeiler in Stahlbeton mit kreuzförmigem Grundriß.
8. Geometrische Darstellung eines Pfeilers.
9. Bewehrungsplan eines Pfeilers. Die oberen Enden der Bewehrungseisen wurden mit den Dachträgern aus Stahl verschweißt.

La Rinascente Department Stores in Rome (1959—61)
Architects: Franco Albini and Franca Helg

Kaufhaus La Rinascente in Rom (1959—61)
Architekten: Franco Albini und Franca Helg

1. Night view from Piazza Firenze. The horizontal stratification of the building is stressed by the concealed facade lighting.
2. Ground floor plan. Key: 1 Staff entrance, 2 Concierge, 3 Emergency exits, 4 Inlet shaft of air-conditioning plant, 5 Air outlet shaft, 6 Bostwick gate, 7 Emergency exit from the basements, 8 Ventilation louvers, 9 Shaft for vitiated air.
3. Longitudinal section.

1. Nachtansicht von der Piazza Firenze. Die Beleuchtung der Fassade durch verdeckt angebrachte Lichtquellen betont die horizontale Schichtung des Gebäudes.
2. Grundriß des Erdgeschosses. Legende: 1 Personaleingang, 2 Pförtner, 3 Notausgang, 4 Zuluftkanal der Klimaanlage, 5 Abluftkanal, 6 Schiebegitter, 7 Notausstieg von den Untergeschossen, 8 Lüftungsgitter, 9 Abluftraum.
3. Längsschnitt.

This building, distinguished by the lucidity of its design, faces the Piazza Firenze opposite the Aurelian Wall, merging without discord with the surrounding buildings. This achievement is partly due to the high standard of architecture and partly to the absence of any pseudo-antique style imitations so often used in such cases. For obvious utility reasons, there are hardly any windows. The facade is dominated by the undulated reddish panels which are in stark contrast with the dark steel beams of the structure. It is only at ground floor level that the building opens up with large show windows. The sales floors extend over six storeys and are reached by escalators and lifts. The technical installations are accommodated in the third basement, the staff changing and wash rooms in the second basement. Administrative offices and buying department are on the top floor.

Das klar konzipierte Gebäude, das an der Piazza Firenze gegenüber der Aurelianischen Mauer steht, fügt sich ohne Bruch in die umliegende Bebauung ein. Dazu tragen die Qualität der Architektur und der Verzicht auf alle, in solchen Fällen sonst häufig anzutreffenden, antikisierenden Stilelemente bei. Die Fassade ist aus funktionalen Überlegungen fast fensterlos. Ihre Struktur wird durch die in einer Art Wellenbewegung gegeneinander versetzten rötlichen Fassadenplatten bestimmt, von denen sich die dunklen Stahlträger der Konstruktion scharf abheben. Nur im Erdgeschoß ist das Gebäude durch große Schaufenster nach außen geöffnet. Die Verkaufsräume sind auf sechs Geschosse verteilt und über Rolltreppen und Aufzüge zu erreichen. Die technischen Einrichtungen wurden im dritten, die Umkleide- und Waschräume für das Personal im zweiten Untergeschoß untergebracht. Das Dachgeschoß enthält die Büros der Verwaltung und der Einkaufsabteilung.

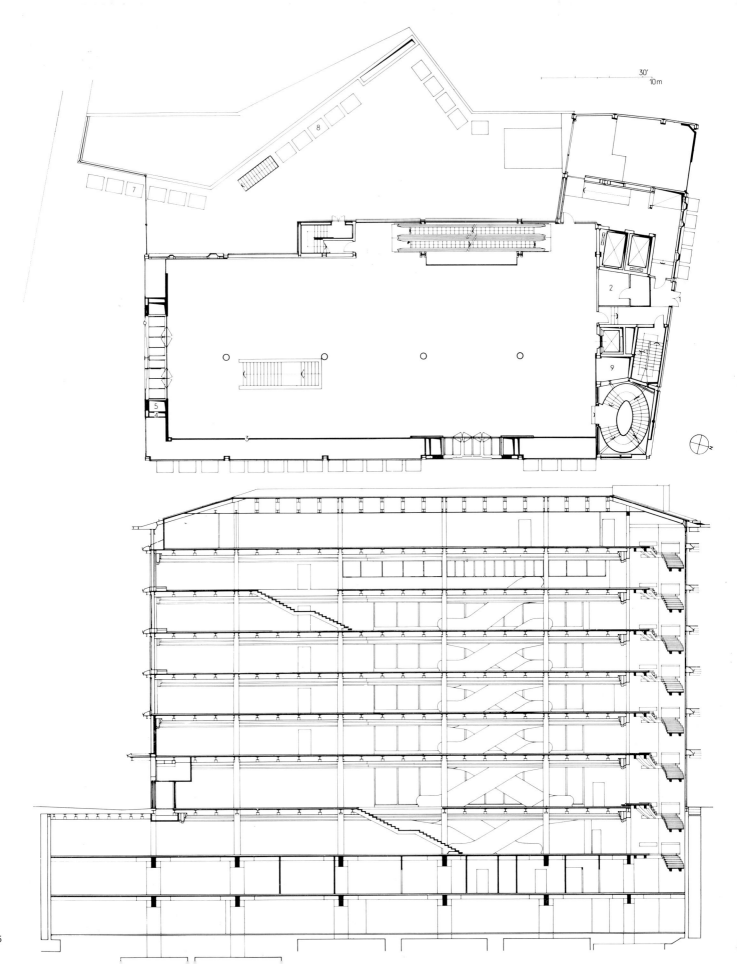

4. Spiral staircase open to the public.
5. The only upper floor windows are on this side facing the Piazza.
6. Facade detail. The facade is enlivened by the undulation of the cladding.

4. Die für die Kunden bestimmte Wendeltreppe.
5. Die einzigen Fenster der Obergeschosse des Gebäudes liegen in der der Piazza zugewandten Fassade.
6. Fassadenausschnitt. Die Wellenbewegung der Fassadenverkleidung wirkt als belebendes Element.

Olivetti Building in Milan (1954)
Architects: Gianantonio Bernasconi, Annibale Fiocchi and Marcello Nizzoli

Bürogebäude der Firma Olivetti in Mailand (1954)
Architekten: Gianantonio Bernasconi, Annibale Fiocchi und Marcello Nizzoli

1. The north side, facing an old garden, is almost completely glazed.
2. View of the south side, covered by sun protection devices. The office block is flanked by two factory buildings which extend right up to the road, thus creating an access yard surrounded by buildings on three sides.

1. Die Nordfassade ist weitgehend verglast und wendet sich gegen einen alten Garten.
2. Ansicht der durch Sonnenschutzvorrichtungen geschützten Südfront. Das Gebäude wird von zwei Fabrikbauten flankiert, die bis zur Straße reichen und so einen dreiseitig umschlossenen Zugangshof schaffen.

The Olivetti Building stands in the centre of the old city, close to the Scala, in the attractive surroundings of the Via Clerici. The building is set back from the road so as to create a visual break and accent against the background of adjacent buildings. The plan is that of a conventional office building: the offices, which can be adapted to changing requirements by the use of removable partitions, are accessible from a central corridor. The south side is covered by a sun protection system of storey-high, movable, vertical blinds. These aluminium blinds are combined in groups; each group is operated by a separate motor and can therefore be placed in a different position, so that the facade has an ever-changing, attractive texture.

Das Olivetti-Bürogebäude steht im Herzen des alten Mailand, ganz in der Nähe der Scala in der reizvollen Umgebung der Via Clerici. Die Architekten setzten das Gebäude von der Straßenfront zurück, um durch diesen Einschnitt optisch eine Unterscheidung und Akzentuierung gegenüber den benachbarten Bauten zu schaffen. Der Grundriß entspricht dem für ein Bürogebäude üblichen: Die Bürofläche, die durch bewegliche Wände den jeweiligen Erfordernissen entsprechend aufgeteilt werden kann, wird über einen Mittelflur erschlossen. Fahrstühle und Treppen sind an den Schmalfronten untergebracht. Die Südfassade ist mit einem Sonnenschutzsystem aus geschoßhohen, beweglichen Vertikallamellen überzogen. Jeweils mehrere dieser Aluminiumlamellen sind zu einer Antriebseinheit zusammengefaßt und geben der Fassade durch ihre verschiedene Stellung eine stets wechselnde, reizvolle Textur.

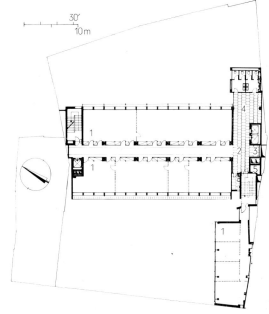

3. Part of the ground floor vestibule is utilised for display purposes.
4. Typical floor plan. Key: 1 Offices, 2 Lobby, 3 Floor porter, 4 Waiting room, 5 Air-conditioning plant.

3. Ein Teil der Eingangshalle im Erdgeschoß wird als Ausstellungsfläche genutzt.
4. Grundriß eines typischen Bürogeschosses. Legende: 1 Bürofläche, 2 Lobby, 3 Bürodiener, 4 Warteraum, 5 Klimaanlage.

Office block in Rome (1964—66)
Architects: Leo Calini and Eugenio Montuori

Bürogebäude in Rom (1964—66)
Architekten: Leo Calini und Eugenio Montuori

This office building, situated at the Via Po, is distinguished by its characteristic framework and by the consistent use of horizontal and vertical modules. The square plan, determined by the shape of the plot, and the desire to minimize the space taken up by columns, led to the concentration of all loads on four internal columns. All piping and wiring is placed inside the cross-ribbed structural floors so that the partitions can be shifted at will. This flexibility is in contrast to the strict rhythm of the facades. All the upper floors are taken up by offices. In the lower basement are technical installations and garage facilities for 36 cars. The upper basement contains archives, changing rooms and the caretaker's flat.

Kennzeichen dieses Bürogebäudes an der Via Po sind die Stützenkonstruktion und die konsequente Anwendung eines Rastermaßes in der Horizontalen und in der Vertikalen. Der quadratische Grundriß, der sich aus der Grundstücksform ergab und die Forderung, die den Raumfluß störenden, vertikal tragenden Elemente auf ein Minimum zu reduzieren, führten zu der Beschränkung auf vier innenliegende Stützen, die sämtliche Lasten aufnehmen. Alle Versorgungsleitungen sind in den verdeckten Kreuzrippendecken geführt. Damit kann die Raumaufteilung der Bürogeschosse flexibel gehalten werden. Diese Flexibilität im Inneren steht im Gegensatz zu dem strengen Rhythmus der Fassadengliederung. Alle Obergeschosse sind mit Büros belegt. Im zweiten Untergeschoß befinden sich technische Räume und Einstellplätze für 36 Wagen. Das erste Untergeschoß enthält Archiv, Umkleideräume und die Hausmeisterwohnung.

1. General view. The cubic block, rising above an almost wholly open ground floor, is enlivened by the facade mesh. For aesthetic reasons, the steel columns are extended upwards to penthouse roof level. A green verge along the edge of the open ground floor surrounds the entrance hall which contains lifts and staircase.
2. The size of the building is in keeping with that of the adjacent buildings.
3. Typical office floor plan. Stairs and lifts are in the centre of the block.
4. Cross-section of the building across the staircase.

1. Gesamtansicht. Über dem offenen Erdgeschoß erhebt sich der kubische Baukörper, gegliedert durch das Netz der Fassadenelemente. Aus formalen Gründen ist die Metallstruktur bis in Höhe des zurückgesetzten Dachgeschosses geführt. Das Erdgeschoß ist im Randbereich bepflanzt. Diese Grünzone umschließt eine Eingangshalle, in deren Mitte Aufzüge und Treppen liegen.
2. Das Gebäude paßt sich vom Volumen her der vorhandenen Bebauung an.
3. Grundriß eines Bürogeschosses. Treppen und Aufzüge liegen im Zentrum des Gebäudes.
4. Schnitt im Bereich der Treppe.

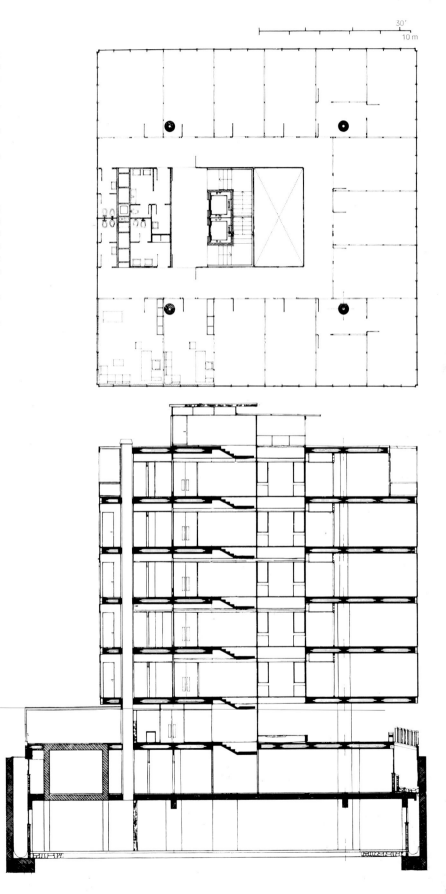

ENI Office Building at San Donato near Milan (1956—58)
Architects: Marcello Nizzoli and Mario Oliveri

Bürogebäude der ENI in San Donato bei Mailand (1956—58)
Architekten: Marcello Nizzoli und Mario Oliveri

This office tower, situated in a large industrial estate in the outskirts of Milan, differs considerably from the conventional type of office building. Its polygonal plan is due to a combination of regular or oblong hexagons, which enables the premises to be partitioned and arranged in many different ways. This interior variegation is matched externally by the sub-division of the tower into several blocks which jut out into the level ground. The curtain wall facades are mainly of glass. As a result, the blocks have a transparency which forms a vivid contrast to the almost window-less staircases placed outside the facade. The geometrical design of the group is accentuated by the horizontality of the white breast panels and the verticality of the staircases.

1. View from the south. The low building at the side, which houses the canteen and other services, helps to mitigate the verticality of the office tower, though matching it with its hexagonal plan and horizontal stratification.

1. Gesamtansicht von Süden. Das niedrig gehaltene Sozialgebäude wirkt als Gegengewicht gegen die Vertikalität des Büroturmes, dem es sich andererseits mit seiner hexagonalen Grundrißform und horizontalen Schichtung anpaßt.

Der Büroturm auf polygonalem Grundriß, der in einem ausgedehnten Industriegelände vor den Toren Mailands steht, unterscheidet sich beträchtlich vom üblichen Typ des Bürogebäudes. Seine Grundrißdisposition ergibt sich aus der Kombination von regelmäßigen oder in die Länge gezogenen Sechsecken, die eine sehr differenzierte Raumeinteilung und -abfolge erlauben. Dieser Vielgestaltigkeit im Inneren entspricht von außen gesehen die Aufgliederung des Gebäudes in mehrere Flügel, die in das ebene Gelände ausgreifen. Die vorgehängten Fassaden bestehen weitgehend aus Glas. Sie geben den Gebäudeflügeln eine Transparenz, zu der die fast völlig geschlossenen, vor die Fassade gestellten Treppenhäuser einen lebhaften Kontrast bilden. Die Horizontale der umlaufenden weißen Brüstungsbänder und die Vertikale der Treppenhäuser betonen die geometrische Form der Anlage.

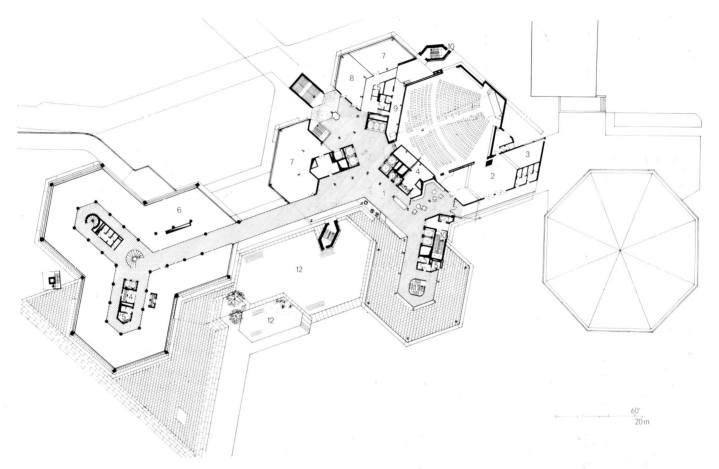

2. Ground floor plan. Key: 1 Vestibule and reception, 2 Main entrance, 3 Cloak room, 4 Hall porters, 5 Changing rooms, 6 Social rooms, 7 Office, 8 Archives, 9 Projector cabin, 10 Emergency stairs, 11 Staff staircase, 12 Water basin.
3. Canteen building and office tower are connected by a wholly glazed covered way.

2. Erdgeschoßgrundriß. Legende: 1 Eingangshalle mit Empfang, 2 Haupteingang, 3 Garderobe, 4 Pförtner, 5 Umkleideräume, 6 Sozialraum, 7 Büro, 8 Archiv, 9 Vorführkabine, 10 Feuertreppe, 11 Personaltreppe, 12 Wasserbecken.
3. Sozialbau und Büroturm sind durch einen verglasten Gang miteinander verbunden.

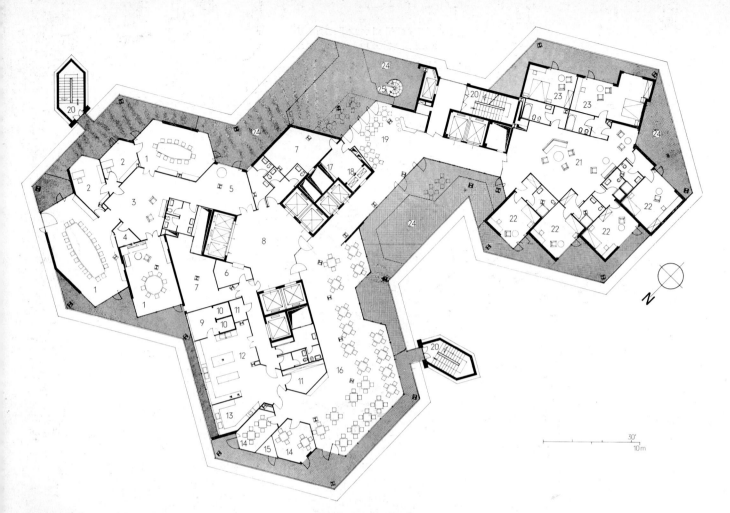

4. Plan of 13th floor. Key: 1 Conference room, 2 Secretarial staff, 3 Foyer, 4 Micro-film projection cabin, 5 Vestibule, 6 Cloak room, 7 Air-conditioning plant, 8 Lobby, 9 Ante-room, 10 Refrigerator room, 11 Store room, 12 Kitchen, 13 Scullery, 14 Small dining room, 15 Aviary, 16 Dining room, 17 Pneumatic mail, 18 Parcel hoist, 19 Bar, 20 Emergency stairs, 21 Guest lounge, 22 Single-bed room, 23 Double-bed room, 24 Terrace with plants, 25 Stairs leading to the roof terrace on the 14th floor.
5. Seen from the office tower, the low building is reflected in the large water basin.
6. West side of the office tower.

4. Grundriß des 13. Obergeschosses. Legende: 1 Konferenzraum, 2 Sekretariat, 3 Foyer, 4 Mikrofilm-Vorführkabine, 5 Vorraum, 6 Garderobe, 7 Klimaanlage, 8 Lobby, 9 Vorzimmer, 10 Kühlraum, 11 Abstellraum, 12 Küche, 13 Spülraum, 14 Kleiner Speisesaal, 15 Voliere, 16 Speisesaal, 17 Rohrpost, 18 Paketaufzug, 19 Bar, 20 Feuertreppe, 21 Aufenthaltsraum für Gäste, 22 Einbettzimmer, 23 Zweibettzimmer, 24 Bepflanzte Terrasse, 25 Treppe zur Dachterrasse im 14. Obergeschoß.
5. Blick vom Büroturm auf das Sozialgebäude, das sich in dem großen Wasserbecken spiegelt.
6. Westansicht des Bürogebäudes.

Velasca Tower in Milan (1956—57)
Architects: Lodovico B. Belgiojoso, Enrico Peressutti and Ernesto N. Rogers

Velasca-Turm in Mailand (1956—57)
Architekten: Lodovico B. Belgiojoso, Enrico Peressutti und Ernesto N. Rogers

Because of its position, rising high above the sprawl of houses in Milan's town centre close to the Cathedral, and because of its unusual shape, the Velasca Tower is among the most discussed post-war buildings in Milan. The plan of the tower, which contains offices and flats, is the usual one for such multi-storey buildings, with the stairs and lifts combined in an inside core. Above the 18th floor, the tower is enlarged on all four sides. This enlargement extends over six storeys which are exclusively taken up by apartments; but the two top floors, with two flats each, are again retracted. With its comparatively large window-less zones interrupted by irregularly spaced windows, with inclined struts supporting the enlarged upper part, and with the castellated shape of its top, the Velasca Tower is clearly reminiscent of a medieval stronghold.

Der Velasca-Turm, der in der Nähe des Domes hoch über das dicht bebaute innerstädtische Zentrum aufragt, gehört wegen seines Standortes und seiner ungewöhnlichen Form zu den meist diskutierten Nachkriegsbauten Mailands. In dem Büro- und Wohngebäude, dessen Grundriß dem für ein Hochhaus üblichen entspricht, sind Treppen und Aufzüge in einem innenliegenden Kern zusammengefaßt. Ab dem 19. Geschoß verbreitert sich der Turm. Diese Volumenerweiterung ist über sechs Geschosse, in denen ausschließlich Wohnungen untergebracht sind, bis zu den beiden zurückgesetzten Dachgeschossen mit Duplexwohnungen durchgehalten. Der verhältnismäßig große Anteil geschlossener Wandfläche, durchbrochen von Fenstern, deren Anordnung keiner strengen Regel folgt, die Stützelemente des auskragenden Turmteils und die zinnenartige Ausbildung des Turmkranzes vermitteln deutlich den Eindruck eines mittelalterlichen Turmes.

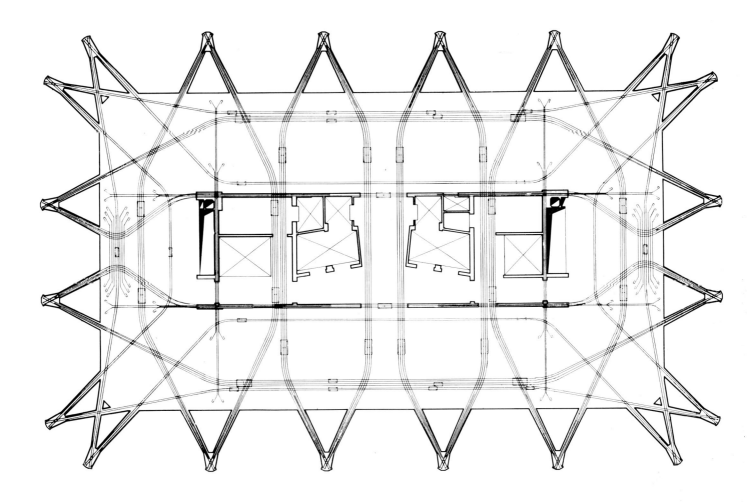

1. South-east side, with Milan Cathedral in the background.
2. Close-up of the struts in the transition zone to the enlarged upper part of the Tower.
3. Horizontal section and reinforcement plan of the bearing elements at 18th floor level.
4. Plan of residential floors (19th to 24th floor).

1. Gesamtansicht von Südosten. Im Hintergrund links der Mailänder Dom.
2. Detailansicht aus dem Bereich des Übergangs der außenliegenden Gebäudestützen zum auskragenden Turmteil.
3. Horizontalschnitt und Armierungsplan der Tragglieder in der Höhe des 18. Obergeschosses.
4. Grundriß eines Wohngeschosses (19.–24. Obergeschoß).

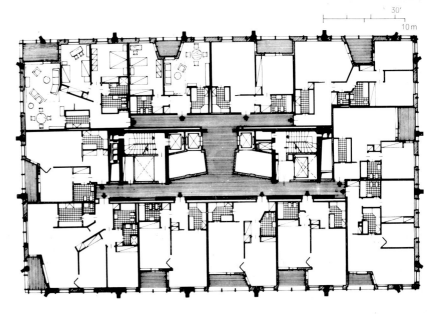

30'

10 m

Galfa Tower in Milan (1957—59)
Architect: Melchiorre Bega

Hochhaus Galfa in Mailand (1957—59)
Architekt: Melchiorre Bega

1. View from the south. Behind the window-less part of the facade is the core of the building containing the stairs and lifts.
2. Facade detail. The verticals of the delicate filigree pattern of the shining curtain walls is adapted to the width of the windows.
3. Cross-section of bearing structure.
4. Standard floor plan. Stairs, lifts and lavatories are concentrated in a core within the rectangular plan.
5. Plan of first basement.

1. Gesamtansicht von Süden. Hinter der geschlossenen Fassadenfläche liegt der Gebäudekern mit Treppen und Aufzügen.
2. Fassadenausschnitt. Der zarte, filigranhafte Raster des glänzenden Curtain-Walls ist in der Vertikalen auf die Fensterbreite abgestimmt.
3. Schnitt durch das konstruktive Gerüst.
4. Grundriß Normalgeschoß. Treppen, Aufzüge und Toiletten wurden innerhalb des rechteckigen Grundrisses zu einem innenliegenden Kern zusammengefaßt.
5. Grundriß erstes Untergeschoß.

The Galfa Tower, containing the offices of a petroleum company, stands at the corner of Via Galvani and Via Fara, not far from the Pirelli Tower. The clear outline of this building which, because of its transparency, appears to float above its surroundings, is due to the strict and consistent arrangement of structural components. Pronounced verticality, mitigated by the horizontal lines of the windows ribbons and parapets, the alternation of glass and aluminium which enlivens the facade, and the tidy treatment of the details are characteristic features of this tower block which is among the most important post-war buildings in Milan.

Das Galfa-Hochhaus, in dem die Büros einer Erdölfirma untergebracht sind, steht an der Ecke Via Galvani und Via Fara, nicht weit entfernt vom Pirelli-Hochhaus. Die klare, fest umrissene Form des Gebäudes, das infolge seiner Transparenz über dem Häusermeer zu schweben scheint, ist das Ergebnis einer strengen und konsequenten Anordnung der konstruktiven Mittel. Betonte Vertikalität, gemildert durch die Horizontale der Fensterbänder und Brüstungen, die Gliederung der Fassadenfläche durch den Wechsel von Glas und Aluminium und die saubere Detaillierung sind kennzeichnende Elemente dieses Hochhauses, das zu den bedeutendsten Mailänder Bauten der Nachkriegszeit gehört.

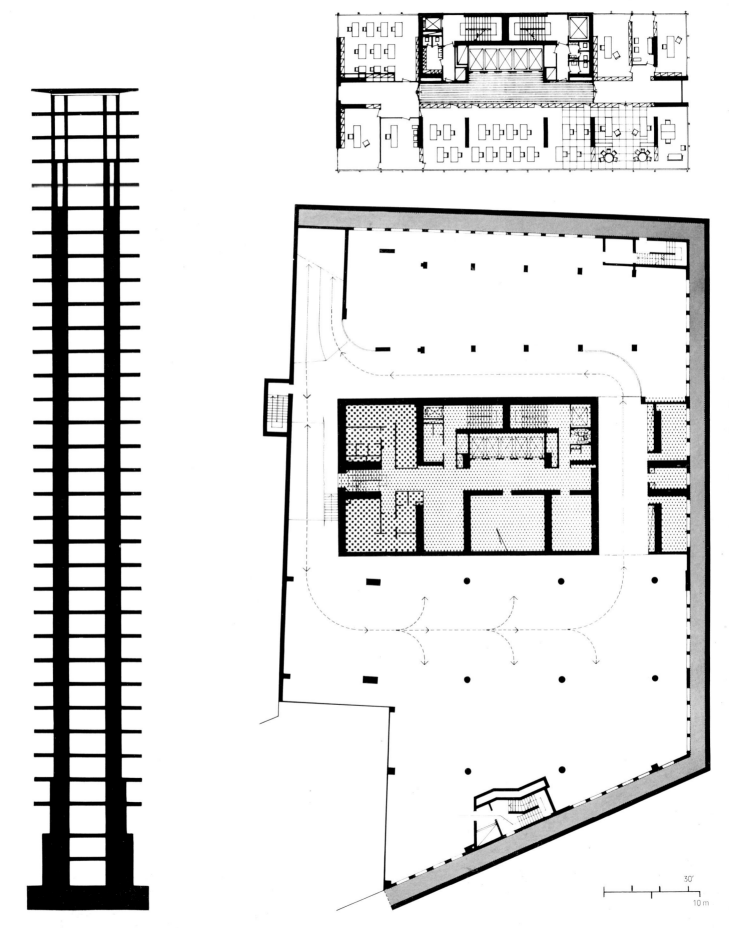

30'

10 m

Pirelli Tower in Milan (1956—59)

Architects: Gio Ponti, Antonio Fornaroli, Alberto Rosselli, Giuseppe Valtolina and Egidio Dell'Orto. Civil Engineers: Arturo Danusso and Pier Luigi Nervi

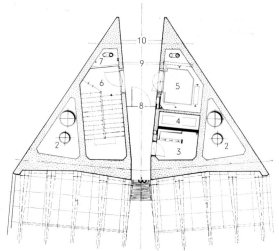

This 124 metres (407 ft.) high reinforced concrete tower, which dominates the station square, represents a novel type of office block. In order to preserve maximum freedom for sub-dividing the floors by removable partitions, the bearing structure has been confined to a small number of units. Between the solid triangular end buttresses and the two pairs of intermediate piers, the structural floors have clear spans of 24 metres (79 ft.) and 14 metres (46 ft.), respectively. In the central span, one-half of the area is taken up by technical installations such as lifts, stairs and toilets. Simplicity and lucidity of design are the outstanding features of this tower which is among the most original architectural creations in post-war Italy.

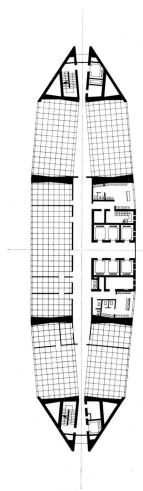

Pirelli-Hochhaus in Mailand (1956—59)

Architekten: Gio Ponti, Antonio Fornaroli, Alberto Rosselli, Giuseppe Valtolina und Egidio Dell'Orto. Statik: Arturo Danusso und Pier Luigi Nervi

Das 124 m hohe, in Stahlbeton ausgeführte Bauwerk, das den Bahnhofsplatz beherrscht, verkörpert durch seine Konstruktion einen neuen Typ des Bürohochhauses. Um eine größtmögliche Freiheit der inneren Aufteilung durch bewegliche Trennwände zu erreichen, wurde die tragende Struktur auf wenige Elemente beschränkt: Zwischen den dreieckigen, massiven Endstützen und zwei Tragpfeilerpaaren spannen sich die Geschoßdecken über 24 beziehungsweise 14 m völlig frei. Im mittleren Feld wird die eine Hälfte von technischen Installationen wie Aufzügen, Treppe und Toiletten eingenommen. Einfachheit und Klarheit im konstruktiven Aufbau sind die wesentlichen Merkmale dieses Hochhauses, das zu den originellsten architektonischen Schöpfungen im Italien der Nachkriegszeit gehört.

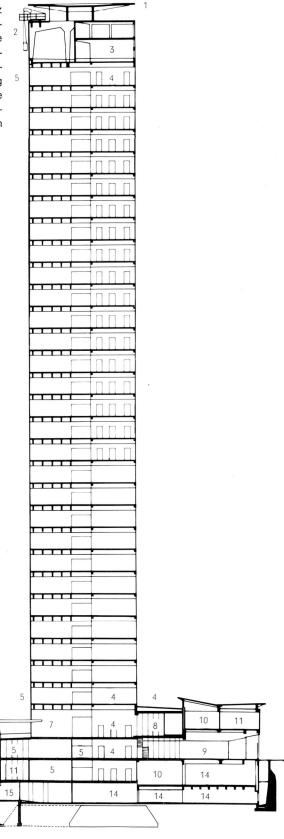

1. Plan of end buttress. Key: 1 Office zone, 2 Air conditioning ducts, 3 Electric switchroom, 4 Flue, 5 Goods elevator, 6 Emergency stairs, 7 Rainwater drain, 8 Fire protection door, 9 Glass partition, 10 Outer balcony.
2. Standard floor plan. The long and narrow plan makes the tower appear remarkably slender but does not make for an efficient utilisation of the floor spaces.
3. General view of the Pirelli Tower which has become a dominant feature in the business centre of Milan. The external appearance is dominated by the pointed ends, by the profile of the pairs of piers, and by the storey-high glass panels.
4. Cross-section. Key: 1 Roof, 2 Window cleaning cradle, 3 Installations room, 4 Lift, 5 Office, 6 Visitors' forecourt, 7,8 Vestibule, 9 Staff entrance, 10,11 Cafeteria, 12,13 Conference room and technical installations, 14 Store room, 15 Gallery, 16 Staff theatre.

1. Grundriß des Giebelfeldes. Legende: 1 Bürozone, 2 Kanäle der Klimaanlage, 3 Elektroschaltraum, 4 Abzugsschacht, 5 Lastenaufzug, 6 Feuertreppe, 7 Regenfallrohr, 8 Feuerschutztür, 9 Glaswand, 10 Außenbalkon.
2. Normalgeschoßgrundriß. Der verhältnismäßig lange und schmale Grundriß verleiht dem Bau zwar eine beachtliche Schlankheit, wirkt sich aber negativ auf die Ausnutzung der Geschoßflächen aus.
3. Gesamtansicht. Das Bürohochhaus, dessen äußeres Bild durch die spitz zulaufenden Giebelscheiben, das Profil der Pfeilerpaare und die geschoßhohen Glasflächen geprägt wird, ist ein bestimmendes Element im Geschäftszentrum der Stadt.
4. Querschnitt. Legende: 1 Dach, 2 Fensterputzgerät, 3 Installationsraum, 4 Aufzug, 5 Büro, 6 Platz vor dem Besuchereingang, 7, 8 Eingangshalle, 9 Angestellteneingang, 10, 11 Café, 12, 13 Versammlungssaal und technische Räume, 14 Lagerraum, 15 Galerie, 16 Theater der Angestellten.

5. Interior of an office floor. The chest-high cupboards on the right separate the working area from the circulation area.
6. One of the conference rooms.
7. Gallery below the roof, extending through the 31st and 32nd floor.

5. Blick in ein Großraumbüro. Die halbhohen Büroschränke (rechts) trennen den Arbeitsbereich von einem Bereich für den Durchgangsverkehr.
6. Blick in einen Konferenzraum.
7. Die zwei Geschosse hohe Galerie im 31. Geschoß unter dem Dach.

Office block of the Zanussi-Rex Company at Pordenone (1959—61)
Architect: Gino Valle. Civil Engineers: R. Novarin and G. Crapiz

Bürogebäude der Firma Zanussi-Rex in Pordenone (1959—61)
Architekt: Gino Valle. Statik: R. Novarin und G. Crapiz

1. View from south-west with the main entrance and the passage leading to the factory buildings in the north.
2. Cross-section.

1. Blick von Südwesten auf den Haupteingang und die Durchfahrt zu den sich im Norden anschließenden Werkhallen.
2. Querschnitt.

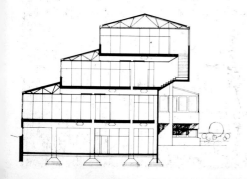

The offices of the Zanussi-Rex Company, manufacturers of household goods, are housed in a longish three-storey block. The design is based on a module of 1.20 metres. Pairs of reinforced concrete frame supports, with centre-to-centre distances of 1.20 metres between the two supports of each pair and 7.20 metres between one pair and the next, are placed cross-wise over the whole length of the building. They carry the upper floors which are, on the north side, staggered inasmuch as the first floor is considerably retracted from the ground floor, and the top floor from the first floor. This stepped-back north facade is wholly glazed. The south facade shows a good deal of exposed concrete, and is highly diversified by projections and recessions. The plan, too, is based on a module of 1,20 metres. The pipes and wires for the offices are covered by the suspended ceiling.

Die Büros der Zanussi-Rex, einer Firma, die Haushaltsartikel herstellt, sind in einem langgestreckten, dreigeschossigen Gebäude untergebracht. Das konstruktive Schema baut auf einem Modul von 1,20 m auf. Quergestellte, paarweise mit einem Zwischenraum von 1,20 m angeordnete Rahmenträger aus Stahlbeton sind im Abstand von 7,20 m von Stützenpaar zu Stützenpaar über die ganze Länge des Gebäudes angeordnet. Darauf ruhen die in der Höhe gestaffelten Geschosse, von denen das erste Obergeschoß und das Dachgeschoß jeweils gegenüber dem darunterliegenden Geschoß beträchtlich zurückgenommen sind. Es entsteht eine gestufte Nordfassade, die weitgehend verglast wurde. Die Südfassade zeigt viel Sichtbeton und ist durch Vor- und Rücksprünge kräftig gegliedert. Auch der Grundriß ist nach dem Modul von 1,20 m gestuft. Die Versorgungsleitungen für die Büros liegen hinter der untergehängten Decke.

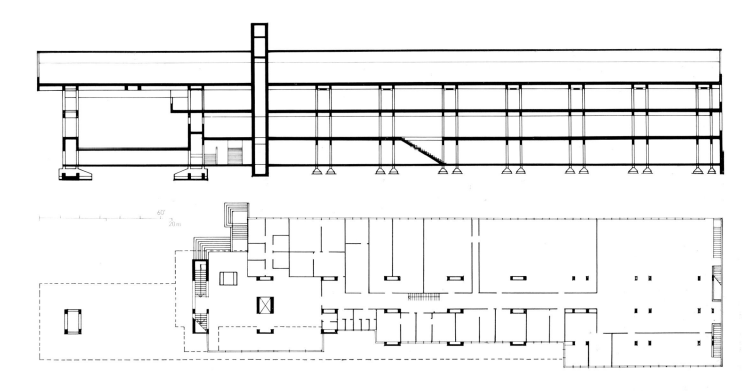

3. Longitudinal section.
4. First floor plan.
5. North facade with the main access to the offices from the factory building.

3. Längsschnitt.
4. Grundriß des ersten Obergeschosses.
5. Ansicht der Nordfassade mit dem Hauptzugang zu den Büros von den Werkhallen her.

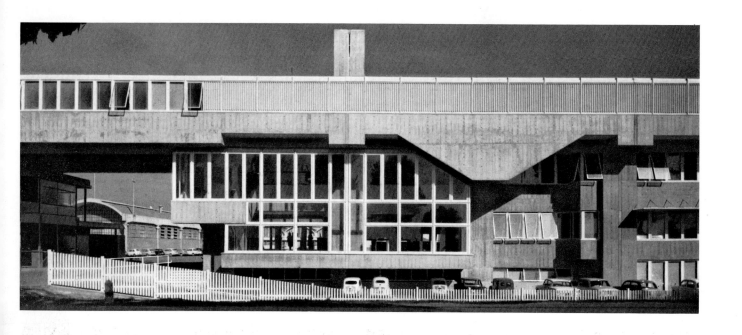

6. South facade. The building is separated from the highway (the Venice-Vienna road) by a low-level car park. Behind the two-storey window frontage is the vestibule.

7. Interior of the vestibule which is partly two-storeyed.

8. The north facade clearly reveals the module division of the building.

9. The design of the south facade differs from that of the remainder of the building. Even here, however, a certain orderliness can be discerned from the alternation of walls and windows and from the arrangement of the facade projections and recessions.

6. Die Südfassade. Das Gebäude ist von der dicht vorbeiführenden Nationalstraße (Venedig-Wien) durch einen vertieft angelegten Parkplatz getrennt. Hinter der zweigeschossigen Fensterfront liegt die Eingangshalle.

7. Blick in die teilweise zweigeschossige Eingangshalle.

8. Die Nordfassade läßt deutlich die modulare Gliederung des Gebäudes erkennen.

9. Die Südfassade zeigt eine vom übrigen Bauwerk abweichende eigene Gestaltung, die jedoch auch in dem Wechsel von Wand- und Fensterflächen und in der Verteilung der Fassadenvor- und -rücksprünge eine bestimmte Ordnung erkennen läßt.

Printing works and offices of the "Corriere della Sera" newspaper, Milan (1962—63)
Architect: Alberto Rosselli

Druckerei- und Bürogebäude der Zeitung »Corriere della Sera«, Mailand (1962—63)
Architekt: Alberto Rosselli

1. General view. The top light ribbon of the ground floor windows, which is repeated in enlarged form by the window ribbon of the top floor, is protected by crossbars.
2. Part of the facade. The glass curtains are enlivened by narrow windows reaching from floor to ceiling. Behind them are slat blinds.

1. Gesamtansicht. Das umlaufende Oberlichtband des Erdgeschosses, das mit der Fensterfront des Dachgeschosses vergrößert wiederholt wird, ist durch ein Gitter geschützt.
2. Fassadenausschnitt. Hinter den durch geschoßhohe, schmale Fenster aufgelockerten Glasfassaden liegen Lamellenjalousien.

The building is situated at the Via Solferino in the old city of Milan. The function of the building as a printing works can, to some extent, be guessed from the light steel framework which is visible from outside. The slender columns and beams divide the translucent glass facade of the first and second floor into panels which, depending on the inside or outside lighting, assume different, attractive colour shades and reflect the image of the houses opposite. The ground floor is mainly bricked up. The partly retracted top floor contains offices.

Das Gebäude liegt in der Mailänder Altstadt, an der Via Solferino. Schon das leichte, von außen sichtbare Stahlskelett verrät etwas von seiner Funktion als graphischer Betrieb. Die schlank dimensionierten Stützen und Träger gliedern die durchscheinende Glasfassade des ersten und zweiten Obergeschosses in Tafeln, die je nach Beleuchtung von innen oder außen verschiedene reizvolle Farbtönungen annehmen und in denen sich die benachbarten Häuser spiegeln. Das gemauerte Erdgeschoß ist weitgehend geschlossen. In dem teilweise zurückgesetzten Dachgeschoß sind Büros untergebracht.

Warehouse at Padua (1960—61)
Architects: A. Mangiarotti, Bruno and Giovanni Morassutti. Civil Engineer: A. Favini
Lagerhalle in Padua (1960—61)
Architekten: Angelo Mangiarotti, Bruno und Giovanni Morassutti. Statik: A. Favini

1. Road frontage with drive. The large sliding doors of glass can be pushed behind the windowless part of the wall which is faced with corrugated aluminium sheeting.

1. Blick auf die der Straße zugekehrte Stirnfront der Halle mit der Autoeinfahrt. Die großen Rolltore sind aus Glas. Sie werden hinter die geschlossenen, mit Well-aluminium verkleideten Wandflächen geschoben.

This warehouse for iron products, situated at the Padua-Venice road, is distinguished by its symmetry and lucid design. The building is divided into two parallel, longitudinal naves. The bearing structure consists of precast reinforced concrete units. The roof is formed by steel tubes of hexagonal cross-section, linked by panels which are guttered in the centre for rain water drainage. The walls are curtained by bricks, aluminium panels and glass.

Diese Lagerhalle für Eisenprodukte, die an der Straße von Padua nach Venedig steht, zeichnet sich durch ihre Symmetrie und klare Konstruktion aus. Das Gebäude ist in zwei parallel zur Längsachse liegende Schiffe gegliedert. Die konstruktiv tragenden Elemente bestehen aus Stahlbetonfertigteilen. Das Dach wird aus Stahlblechrohren mit hexagonalem Querschnitt gebildet, die durch Dachplatten miteinander verbunden sind, in die in der Mitte eine Rinne zur Ableitung des Regenwassers eingefaltet ist. Für die Ausfachung der Wände wurden Backsteine, Aluminiumplatten und Glas verwendet.

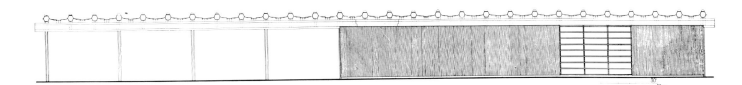

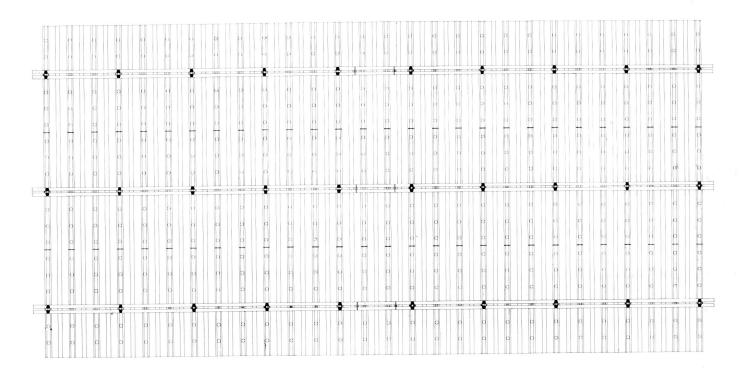

2. Section.
3. The roof as seen from below. The approx. 3 ft. high honeycomb-shaped roof joists carry Plexiglass domes from which the daylight enters the hall through sheet metal cylinders.
4. Part of the brick-panelled long side. The wall panels conform to the rhythm of the roof which has a cantilever of 8.10 metres (29½ ft.).

2. Schnitt.
3. Untersicht des Daches. Auf die wabenförmigen, 92 cm hohen Dachträger sind Plexiglaskuppeln aufgesetzt, deren Licht durch Blechzylinder in die Halle strahlt.
4. Detail der Längsfront, die mit Backsteinen ausgefacht ist. Die Wandfelder wiederholen die Gliederung des Daches, das 8,10 m auskragt.

1. East side of the office building.

1. Ostansicht des Büroblocks.

The group consists of two parts, viz. the factory proper and the office and administration building which, though physically separated from each other, are functionally and aesthetically combined. The modular framework and the shed-type roof of the factory hall facilitate a future extension which has already been taken into account in the original design. The office and administration building, situated between the factory proper and the main road, can likewise be extended without difficulty. Its bearing structure is projected in front of the facade. The regular pattern of the vertical units is merely interrupted by the spiral stairs inserted between them.

Die Anlage setzt sich aus zwei Teilen zusammen, der Fabrikationshalle und dem Verwaltungs- und Bürogebäude, die zwar räumlich voneinander getrennt, jedoch funktional und formal zu einer Einheit verbunden sind. Modular gestufte Skelettkonstruktion und Sheddach der Fabrikationshalle erlauben ohne große Schwierigkeiten eine Erweiterung, die schon im Entwurf eingeplant wurde. Der Büro- und Verwaltungsbau liegt an der der Straße zugekehrten Stirnseite der Halle. Auch er läßt sich bei Bedarf leicht vergrößern. Seine tragende Struktur ist vor die Fassade genommen. Den regelmäßigen Raster der vertikalen Elemente unterbrechen nur die dazwischengeschobenen, zylindrischen Treppenhäuser.

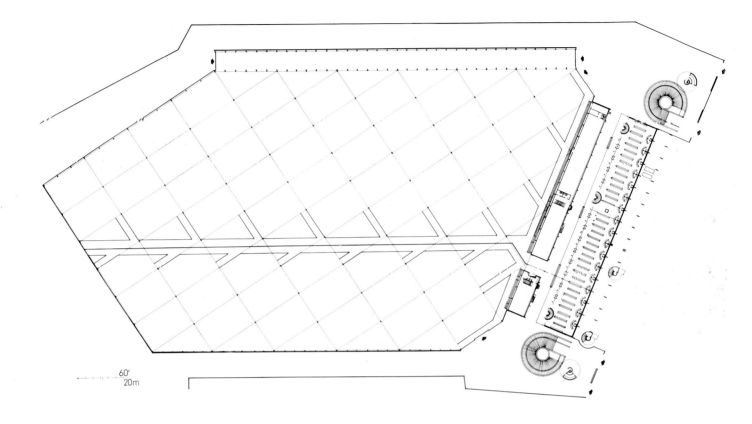

2. Ground floor plan of the entire group of buildings.
3. Aerial photograph. The group is so arranged that future extensions are possible in two directions.

2. Erdgeschoßgrundriß des Gesamtkomplexes.
3. Luftaufnahme. Der Komplex ist so gegliedert, daß er später in zwei Richtungen erweitert werden kann.

4. West side of the office building. The bearing structure is clearly separated from the facade.
5. Interior of one of the spiral stairs which have no roof.
6. Ramp leading to the low-level garages. In the background is the office building.
7. Cross-section and parts of the ground floor plan of the office and administration building. Top to bottom: First floor, first basement, second basement.

4. Ansicht des Bürogebäudes von Westen. Das tragende Gerüst hebt sich deutlich von der Fassade ab.
5. Blick in eines der zylindrischen Treppenhäuser, die oben offen sind.
6. Blick auf die Rampe zu den Tiefgaragen. Im Hintergrund das Bürogebäude.
7. Querschnitt und Grundrißausschnitte des Büro- und Verwaltungsgebäudes. Von oben nach unten: Erstes Obergeschoß, Erdgeschoß, erstes und zweites Untergeschoß.

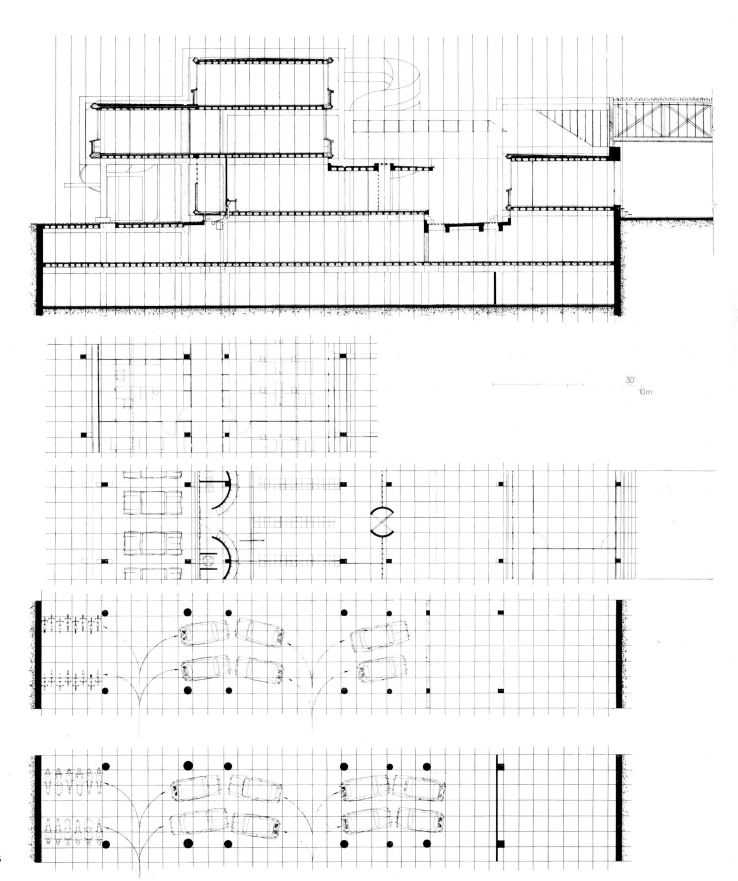

Marxer Laboratories at Ivrea, Turin (1960—62)
Architect: Alberto Galardi. Civil Engineer: Antonio Migliasso

Marxer-Laboratorien in Ivrea, Turin (1960—62)
Architekt: Alberto Galardi. Statik: Antonio Migliasso

1. General view of the laboratory building, seen from north-west. A screen-like system of sun protection blinds is inserted between the cantilevered floor slabs.
2. Site plan.

1. Gesamtansicht des Laborgebäudes von Nordwesten. Zwischen die auskragenden Geschoßdecken ist ein screenartiger Sonnenschutzraster gespannt.
2. Lageplan.

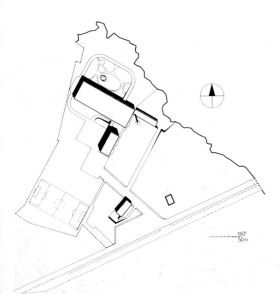

160'
50m

The Research Institute, occupying part of an extensive plot at the outskirts of the town, is concerned with bacteriological research, and with the production of certain drugs. It consists of four separate buildings. The largest of them is the two-storey production shop, containing production rooms in the ground floor and store rooms in the basement. The research building has three storeys, including a semi-basement with the bacteriological research laboratories. In a smaller building removed from the others are the electric substation and the porter's lodge. The bearing structures of all buildings are of exposed reinforced concrete, standing on a semi-basement of plain concrete. The Sekurit windows have aluminium frames. In front of the windows is a sun protection grille of concrete blinds.

Das Forschungsinstitut, das auf einem ausgedehnten Gelände am Stadtrand liegt, beschäftigt sich mit bakteriologischen Untersuchungen und stellt im Zusammenhang damit bestimmte Medikamente her. Es besteht aus vier Einzelgebäuden. Das größte davon ist zweigeschossig und enthält im Erdgeschoß Produktionsräume und im Untergeschoß Lagerräume. Das Forschungsgebäude hat zusammen mit dem Sockelgeschoß, in dem die Laboratorien für bakteriologische Untersuchungen untergebracht sind, drei Geschosse. In einem kleineren, abseits liegenden Bau befindet sich die Energiezentrale, an die sich das Pförtnerhaus anschließt. Alle Gebäude sind schalungsroh belassene Stahlbetonkonstruktionen auf einem Sockelgeschoß aus Beton. Die Sekuritfenster haben Aluminiumrahmen. Den Fensterfronten ist ein Sonnenschutzgitter aus Betonelementen vorgeschaltet.

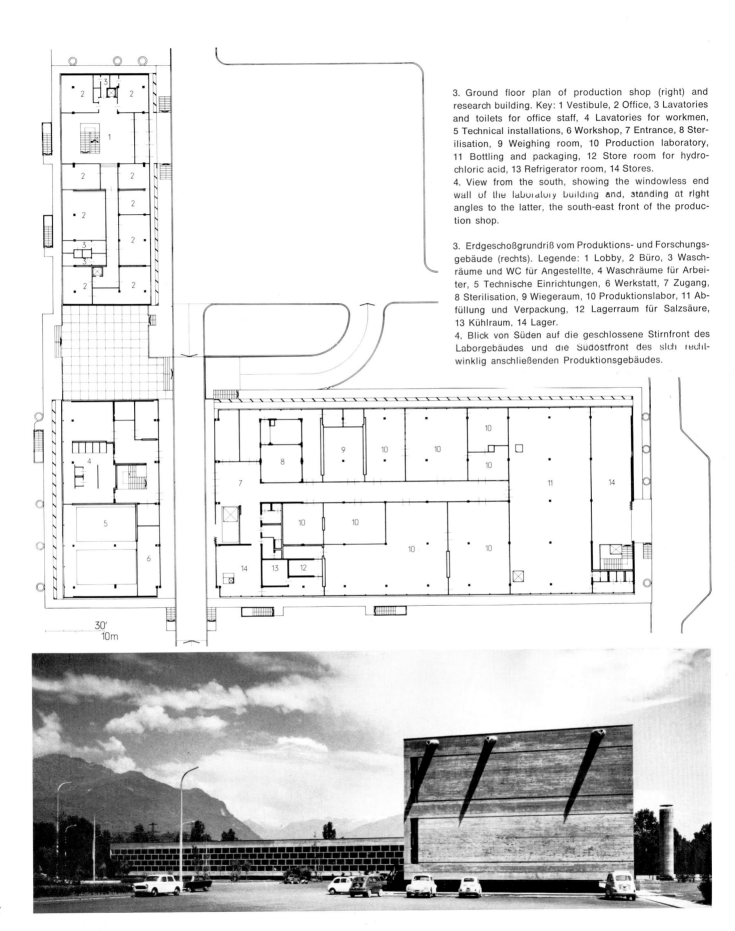

3. Ground floor plan of production shop (right) and research building. Key: 1 Vestibule, 2 Office, 3 Lavatories and toilets for office staff, 4 Lavatories for workmen, 5 Technical installations, 6 Workshop, 7 Entrance, 8 Sterilisation, 9 Weighing room, 10 Production laboratory, 11 Bottling and packaging, 12 Store room for hydrochloric acid, 13 Refrigerator room, 14 Stores.
4. View from the south, showing the windowless end wall of the laboratory building and, standing at right angles to the latter, the south-east front of the production shop.

3. Erdgeschoßgrundriß vom Produktions- und Forschungsgebäude (rechts). Legende: 1 Lobby, 2 Büro, 3 Waschräume und WC für Angestellte, 4 Waschräume für Arbeiter, 5 Technische Einrichtungen, 6 Werkstatt, 7 Zugang, 8 Sterilisation, 9 Wiegeraum, 10 Produktionslabor, 11 Abfüllung und Verpackung, 12 Lagerraum für Salzsäure, 13 Kühlraum, 14 Lager.
4. Blick von Süden auf die geschlossene Stirnfront des Laborgebäudes und die Südostfront des sich rechtwinklig anschließenden Produktionsgebäudes.

5. Production shop, seen from the laboratory building. The sun protection grille, placed at a distance of 1.31 metres (4'4") from the windows, consists of precast concrete blinds. The vertical and horizontal units are placed at an angle so as to obtain most effective sun protection.

6,7. Interior and cross-section of the production shop.

8. West wall of the production shop. The facade is enlivened by the sculptured water spouts and the notches serving as panel partitions.

5. Blick vom Labor- auf das Produktionsgebäude. Das Sonnenschutzgitter, das in einem Abstand von 1,31 m vor der Fensterwand angebracht wurde, besteht aus Betonfertigteilen. Die vertikalen und horizontalen Elemente sind schräggestellt, um einen möglichst guten Sonnenschutz zu erreichen.

6,7. Innenansicht und Querschnitt des Produktionsgebäudes.

8. Detail der Westfassade des Produktionsgebäudes. Die Fassade wird durch die plastisch geformten Wasserspeier und die graphische Felderteilung mittels Einkerbungen belebt.

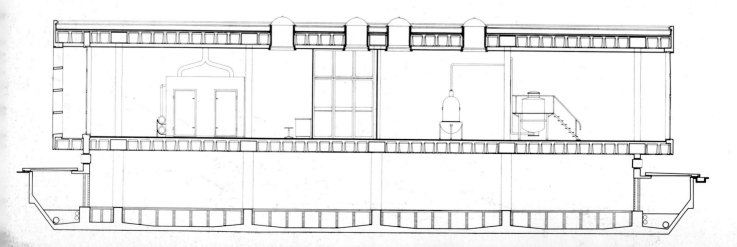

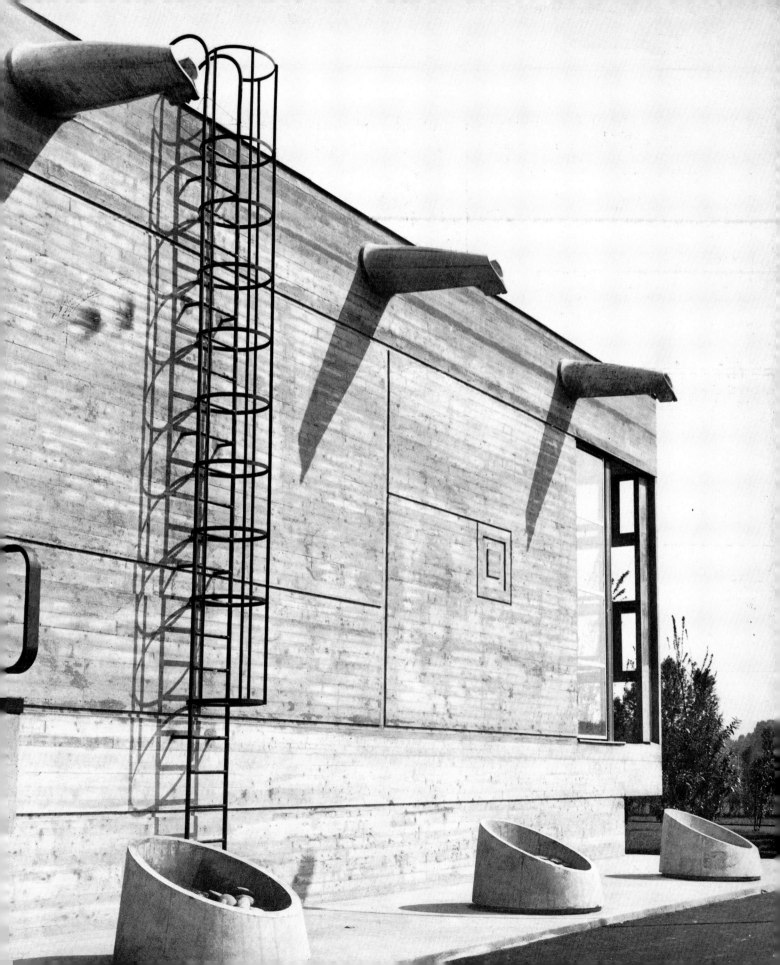

Pozzi Ceramics Factory at Sparanise, Caserta (1960—63)
Architects: Luigi Figini and Gino Pollini. Civil Engineers: G. L. Papini and S. Zorzi

Keramikfabrik Pozzi in Sparanise, Caserta (1960—63)
Architekten: Luigi Figini und Gino Pollini. Statik: Gian Luca Papini und Silvano Zorzi

This industrial estate represents one of the most extensive and complex projects hitherto realized by the architects Figini and Pollini. The buildings, though arrayed in accordance with a strictly ordered plan, are distinguished by individual features derived from functional considerations. Although, due to the richness of architectural expression, each separate building thus clearly presents itself as a remarkable achievement, the diversity in the design of the individual buildings tends to impair the — no doubt intended — integrity of the group as a whole. Despite these qualifications, the head office building placed in the centre of the estate represents, with its balanced and single-minded design, one of the most convincing works of the architects in recent years. The dimensional rhythm of the load-bearing structure is felicitously matched and enhanced by the aesthetic interpretation of the facade.

Dieser Fabrikkomplex ist eines der umfangreichsten und kompliziertesten Projekte, die von den Architekten Figini und Pollini bis heute realisiert wurden. Innerhalb der streng gegliederten Gesamtanlage unterscheiden sich die Gebäude voneinander durch ihren funktionsbedingten, eigenständigen Charakter. Diese Vielfalt im architektonischen Ausdruck läßt zwar in jedem Fall das einzelne Gebäude als eine bemerkenswerte Leistung hervortreten, aber die dadurch bedingte Verschiedenartigkeit der Bauten untereinander beeinträchtigt die offensichtlich für die Gesamtanlage angestrebte Einheitlichkeit. Trotz dieser Einschränkung ist der im Zentrum liegende Verwaltungsbau in seiner ausgewogenen Geschlossenheit eine der überzeugendsten Arbeiten der Architekten aus den letzten Jahren. Das von den Konstruktionsgliedern gebildete plastische Volumen wird durch die formale Interpretation der Fassade harmonisch ergänzt und gesteigert.

1. Head office building. With its symmetric design and layout and the conspicuous flight of steps, the building has classicist overtones. The balcony balustrade which surrounds the entire building consists of prefabricated no-fines concrete panels.

1. Ansicht des Verwaltungsgebäudes. Die Symmetrie in Anlage und Aufbau und die große Freitreppe geben dem Gebäude eine leicht klassizistische Note. Die rundum geführten Balkonbrüstungen sind aus vorgefertigten Waschbetonplatten zusammengesetzt.

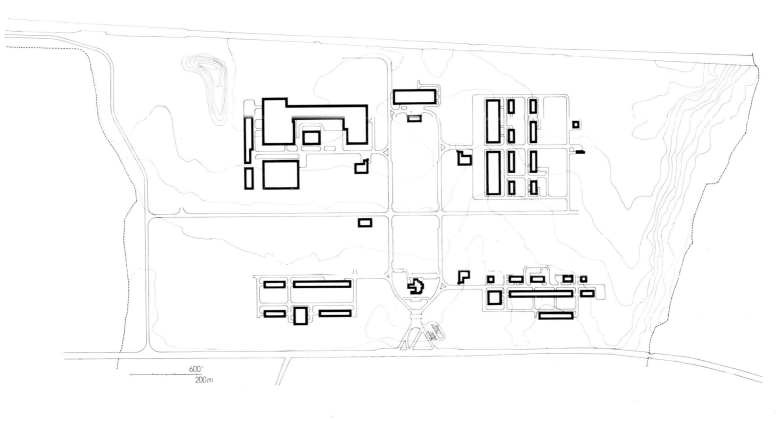

2. Plan of the estate.
3. One of the buildings in the Ceramics Department.
All the buildings are erected in exposed concrete.

2. Lageplan des Gesamtkomplexes.
3. Ein Gebäude der Keramikabteilung. Alle Bauten sind
in Sichtbeton errichtet.

4. The fire escape stairs represent an important design feature accentuating the individual buildings.

5. The roof of the Varnishing Department is surrounded by a crown of V-shaped precast concrete units which has a remarkable plastic effect.

6. Together with the roof units, the stairs conspicuously showing their separate functional components (integrally cast flights of steps and solid balustrades, both left in exposed concrete) convey an impression of forceful elegance.

4. Die Feuertreppen dienen als wichtiges gestalterisches Element und setzen an den einzelnen Gebäuden Akzente.

5. Rings um das Dach der Abteilung für Lackarbeiten zieht sich ein Kranz von V-förmigen Betonfertigteilen. Das Spiel dieser Elemente gibt dem Gebäude einen betont plastischen Abschluß.

6. Die in ihre Funktionsglieder (Stufenplatte und massive Brüstung) zerlegte Treppe aus Sichtbeton vermittelt zusammen mit den Firstziegeln am Dachrand den Eindruck kraftvoller Eleganz.

1. General view with the reactor building on the left and the generator hall and the control centre on the right.

1. Gesamtansicht. Links Reaktorbau, rechts Generatorenhalle und Steuerzentrale.

The power station consists, essentially, of three units, viz., the reactor building, the generator hall, and the stores building. The reactor is housed in a spheroidal metal casing with a diameter of 50 metres so that it dominates the appearance of the entire plant. The spherical shape was mainly adopted for safety reasons so as to prevent the escape of radioactive steam in case of accidents. In the case of the generator hall, too, safety precautions against radioactivity had to be adopted. The hall was therefore constructed as a window-less reinforced concrete building, but its monolithic appearance is mitigated by the plastic treatment of the roof trusses.

Das Kraftwerk besteht im wesentlichen aus den drei Baukörpern: dem Reaktorbau, der Generatorenhalle und dem Lagergebäude. Der Reaktor ist in einem kugelförmigen Metallgehäuse mit einem Durchmesser von fünfzig Metern untergebracht, das durch seine Ausmaße das Bild der ganzen Anlage bestimmt. Die Kugelform wurde hauptsächlich aus Sicherheitsgründen, als vorbeugende Maßnahme gegen das Ausströmen radioaktiven Wasserdampfes im Katastrophenfall gewählt. Auch für die Generatorenhalle waren Sicherheitsvorschriften gegen Radioaktivität zu beachten. Sie wurde deshalb als fensterloser Stahlbetonbau errichtet, dessen blockhafte Geschlossenheit durch die plastisch hervortretenden Dachbinder aufgelockert wird. Dagegen hat die Steuerzentrale die für einen Bürobau üblichen Fensterfronten.

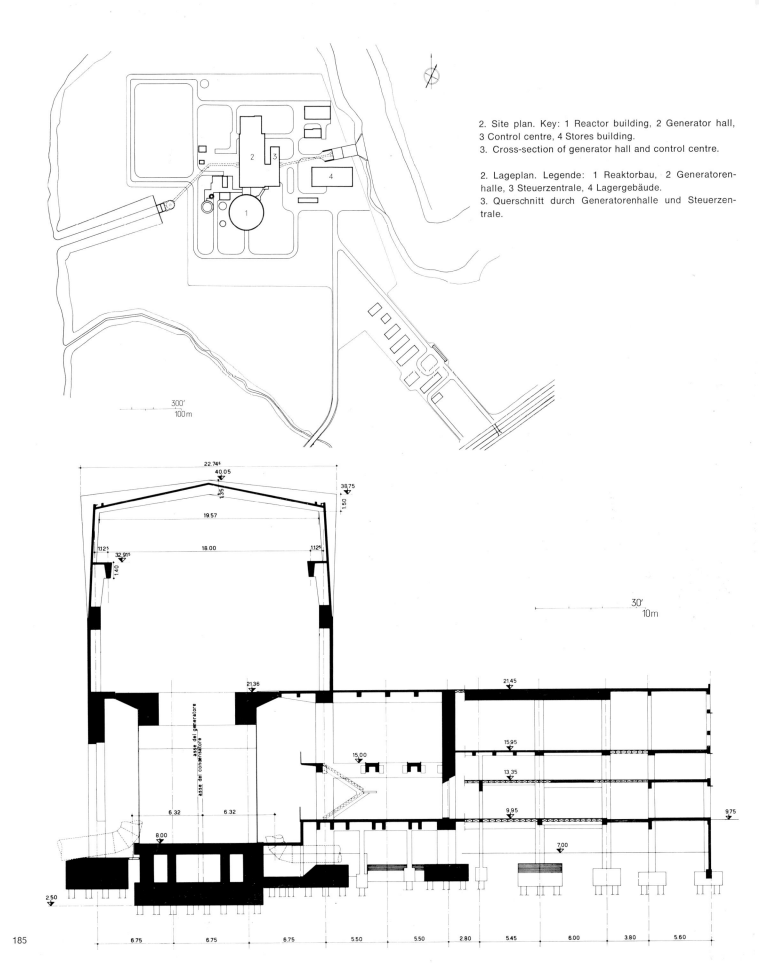

2. Site plan. Key: 1 Reactor building, 2 Generator hall, 3 Control centre, 4 Stores building.
3. Cross-section of generator hall and control centre.

2. Lageplan. Legende: 1 Reaktorbau, 2 Generatorenhalle, 3 Steuerzentrale, 4 Lagergebäude.
3. Querschnitt durch Generatorenhalle und Steuerzentrale.

Burgo paper factory at Mantua (1960—62)
Architect: Pier Luigi Nervi. Civil Engineer for steelwork: G. Covre

Papierfabrik Burgo in Mantua (1960—62)
Architekt: Pier Luigi Nervi. Entwurf der Stahlkonstruktion: G. Covre

1. Partial view of the group of buildings. The facade of the factory building is reinforced by vertical ribs.

1. Teilansicht des Komplexes. Die Fassade der Fabrikationshalle ist mit Vertikalrippen ausgesteift.

The building is situated at the outskirts of Mantua. Covering an area of some 80 000 sq.ft., it houses a large modern production line for paper manufacture. The choice of the structural system for roofing this area was governed by the need for a clear span of 160 metres (525 ft.), also with a view to a future extension. It is envisaged to install one or more identical production lines parallel to the first. The roof consists of a steel frame suspended from steel cables. The span between the suspension points is 163 metres (535 ft.), but the roof frame extends another 43 metres (141 ft.) to either side. It has a constant width of 30 metres (98 ft.). The cables carrying the roof are supported by two reinforced concrete pylons of 50 metres (164 ft.) height.

Das Gebäude steht am Stadtrand von Mantua. Es bedeckt eine Fläche von 8000 m² und nimmt ein großes, modernes Fertigungsband für die Papierherstellung auf. Die Wahl des Konstruktionssystems für die Überdeckung dieser Fläche war hauptsächlich von der Notwendigkeit bestimmt, eine freie Spannweite von 160 m zu gewinnen, die zugleich spätere Erweiterungen erleichtert. Es ist vorgesehen, ein oder mehrere gleichartige Fertigungsbänder parallel zum ersten aufzubauen. Die Überdeckung besteht aus einem Metallgerüst, das an vier Stahlkabeln aufgehängt ist. Die Spannweite zwischen den Aufhängepunkten beträgt 163 m mit zwei Kragenden von je 43 m. Die Breite ist gleichbleibend 30 m. Die Tragkabel der Dachstruktur werden von zwei 50 m hohen Pylonen aus Stahlbeton aufgenommen.

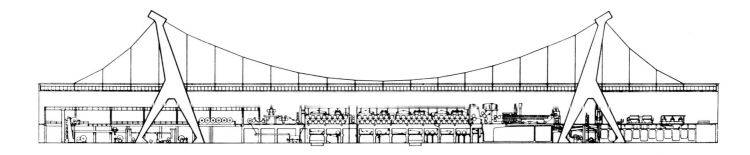

2. Longitudinal section.
3. Plan at intermediate floor level. The beams shown in black are prefabricated.
4. Interior of the factory building with the production line machinery.

2. Längsschnitt.
3. Grundriß der Zwischendecke. Die schwarz dargestellten Träger sind vorgefertigt.
4. Blick in die Fabrikationshalle mit dem großen Fertigungsband.

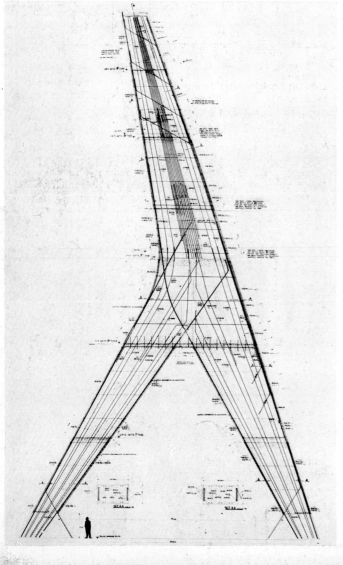

5. Overall view by night.
6. Reinforcement plan of one of the pylons.
7. The pylons were built up from precast reinforced concrete slabs of 7 cm (2.3/4″) thickness, assembled by means of connecting ribs of in-situ cast concrete. They thus formed a self-supporting hollow structure able to withstand the pressure of the in-situ cast concrete with which the interior of the structure is filled.

5. Gesamtansicht bei Nacht.
6. Bewehrungsplan eines Pylonen.
7. Für die Herstellung der Pylonen sind vorgefertigte Stahlbetonplatten von 7 cm Dicke verwendet worden. Diese Platten wurden montiert und durch in Ortbeton eingebrachte Verbindungsrippen miteinander verklammert. Sie bildeten so eine selbsttragende Hohlstruktur, die den Druck des Ortbetons aufnehmen konnte, mit dem die Struktur im Inneren ausgefüllt wurde.

Arno Bridge at Incisa near Florence (1961—63)
Architects: Giorgio Macchi and Silvano Zorzi

Brücke über den Arno bei Incisa, Florenz (1961—63)
Architekten: Giorgio Macchi und Silvano Zorzi

1. Under-view of the central arch.
2. Part of the box girder section of the bridge.
3. The structure, reduced in volume to the minimum load-bearing requirements, blends elegantly with the landscape.
4. General view.

1. Untersicht des mittleren Bogens.
2. Ausschnitt mit den Kastenträgern der Fahrbahn.
3. Die auf die statisch erforderlichen Mindestquerschnitte reduzierte Konstruktion fügt sich elegant in die Landschaft ein.
4. Gesamtansicht.

At Incisa, the Autostrada del Sole crosses the Arno valley on two parallel bridges, each carrying a roadway of 11 metres (36 ft.) width. The volume of the arches forming the central spans of the bridges has been reduced to the minimum required for load-bearing purposes; the side spans of the bridges are box girders resting on T-shaped columns. All the structural components are of prestressed concrete. The bridges have an overall length of 232 metres (761 ft.), including the central span of 104 metres (341 ft.). Compared with bridges exclusively consisting of arches, the combination of arches and columns has permitted a significant reduction in deadweight and hence in the pressure exerted on the foundations which are placed directly on the soil. The central arches of the two bridges were cast one by one, using the same centering.

Die Autostrada del Sole überquert das Arnotal mit zwei parallel geführten Brücken von jeweils 11 m Fahrbahnbreite. Die Konstruktion besteht im mittleren Bereich aus einem Bogenstück, das bis auf die statisch notwendige Masse ausgemagert wurde, und in den Seitenbereichen aus T-förmigen Stützen, sämtliche aus vorgespanntem Beton. Bei einer Gesamtlänge von 232 m hat der Mittelbogen eine Spannweite von 104 m. Die Kombination von Bögen und Stützpfeilern bot gegenüber einer Lösung mit reinen Bögen die Möglichkeit, mit kleinerem Eigengewicht zu arbeiten und zudem den Druck auf die Fundamente erheblich zu verringern; diese ruhen direkt auf dem Erdboden. Die Bögen des Mittelteils wurden mit dem gleichen Lehrgerüst nacheinander betoniert.

Bibliography of the most important Italian publications on Italian Architecture since the end of the 19th century

Bibliographie der wichtigsten italienischen Veröffentlichungen über die italienische Architektur vom Ende des 19. Jahrhunderts bis heute

Architecture at the turn of the century
Architektur um die Jahrhundertwende

Annoni, Ambrogio: Gaetano Moretti, Luca Beltrami, Camillo Boito. In «Metron», anno VI, n. 37.
Armato O. P., Maria Michele: Luca Beltrami. Sansoni, Firenze 1952.
Boito, Camillo: Questioni pratiche di belle arti. Hoepli, Milano 1893.
Calzavara, Maurizio: L'architetto Gaetano Moretti. In «Casabella-Continuità», n. 218.
Deon, B. A.: Camillo Boito. Società Anonima Arti Grafiche, Reggio Emilia 1915.
Grassi, Liliana: Camillo Boito. Ed. Il Balcone, Milano 1959.
Zevi, Bruno: Eredità dell'ottocento. In «Metron», anno VI, n. 37.

Art Nouveau
Jugendstil

Angelini, Luigi: Giuseppe Sommaruga. In «Emporium», anno XXII, n. 276.
Basile, Ernesto: Studi e schizzi. Crudo, Torino 1911.
Battaglia, Carlo: Il «Kursaal Biondo» dell'architetto Ernesto Basile. In «Emporium», anno XX, n. 244.
Bini, Vittorio: L'Art Nouveau. Tipografia De Silvestri di Baldini e Ghezzi, Milano 1957.
Caronia-Roberti, Salvatore: Ernesto Basile e cinquant'anni di architettura in Sicilia. Ciuni, Palermo 1935.
Cremona, Italo: Discorso sullo stile Liberty. In «Selearte», anno I, n. 3.
Monneret de Villard, Ugo: L'architettura di Giuseppe Sommaruga. Bestetti & Tumminelli, Milano, s. d.
Nicoletti, Manfredi: Raimondo D'Aronco. Ed. Il Balcone, Milano 1955.
Piacentini, Marcello: L'opera di Raimondo D'Aronco. In «Emporium», anno XIX, n. 220.
Pica, Agnoldomenico: Revisione del Liberty. In «Emporium», anno XLVII, n. 560.
Rossi, Aldo: A proposito di un recente studio sull'Art Nouveau. In «Casabella-Continuità», n. 225.
Tentori, Francesco: Contributo alla storiografia di Giuseppe Sommaruga. In «Casabella-Continuità», n. 217.
Torres, Duilio: Commemorazione dell'architetto Raimondo D'Aronco. Arti Grafiche Friulane, Udine 1936.

Futurism
Futurismus

Angelini, Luigi: L'architetto Antonio Sant'Elia. In «Emporium», anno XXIII, n. 266.

Arata, Giulio U.: L'Architettura futurista. In «Pagine d'arte», anno II, n. 14.
Argan, Giulio Carlo: Il pensiero critico di Antonio Sant'Elia. In «Dopo Sant'Elia», Domus, Milano 1935.
Argan, Giulio Carlo: Il pensiero critico di Antonio Sant'Elia. In «L'Arte», anno XXXII, n. 9.
Banham, Reyner: Poetica di Sant'Elia e ideologia futurista. In «L'Architettura», anno II, n. 15.
Calvesi, Maurizio: Sant'Elia, Marinetti e Boccioni. In «L'Architettura», anno II, n. 17.
Costantini, Vincenzo: Sant'Elia. In «L'Italia letteraria», 12 ottobre 1930.
Fillia, Luigi Colombo: Futurismo e Fascismo. In «La città futurista», Roma, aprile 1929.
Marchi, Virgilio: Architettura futurista. Franco Campitelli Editore, Foligno 1924.
Mariani, Leonardo: Altri disegni inediti di Sant'Elia. In «L'Architettura», anno I, n. 5.
Marinetti, F. T.: Movimento futurista. Bilancio ad un anno di dictanza. In «La fiera letteraria», 10 aprile 1927.
Marinetti, F. T.: Primato italiano. In «La città futurista», Roma, giugno 1929.
Marinetti, F. T., Prampolini, E. e Escodame': Sant'Elia e l'architettura futurista mondiale. Ed. Morreale, Milano 1931.
Marinetti, F. T.: Sant'Elia e la nuova architettura. In «Oggi e domani», Roma, 29 settembre 1930.
Nebbia, Ugo: I futuristi e il manifesto di Sant'Elia. In «L'Espresso», anno II, n. 50.
Nezi, Antonio: Dal futurismo italiano al razionalismo internazionale. Antonio Sant'Elia in luce. In «Emporium», anno XXXVII, n. 436.
Orazi, Vittorio: Stile futurista e stile fascista. In «La città futurista», Roma, aprile 1929.
Persico, Edoardo: L'esempio di Sant'Elia. In «Casabella», n. 82.
Sartoris, Alberto: Sant'Elia e l'architettura futurista. Ed. O.E.T., s.l., 1944.
Sartoris, Alberto: Antonio Sant'Elia. In «La città nuova», 20 febbraio 1934.
Sartoris, Alberto: Antonio Sant'Elia. In «Futurismo», 5 febbraio 1933.
Tagliaventi, Ivo: Sant'Elia e l'architettura futurista. In «Documenti di architettura e industria edilizia», nn. 10-11-12.
Tentori, Francesco: Le origini del Liberty di Antonio Sant'Elia. In «L'Architettura», anno I, n. 2.
Terragni, Giuseppe: L'architettura di Sant'Elia invano rosicchiata da Ugo Ojetti. In «Origini», anno VI, n. 5.
Veronesi, Giulia: L'architetto Sant'Elia non era un futurista. In «La Nazione», Firenze, 5 febbraio 1957.
Zanzi, Emilio: L'architettura dell'avvenire è nata a Como. In «Nord», Milano, ottobre 1930.
Zevi, Bruno: Ancora su Sant'Elia. In «L'Espresso», anno III, n. 16.
Zevi, Bruno: Poetica di Sant'Elia e ideologia futurista. Il messaggio di Antonio Sant'Elia e il manifesto dell'architettura futurista. In «L'Architettura», anno II, n. 13.
Zevi, Bruno: I disegni smentiscono il manifesto futurista. In «L'Espresso», anno II, n. 44.
Zevi, Bruno: Sant'Elia non era futurista. In «L'Espresso», anno II, n. 36.
Zevi, Bruno: La Milano del duemila dell'architetto futurista. In «L'Espresso», anno I, n. 10.

Architecture of rationalism
Architektur des Rationalismus

Betta, Pietro: Il «Gruppo 7» e l'architettura nuova. In «L'Architettura italiana», anno XXII, n. 2.

Canino, Marcello: Il senso dell'architettura italiana. In «Il Mattino», Napoli, 23 maggio 1931.

Costantini, Vincenzo: Memoria di tre scomparsi. In «L'illustrazione italiana», 14 ottobre 1945.

Gatto, Alfonso: Amici perduti. In «Domus», anno XVIII, n. 1.

Koenig, Giovanni Klaus: Il consumo del razionalismo italiano. In «L'Architettura», anno VII, n. 9.

Labò, Mario: Giuseppe Terragni. Ed. Il Balcone, Milano 1947.

Lancellotti, A.: La mostra di architettura razionale. In «La Casa Bella», n. 5.

Levi-Montalcini, Gino: Giuseppe Pagano. In «Agorà», novembre 1945.

Libera, Adalberto: Arte e Razionalismo. In «La Rassegna italiana», marzo 1928.

Marchi, Virgilio: Architettura razionale. In «L'Impero», quotidiano futurista, 27 aprile 1928.

Melograni, Carlo: Giuseppe Pagano. Ed. Il Balcone, Milano 1955.

Morozzo della Rocca, Robaldo: Architettura razionale — valore di una parola. In «Il giornale di Genova», 22 maggio 1931.

Ojetti, Ugo: Il Concorso per la stazione di Firenze. In «Il Corriere della Sera», marzo 1933.

Oppo, Cipriano Efisio: La prima mostra di architettura razionale. In «La Tribuna», Roma, 29 marzo 1928.

Pagano, Giuseppe: Edoardo Persico. In «Casabella», n. 109.

Palanti, Giancarlo: Giuseppe Pagano Pogatschnig. Architetture e scritti. Ed. Domus, Milano 1947.

Papini, Roberto: Architettura giovane. In «Il Corriere della Sera», 14 maggio 1928.

Persico, Edoardo: Profezia dell'architettura. Muggiani, Milano 1945.

Persico, Edoardo: Scritti critici e polemici. Alfonso Gatto, Rosa e Ballo, Milano 1947.

Piacentini, Marcello: La mostra di Architettura nelle sale della ENAPI. In «La Tribuna», Roma, 22 giugno 1932.

Podestà, Attilio: Omaggio a Terragni. In «Emporium», anno LIII, n. 640.

Polistina, Sam: Giuseppe Pagano. In «Avanti!», Milano, 29 settembre 1945.

Ragghianti, Carlo Ludovico: Ricordo di Pagano. In «Metron», anno VII.

Tridenti, Carlo: La prima mostra italiana di architettura razionale. In «Il Giornale d'Italia», 19 marzo 1928.

Veronesi, Giulia: Difficoltà politiche dell'architettura in Italia. 1920–1940. Tamburini, Milano 1953.

Architecture after the Second World War
Architektur nach dem Zweiten Weltkrieg

Aloi, Roberto: Nuove architetture a Milano. Hoepli, Milano 1959.

Bottoni, Piero: Edifici moderni in Milano. Domus, Milano 1955.

Centro di studio e informazione per l'architettura sacra:

Dieci anni di architettura sacra in Italia 1945–1955. Ed. dell'Ufficio tecnico organizzativo arcivescovile, Bologna 1956.

Dezzi Bardeschi, Marco: Il senso della storia nell'architettura italiana degli ultimi anni. In «Comunità», anno XIX, n. 130.

Moretti, Luigi: L'Architecture italienne d'aujourd'hui. Tip. In. Gra. Do., Roma 1960.

Paci, Enzo: Problematica dell'architettura contemporanea. In «Casabella-Continuità», n. 209.

Pagani, Carlo: Architettura italiana d'oggi. Hoepli, Milano 1956.

Perogalli, Carlo: Aspetti dell'architettura contemporanea. Salto, Milano 1952.

Pica, Agnoldomenico: Architettura italiana ultima. Edizioni del Milione, Milano 1959.

Portoghesi, Paolo: Tendenze delle nuove generazioni di architetti. In «Comunità», anno XVII, n. 115.

Samonà, Alberto: Il dibattito architettonico urbanistico oggi in Italia. In «Comunità», anno XVII, n. 115.

Tentori, Francesco: Quindici anni di architettura. In «Casabella-Continuità», n. 251.

Veronesi, Giulia: L'architettura dei grattacieli a Milano. In «Comunità», anno XIII, n. 74.

General publications
Allgemeine Veröffentlichungen

Argan, Giulio Carlo: Gardella. Ed. di Comunità, Milano 1959.

Argan, Giulio Carlo: Pier Luigi Nervi. Ed. Il Balcone, Milano 1954.

Bargellini, P. e Freyrie, E.: Nascita e vita dell'architettura moderna. Arnaud, Firenze 1947.

Beltrami, Luca: Gaetano Moretti. Costruzioni, Concorsi, Schizzi. Bestetti & Tumminelli, Milano 1912.

Benevolo, Leonardo: Una introduzione all'architettura. Laterza, Bari 1960.

Blasi, Cesare: Figini e Pollini. Ed. di Comunità, Milano 1963.

Boaga, Giorgio e Boni, Benito: Riccardo Morandi. Ed. di Comunità, Milano 1962.

Brizio, Anna Maria: Ottocento-Novecento. U.T.E.T., Torino 1939.

Caracciolo, Edoardo: L'architettura moderna in Sicilia. In «Metron», anno IV, n. 29.

Caronia, Giuseppe: Introduzione allo studio dei caratteri dell'architettura moderna. Ed. S. F. Flaccovio, Palermo, s. d.

De Carlo, Giancarlo: Il contributo dell'architettura italiana alla cultura internazionale. In «L'Architettura», anno IV, n. 33.

Figini, Luigi e Pollini, Gino: Origini dell'architettura moderna in Italia. In «L'Architecture d'aujourd'hui», anno XXII, n. 41.

Gentili Tedeschi, Eugenio: Figini e Pollini. Il Balcone, Milano 1959.

Grassi, Liliana: Motivi per una storiografia dell'architettura. Edizioni Universitarie Bignami, Milano 1956.

Kirchmayr, Mario: L'architettura italiana dalle origini ai giorni nostri. Vol. I e vol. II, S.E.I., Torino 1957–58.

Magagnato, Licisco: Esperienza storica e architettura moderna. In «Comunità, anno XIII, n. 59.

Nervi, Pier Luigi: Nuove strutture. Ed. di Comunità, Milano 1963.
Pane, Roberto: La cultura architettonica italiana nel mondo moderno. In «L'Architettura», anno IV, n. 34.
Pica, Agnoldomenico: Architettura moderna in Italia. Hoepli, Milano 1941.
Reggiori, Ferdinando: Milano 1800–1943. Edizioni del Milione, Milano 1947.
Rogers, Ernesto N.: La tradizione dell'architettura moderna italiana. In «Casabella-Continuità», n. 206.
Semerani, Luciano: Una introduzione all'architettura. In «Casabella-Continuità», n. 244.
Tafuri, Manfredo: Ludovico Quaroni e la cultura architettonica italiana. In «Zodiac», anno VI, n. 11.
Tentori, Francesco: Introduzione allo studio dei caratteri dell'architettura moderna. In «Casabella-Continuità», n. 229.
Tintori, Silvano: Figini e Pollini. In «Casabella-Continuità», n. 232.

Also included under the heading of "General publications" are the monographs of those architects whose works belong to different stylistic periods.

In die Rubrik »Allgemeine Veröffentlichungen« sind auch Monographien über die Architekten aufgenommen, deren Arbeiten in verschiedene Stilperioden gehören.

Periodicals dealing with Arts and Architecture published in Italy since 1888

Abitare — Milan
Published monthly. First published in January 1961 under the title "Casa Novità". After five issues, the journal was renamed "Abitare" in June 1961 though Piera Peroni remained the editor. Published by "Abitare", 18 Foro Buonaparte, Milan.

Acciaio — Milan
Monthly edition in Italian of the journal "Acier-Stahl-Steel". First published in January 1960 under the editorship of F. Bittasi. He was followed in December 1962 by F. Saverio Scultheis-Brandi who, in his turn, was replaced in December 1963 by Giulia Affer. Published by UISAA, 8 Piazza Velasca, Milan.

Architettura — Milan-Rome
Journal of the National Fascist Union of Architects. First published in January 1932 as a successor to the journal "Architettura e Arti decorative". Published monthly by Treves-Treccani-Tumminelli, Milan, and edited by Marcello Piacentini until the end of 1942 when it ceased publication. Succeeded in the following year by "Architettura — Rassegna di Architettura", which see below.

Architettura e Arti decorative — Milan-Rome
Organ of the National Union of Architects. First published in May 1921, at bi-monthly intervals, by Editrice d'arte Bestetti & Tumminelli, Milan-Rome. Ceased publication in December 1931. Re-appeared title in the following year as "Architettura".

Architettura Cantiere — Milan
Journal for Architecture, Civil Engineering and Building Industry. First published in 1952 under the patronage of the Architectural Faculty of Milan Technical University, edited by Libero Guarnieri and published quarterly by Görlich, Milan. The last issue was that of No. 25/26 in 1963, edited by G. G. Görlich.

Architettura, Rassegna di Architettura — Milan
Organ of the National Fascist Union of Architects. Published in 1943 by Garzanti as a successor to "Architettura", appearing first monthly and later at irregular intervals; edited by Marcello Piacentini. The last issue of the journal was that of January/April, 1944.

Archivio Storico dell'Arte — Rome
Illustrated monthly journal, edited by Domenico Gnoli. First published in January 1888 by Loreto Pasqualucci, Rome. Contributors included important personalities of contemporary Italian cultural life, such as Luca Beltrami, Camillo Boito, Corrado Ricci, Giuseppe Sacconi, Adolfo Venturi as well as renowned English, French, German and Austrian art historians. From January 1889 to September 1892, the journal was published by Ermanno Loescher & Co., Rome. From November 1892 onwards, it was published by Michele Danesi, Rome. From 1891 to the end, six issues per annum were published. The second series of the journal commenced publication in January 1895, with the same publishers and editors.

Publication of the journal ceased with the November/December number, 1897. In the new year, it became the journal "L'Arte".

Arte italiana decorative e industriale — Venice
A monthly journal published by Ferdinando Ongania, Venice, and sponsored by the Ministry for Agriculture, Industry and Commerce. First published in 1890 under the editorship of the publishers. From January 1892 onwards, Camillo Boito was the editor. Later, the journal was edited by Fratelli Cattaneo-Gaffuri and Ratti, Milan, and published by Hoepli and Edizioni Arti Grafiche, Bergamo, until publication ceased in December 1911.

Casabella — Milan
First published under the title of "La casa bella", edited by Guido Marangoni (1928 – 1930) and later by Giuseppe Pagano. In 1933, the journal assumed the title "Casabella" and was edited by Giuseppe Pagano and Edoardo Persico. In 1938, the journal was renamed "Casabella-costruzioni" and in 1940 "Costruzioni-Casabella". After an interval of two years (1944 – 1945), the journal re-appeared under the editorship of Franco Albini and Giancarlo Palanti. In 1954, E. N. Rogers became editor-in-chief, and the journal was renamed "Casabella-Continuità". The journal ceased publication from February to August 1965 but was then again published under the editorship of Gianantonio Bernasconi under the title "Casabella". Published by Domus, Milan.

Case d'oggi — Milan
Monthly journal published by "La casa", Milan, and sponsored by the Civil Engineering Section of the Fascist Union of Engineers, Milan. There was an editorial committee consisting of A. Goldstein, E. Frisia, G. Vinaccia, L. Lenzi, G. Lenzi and M. Cavallè. The journal first appeared in January 1935 and ceased publication with the December issue, 1944.

Comunità — Milan
First published in March 1946, under the title "Giornale mensile di politica e cultura", by Edizioni di Comunità, Rome, under the editorship of Adriano Olivetti. From April, 1947, onwards, the journal was published weekly by Taurinia, Turin until No. 18 of 6th September when it became a fortnightly review. Publication temporarily ceased at the end of 1947 and was only resumed in 1949. During the year 1948, however, there appeared two issues of the journal "Movimento Comunità", a regional supplement to the newspaper "Comunità", edited by Adriano Olivetti. "Comunità" re-appeared in January 1949 as a bi-monthly review of the "Movimento Comunità", again under the editorship of Adriano Olivetti and published by Edizioni di Comunità. From No. 11 of June, 1951 onwards, the journal appeared every three months, from No. 17 of January/February 1953 every two months, and finally from No. 32 of September 1955 every month. With No. 72 of July 1959, it assumed the new title "Comunità — Rivista mensile di cultura ed informazione". After Adriano Olivetti's death, Renzo Zorzi became in March, 1961, the new editor. Since January 1961, the journal has appeared unter the new title "Comunità — Rivista mensile di informazione culturale", and it is still appearing under this title.

Costruire — Rome
Journal for architecture and technology of the ANDIL, edited by Mario Cantelli, appearing at four-monthly intervals from January 1959 onwards. The intervals were reduced to three months in 1962 and to two months in 1963. Published by ANDIL, 71 Via Cavour, Rome.

Dibattito urbanistico — Milan
Bi-monthly journal for town planning studies. First published in September 1965 under the editorship of L. Bellini. Published by Officine Grafiche Vallecchi di Firenze, 4 Piazza Sant'Alessandro, Milan.

Domus — Milan
Published from January 1928 to the end of 1940 under the title of "Rivista d'architettura e arredamento dell'abitazione moderna in città e in campagna" by Domus, Milan, and edited by Gio Ponti. With the January issue, 1941, the editorship was taken over by Massimo Bontempelli, Giuseppe Pagano and Melchiorre Bega, joined in September 1942 by Guglielmo Ulrich. From January 1943 onwards, the editors were Melchiorre Bega and Guglielmo Ulrich, and from October 1943 to the end of 1944, Melchiorre Bega alone. The journal did not appear throughout the year 1945 but publication was resumed in January 1946 under the editorship, until December 1947, of E. N. Rogers. Since January 1948, Gio Ponti has been the editor.

Edilizia moderna — Milan
Published by the Linoleum Association. First published as a quarterly in March 1931 under the editorship of Ernesto Giorgi, who was replaced in December 1938 by Giuseppe Luraghi. Ceased publication in December 1940 but re-appeared from April to December 1942. After another interval, the journal finally re-appeared in December 1948 with Vittorio Beltrami as editor-in-chief. He was followed by Renato Bisignani (June 1950), Emilio Romanini (June 1953), and Dino Bernardi (April 1955).

Edilizia Popolare — Rome
Bi-monthly journal of the Italian Federation of Housing Associations under the editorship of Camillo Ripamonti. First appeared in November/December 1954. Published by Edilizia Popolare, 58 Via XX Settembre, Rome.

Emporium — Bergamo
Illustrated monthly journal for arts, literature, science and entertainment, published by Istituto Italiano d'Arti Grafiche, Bergamo. First published in January 1895 under the editorship of Paolo Testa who continued until May 1911. He was succeeded by Giuseppe Monticelli who continued until June 1924. Then followed Luigi Pelandi up to the end of 1925, and Ezio Sangiovanni from January 1926 to August 1941. Luigi Pelandi then resumed the editorship until the end of 1942, finally succeeded by Attilio Podestà up to the end of 1964, when the journal ceased publication.

Il Vetro — Milan
Monthly journal of the National Fascist Association of Glass Manufacturers. First published in 1938 under the editorship of Pietro Bergonzi as a successor to the journal "L'Industria del vetro e della ceramica". When

the journal was sold by the publishers "Officio periodici Tumminelli", Rome, it ceased publication in 1943.

Lacerba – Florence
Fortnightly journal for cultural affairs, edited by Guido Pogni. First published in January 1913 in Florence. Contributors included some of the most outstanding representatives of contemporary Italian culture such as Soffici, Papini, Palazzeschi, Marinetti. This review of clearly anti-traditional and anti-conformist character was a collection of satirical contributions, critical essays, short poems, drawings (by Picasso, Rosai, Carrà, etc.) as well as French and English contributions by representatives of European Futurism. In November 1914, Pietro Gramigni became editor-in-chief. The journal ceased publication in May 1915.

L'Architettura, Cronache e storia – Milan
Monthly journal published, since 1955, by ET/AS Kompass, Milan, under the editorship of Bruno Zevi.

L'Architettura Italiana – Turin
Monthly journal for architecture and building, first published in 1905 by Crudo e Lattuada, Turin. The first editors were Carlo Bianchi and Antonio Cavallassi, followed by G. Lavini. Ceased publication in 1943.

L'Arte – Rome-Milan
Illustrated bi-monthly journal first published in 1898, under the editorship of Domenico Gnoli and Adolfo Venturi, by Michele Danesi, Rome, as successor to "Archivio Storico dell'Arte". In 1900, the journal assumed the title "Periodico di Storia dell'Arte medioevale e moderna e d'arte decorativa"; it was then edited by Adolfo Venturi and published by Michele Danesi, Rome and Ulrico Hoepli, Milan. The journal appeared at irregular intervals. The year 1904 saw the beginning of a new bi-monthly series with the same editors and publishers. From 1905 onwards, the journal was published by Casa editrice de l'Arte, Rome. A new series, edited by Adolfo and Lionello Venturi, appeared in 1930, printed by Ajani e Canale, Turin. From July 1935 onwards, Adolfo Venturi was the sole editor; with the January number of 1936, the journal became a quarterly. From January 1935 onwards, it was published by Industrie Grafiche Italiane Stucchi, Milan. From 1943 onwards, the numbers appeared at irregular intervals so that there was one issue in 1943, one in 1944, none in 1945 and only one in 1946, with Aurelio Minghetti acting as editor-in-chief. The next issue only appeared in 1948, followed by a supplement in 1949. No number was published in 1950. In 1951, Giorgio Nicodemi became editor-in-chief. There was only one issue in 1952, none in 1953, one in 1954, none in 1955. From January 1956, the periodical appeared bi-annually. From January 1958, it appeared quarterly, from 1959 to 1961 three times per annum, and in 1962 twice. The journal ceased publication at the end of that year.

L'Edilizia moderna – Milan
Monthly journal for practical architecture and building, published by Arturo Demarchi, Milan. First published in April 1892 under the editorship of Luca Beltrami, Andrea Ferrari, Federico Jorini, Carlo Mina and Gaetano Moretti.

Later, Carlo Formenti and Francesco Magnoni became the editors. The journal ceased publication in December 1916.

L'Industria italiana del Cemento – Rome
Monthly journal published by the Association for the Promotion of Cement Utilisation (SIAC) from January 1930 to December 1943. After an interval of three years, the journal re-appeared in September 1946, published by the Italian Cement, Asbestos Cement, Lime and Plaster Industry. With the January issue, 1962, the journal assumed its present typographical appearance, under the editorship of Gaetano Bologna, Rome.

La nuova città – Florence
Monthly journal for architecture, town planning and interior design, published 1946–54. Editor was G. Michelucci.

Lineestruttura – Naples
Quarterly review for architecture, design and the plastic arts. First published in May 1966 with Lea Vergine as editor-in-chief. Nino del Papa was responsible for architecture and town planning, Enzo Mari for design, and Lea Vergine for plastic arts. Published by Diaframma, Naples.

Metron – Rome
International monthly journal for architecture, published by Sandron, Rome. First published in August 1945. Editors: Luigi Piccinato (for town planning) and Mario Ridolfi (for architecture). Seven issues appeared in 1946, ten in 1947. With No. 25, published in 1948, format and volume were changed, with a greater emphasis on service to readers and on illustrations. Editors of the new journal were Luigi Piccinato, Mario Ridolfi, Silvio Radiconcini and Bruno Zevi. Eight issues were published in 1948, six in 1949. From July, 1950 onwards, the journal was published at bi-monthly intervals by Comunità under the editorship of Riccardo Musatti, Luigi Piccinato, Silvio Radicincini and Bruno Zevi. Four issues each were published in 1951 and 1952, one in 1953, six in 1954. No. 54 of November/December of that year was the last issue of this journal.

Pagine d'Arte – Milan
Published by Alfieri e Lacroix with Antonio Bonfanti as editor-in-chief. This "Chronicle and review of ancient and modern art" was first published in 1913, at fortnightly intervals from October to June and at monthly intervals from July to September. From January 1917, it was published as a monthly until publication ceased with the December issue, 1919.

Pagine d'Arte (second series) – Milan
Published monthly under the editorship of Marisa Romano and Innocenza Papetti from April 1951 onwards, and printed by Fattori, Rome. Later, the journal appeared at irregular intervals until it finally ceased publication in December 1952.

Prefabbricare – Milan
Bi-monthly journal of the Italian Association for the Research into Development in the Sphere of Prefabri-

cated Materials and Systems. First published in January 1958 under the editorship of Sergio Mulitsch. With No. 3/4 of December 1958/February 1959, the editorship went to Ete Stucchi. From No. 4 October/December 1959 onwards, the journal appeared bi-monthly; since 1961, it has been published by the Italian Association for Prefabrication. In 1964, the editorship was taken over by Arardo Spreti, 1 Galleria Passarella, Milan.

Prospettive — Milan
Quarterly review for architecture and interior design, edited by C. E. Rava and published by Görlich, Milan. First published in 1963. From No. 13 of December 1956, onwards, the journal appeared at bi-monthly intervals. With No. 26/27 of June 1963, the journal ceased publication.

Quadrante — Milan
Monthly journal for architecture and interior design, edited by Massimo Bontempelli and Pietro Maria Bardi. Published from May 1932 to October 1936.

Rassegna di Architettura — Milan
Monthly journal for architecture and interior design, published by the architectural review group. First published in January 1929 with Giovanni Rocco as editor-in-chief. From January to December 1940, A. Cassi-Ramelli was the editor. The journal ceased publication at the end of 1940.

Rassegna d'Arte — Milan
Monthly journal published by G. Martinelli & Co., Milan, with Cesare Ostini as editor-in-chief. First published in January 1901. The Editorial Committee comprised some of the leading personalities of contemporary Italian cultural life, including Luca Beltrami, Gaetano Moretti, Lodovico Pogliaghi and Virginio Muzio. In May 1902, Ostini was superseded by Amos Mantegazza who was, in his turn replaced by Emilio Magni in July 1902. At the same time, the journal was taken over by Menotti, Bassani & Co., Milan. In January 1903, an Editorial Committee was constituted, comprising Solone Ambrosoli, Guido Cagnola, Francesco Malaguzzi-Valeri, Corrado Ricci and G. B. Vittadini. Editor-in-chief was Emilio Magni who was replaced, in April of that year, by Battista Biassoni. In January 1904, G. Cagnola, Francesco Malaguzzi-Valeri and Corrado Ricci became the editors with Battista Biassoni as editor-in-chief. From January 1905, "Rassegna d'Arte" appeared under the editorship of Guido Cagnola and Francesco Malaguzzi-Valeri, together with the previous editor-in-chief who was, however, replaced by Andrea Moretti in June 1906. From January onwards, the journal was published by Alfieri e Lacroix, Milan, with Antonio Bonfanti, though Guido Cagnola and Francesco Malaguzzi-Valeri remained the editors. From January 1915 to December 1916, Guido Cagnola was the sole editor. Subsequently, the journal was merged with "Rassegna d'Arte antica e moderna".

Rassegna d'Arte antica e moderna — Milan
First published in January 1914 as a monthly journal, under the editorship of Guido Cagnola and Francesco Malaguzzi-Valeri, by Alfieri e Lacroix, Milan, with the sub-title "Vita d'Arte", the journal appeared in monthly alternation in two series, viz. "Rassegna d'Arte antica e

moderna — Vita d'Arte" and "Rassegna d'Arte antica e moderna — Rassegna d'Arte antica", the latter under the editorship of Guido Cagnola, the former under that of F. Bargagli-Petrucci. In 1920, both series were combined under the title "Rassegna d'arte antica e moderna" with Corrado Ricci as editor and Alfiere e Lacroix, with Antonio Bonfanti, as publishers. The latter retained his responsibility until January 1921 when he was replaced by Carlo Zacchetti who was in turn replaced in April 1922 by Cesare Castelli. The journal ceased publication in December 1922.

Sele arte — Ivrea
Bi-monthly review for culture and international arts communications. First published in July 1952, under the editorship of Carlo L. Ragghinati, by "Ufficio Stampa della Ing. C. Olivetti & Co., S.p.A.", Ivrea. The journal ceased publication in June 1966.

Spazio — Rome
Monthly review for arts and architecture. First published in July 1950 under the editorship of Luigi Moretti. Ceased publication with the January issue, 1953.

Stile — Milan
First published in January 1941 under the title "Stile nella casa e nell'arredamento", edited by Gio Ponti and published by Garzanti. Ceased publication with the December issue, 1947.

Urbanistica — Turin
First published in January 1932 under the title "Bollettino della Sezione Regionale Piemontese Istituto Nazionale di Urbanistica" under the editorship of Pietro Betta, the publishers being F. Casanova & Co., Turin. In July 1932, Armando Melis became the editor. In January 1934, the journal changed its title to "Rivista dell'Istituto Nazionale di Urbanistica". From January 1947 to December 1948, Mario Zocca was editor-in-chief. From July 1949, the journal appeared at bi-monthly intervals with Adriano Olivetti as editor and assumed its present-day typographical appearance. Since 1950, the journal has appeared at quarterly intervals. In December 1953, Giovanni Astengo became the editor.

Vitrum — Milan
First published in November 1949 as a monthly journal under the title "Lastre di vetro e cristallo", sponsored by the Information and Research Centre for the Utilisation of Glass in Buildings and Equipment (CISAV), and edited by Giulio Benelli. With No. 10 of August 1950, Luigi Gandini became the editor. The title of the journal was changed, with No. 15 of January 1951, to "Vitrum — Lastre di vetro e cristallo". Since January 1959, the journal has appeared at bi-monthly intervals and has assumend its present-day typographical appearance. It is published by CISAV, 5 Via Hoepli, Milan.

Zodiac — Milan
International review for contemporary architecture, founded by Adriano Olivetti. First published in October 1957 under the editorship of Bruno Alfieri, by Comunità. Since 1964, the editorship has been in the hands of Pier Carlo Santini.

Von 1888 bis heute in Italien veröffentlichte Kunst- und Architektur-Zeitschriften

Abitare — Mailand
Erscheint monatlich. Kam erstmals im Januar 1961 unter dem Titel »Casa Novità« heraus. Nach fünf Nummern wurde sie im Juni 1961 in »Abitare« umbenannt, doch blieb die Schriftleitung in Händen von Piera Peroni. Erscheint im Verlag »Abitare«, Mailand, Foro Buonaparte 18.

Acciaio — Mailand
Monatlich erscheinende italienische Ausgabe der Zeitschrift »Acier-Stahl-Steel«, bei UISAA verlegt. Sie kam im Januar 1960 unter der Schriftleitung von F. Bittasi heraus. Im Dezember 1962 folgte ihm F. Saverio Scultheis-Brandi, der im Dezember 1963 von Giulia Affer abgelöst wurde. Verlag UISAA, Mailand, Piazza Velasca 8.

Architettura — Mailand-Rom
Zeitschrift der Nationalen Faschistischen Architekten-Gewerkschaft. Kam im Januar 1932 als Nachfolgerin der Zeitschrift »Architettura e Arti decorative« heraus. Erschien monatlich im Verlag Treves-Treccani-Tumminelli, Mailand, unter der Schriftleitung von Marcello Piacentini bis Ende 1942 und stellte dann ihr Erscheinen ein. Sie wurde im darauffolgenden Jahr durch »Architettura — Rassegna di Architettura« ersetzt.

Architettura e Arti decorative — Mailand-Rom
Organ der Nationalen Architekten-Gewerkschaft. Kam im Mai 1921 heraus, erschien zweimonatlich im Verlag Editrice d'arte Bestetti & Tumminelli, Mailand-Rom, und stellte ihr Erscheinen im Dezember 1931 ein. Im folgenden Jahr änderte sie ihren Titel in »Architettura« um.

Architettura Cantiere — Mailand
Zeitschrift für Architektur, Bautechnik und Bauindustrie. Kam 1952 unter der Schirmherrschaft der Architektur-Fakultät des Polytechnikums in Mailand heraus und erschien vierteljährlich unter der Schriftleitung von Libero Guarnieri im Verlag Görlich, Mailand. Für die Nr. 25/26 des Jahres 1963 hatte G. G. Görlich die Schriftleitung, und mit dieser Nummer stellte das Blatt sein Erscheinen ein.

Architettura, Rassegna di Architettura — Mailand
Organ der Nationalen Faschistischen Architekten-Gewerkschaft. Kam 1943 als Nachfolgerin von »Architettura« heraus und erschien zunächst monatlich, später in unregelmäßigen Zeitabständen, im Verlag Garzanti. Schriftleiter war Marcello Piacentini. Mit der Januar/April-Nummer stellte die Zeitschrift ihr Erscheinen ein.

Archivio Storico dell'Arte — Rom
Illustrierte Monatszeitschrift unter der Chefredaktion von Domenico Gnoli. Kam im Januar 1888 im Verlag Loreto Pasqualucci, Rom, heraus. Mitarbeiter waren bedeutende Persönlichkeiten der italienischen Kultur jener Zeit, darunter Luca Beltrami, Camillo Boito, Corrado Ricci, Giuseppe Sacconi, Adolfo Venturi und bekannte englische, französische, deutsche und österreichische Kunsthistoriker. Von Januar 1889 bis September 1892 wurde die Zeitschrift vom Verlag Ermanno Loescher & C., Rom, herausgegeben. Ab November 1892 war Michele Danesi, Rom, neuer Verleger. Von 1891 bis zu ihrer Einstellung erschienen jährlich sechs Hefte. Im Januar 1895 begann die zweite Folge im gleichen Verlag und unter derselben Schriftleitung. Mit dem November/Dezember-Heft des Jahres 1897 stellte die Zeitschrift ihr Erscheinen ein. Sie wurde dann im neuen Jahr zur Zeitschrift »L'Arte«.

Arte italiana decorativa e industriale — Venedig
Unter der Schirmherrschaft des Ministeriums für Landwirtschaft, Industrie und Handel erscheinende Monatszeitschrift im Verlag Ferdinando Ongania, Venedig. Kam erstmals 1890 unter der Schriftleitung des Verlegers heraus. Vom Januar 1892 an war Camillo Boito Schriftleiter. Später wurde sie von Fratelli Cattaneo-Gaffuri und Ratti, Mailand, herausgegeben und bei Hoepli und Edizioni Arti Grafiche, Bergamo, verlegt, bis sie im Dezember 1911 ihr Erscheinen einstellte.

Casabella — Mailand
Erschien erstmals als »La casa bella« unter der Schriftleitung von Guido Marangoni (1928–1930) und dann von Giuseppe Pagano. Im Januar 1933 erhielt sie den Titel »Casabella«. Die Schriftleitung hatten Giuseppe Pagano und Edoardo Persico. Im Jahr 1938 wurde sie in »Casabella-costruzioni« und im Jahr 1940 in »Costruzioni-Casabella« umbenannt. Nach zweijähriger Pause (1944 bis 1945) erschien sie unter der Schriftleitung von Franco Albini und Giancarlo Palanti wieder. 1954 wurde E. N. Rogers Chefredakteur, und der neue Titel der Zeitschrift hieß »Casabella-Continuità«. Von Februar bis August 1965 stellte sie ihr Erscheinen ein, kam dann jedoch unter der Schriftleitung von Gianantonio Bernasconi als »Casabella« wieder heraus. Verlag Domus, Mailand.

Case d'oggi — Mailand
Monatszeitschrift, die bei »La casa«, Mailand, verlegt und von der Baugruppe der Faschistischen Ingenieur-Gewerkschaft, Mailand, herausgegeben wurde. Der Schriftleitungsausschuß bestand aus A. Goldstein, E. Frisia, G. Vinaccia, L. Lenzi, G. Lenzi und M. Cavallè. Sie erschien erstmals im Januar 1935 und wurde mit der Dezember-Nummer 1944 eingestellt.

Comunità — Mailand
Die Zeitschrift kam im März 1946 als »Giornale mensile di politica e cultura« unter der Schriftleitung von Adriano Olivetti beim Verlag Edizioni di Comunità, Rom, heraus. Von April 1947 an erschien sie wöchentlich im Verlag »Taurinia«, Turin, bis zur Nr. 18 vom 6. September, von da an vierzehntäglich. Mit dem Jahresende 1947 stellte die »Comunità« zeitweise ihr Erscheinen ein; erst 1949 kam sie wieder heraus. 1948 erschienen jedoch zwei Nummern der Zeitschrift »Movimento Comunità«, unter der Schriftleitung von Adriano Olivetti, als regionale Beilage der Zeitung »Comunità«. Im Januar 1949 erschien die »Comunità« als zweimonatliche Zeitschrift der »Movimento Comunità« wieder, ebenfalls unter der Schriftleitung von Adriano Olivetti und im Verlag Edizioni di Comunità. Ab Heft 11 vom Juni 1951 kam die Zeitschrift vierteljährlich heraus, ab Heft 17 vom Januar/Februar 1953 zweimonatlich und schließlich ab Nr. 32

vom September 1955 monatlich. Mit der Nr. 72 vom Juli 1959 bekommt sie den neuen Titel »Comunità – Rivista mensile di cultura ed informazione«. Nach Adriano Olivettis Tod wird Renzo Zorzi im März 1961 verantwortlicher Schriftleiter. Ab Januar 1961 heißt der neue Titel »Comunità – Rivista mensile di informazione culturale«, und unter diesem Titel erscheint die Zeitschrift auch heute noch.

Costruire – Rom
Zeitschrift für Architektur und Technik der ANDIL, Schriftleitung Mario Cantelli, die ab Januar 1959 alle vier Monate herauskam. Im Jahr 1962 erschien sie vierteljährlich, seit 1963 jeden zweiten Monat. Verlag ANDIL, Rom, Via Cavour 71.

Dibattito urbanistico – Mailand
Zweimonatszeitschrift für städtebauliche Studien. Erschien erstmals im September 1965 unter der Schriftleitung von L. Bellini. Sie wird herausgegeben von Officine Grafiche Vallecchi di Firenze, Mailand, Piazza Sant'Alessandro 4.

Domus – Mailand
Kam vom Januar 1928 an bis Ende 1940 als »Rivista d'Architettura e Arredamento dell'abitazione moderna in città e in campagna« im Verlag Domus, Mailand, unter der Schriftleitung von Gio Ponti heraus. Mit der Januar-Nummer des Jahres 1941 übernahmen Massimo Bontempelli, Giuseppe Pagano und Melchiorre Bega die Schriftleitung. Von 1942 an waren Massimo Bontempelli und Melchiorre Bega die Schriftleiter, zu denen sich im September 1942 Guglielmo Ulrich gesellte. Von Januar 1943 an bestand die Chefredaktion aus Melchiorre Bega und Guglielmo Ulrich, von Oktober 1943 bis Ende 1944 war Melchiorre Bega allein maßgeblich. Das ganze Jahr 1945 über ruhte das Erscheinen der Zeitschrift, von Januar 1946 bis Dezember 1947 kam sie unter E. N. Rogers, wieder heraus. Seit Januar 1948 ist Gio Ponti Schriftleiter.

Edilizia moderna – Mailand
Herausgegeben von der Linoleum-Gesellschaft. Erschien ab März 1931 als Vierteljahreszeitschrift unter der Schriftleitung von Ernesto Giorgi, an dessen Stelle im Dezember 1938 Giuseppe Luraghi trat. Im Dezember 1940 stellte sie ihr Erscheinen ein und kam erst wieder von April bis Dezember 1942 heraus. Darauf folgte eine neue Pause und dann das endgültige Wiedererscheinen im Dezember 1948 unter der Chefredaktion von Vittorio Beltrami. Die nächsten Schriftleiter waren Renato Bisignani (im Juni 1950), Emilio Romanini (im Juni 1953) und Dino Bernardi (im April 1955).

Edilizia Popolare – Rom
Zweimonatszeitschrift der Italienischen Vereinigung der Genossenschaften für den Bau von Wohnblöcken unter der Schriftleitung von Camillo Ripamonti. Erscheinungsbeginn: November/Dezember 1954. Verlag Edilizia Popolare, Rom, Via XX Settembre 58.

Emporium – Bergamo
Illustrierte Monatszeitschrift für Kunst, Literatur, Wissenschaft und Unterhaltung, herausgegeben vom Verlag Istituto Italiano d'Arti Grafiche, Bergamo. Erschien erstmals im Januar 1895 unter Paolo Testa, der die Schriftleitung bis Mai 1911 innehatte. Er wurde abgelöst von Giuseppe Monticelli, der die Schriftleitung bis Juni 1924 behielt. Von diesem Zeitpunkt an bis Ende 1925 war Luigi Pelandi, von Januar 1926 bis August 1941 Ezio Sangiovanni Chefredakteur. Dann übernahm wieder Luigi Pelandi bis Ende 1942 und schließlich Attilio Podestà bis Ende 1964 die Schriftleitung. 1964 stellte die Zeitschrift ihr Erscheinen ein.

Il Vetro – Mailand
Monatszeitschrift des amtlichen Organs des Nationalen Faschistischen Bundes der Glasindustriellen. Erschien erstmals 1938 unter der Schriftleitung von Pietro Bergonzi als Nachfolgerin der Zeitschrift »L'Industria del vetro e della ceramica«. Nachdem das Ufficio periodici Tumminelli, Rom, sie verkaufte, stellte sie ihr Erscheinen im Jahr 1943 ein.

Lacerba – Florenz
Vierzehntäglich erscheinende Zeitschrift für Kultur mit Guido Pogni als verantwortlichem Herausgeber. Erschien erstmals im Januar 1913 in Florenz. Mitarbeiter waren einige der markantesten Vertreter der modernen italienischen Kultur jener Zeit wie Soffici, Papini, Palazzeschi, Marinetti. Diese Zeitschrift mit eindeutig antitraditionellem und antikonformistischem Charakter war eine Sammlung satirischer Beiträge, kritischer Essays, kurzer dichterischer Aufsätze, Zeichnungen (von Picasso, Rosai, Carrà usw.) und auch französischer und englischer Artikel von Vertretern des europäischen Futurismus. Im November 1914 wurde Pietro Gramigni verantwortlicher Herausgeber. Die Zeitschrift stellte im Mai 1915 ihr Erscheinen ein.

L'Architettura, Cronache e storia – Mailand
Monatszeitschrift, die seit 1955 unter der Schriftleitung von Bruno Zevi herauskommt. Sie wird vom Verlag ET/AS-Kompass, Mailand, herausgegeben.

L'Architettura Italiana – Turin
Monatszeitschrift für Architektur und Bauwesen, die erstmals im Jahr 1905 erschien; Verlag: Crudo e Lattuada, Turin. Schriftleitung: zunächst Carlo Bianchi und Antonio Cavallassi, dann G. Lavini. Sie stellte ihr Erscheinen im Jahr 1943 ein.

L'Arte – Rom-Mailand
Illustrierte Zweimonatszeitschrift, die im Jahr 1898 erstmals herauskam, unter der Schriftleitung von Domenico Gnoli und Adolfo Venturi stand und als Nachfolgerin der »Archivio Storico dell'Arte« bei Michele Danesi, Rom, verlegt wurde. 1900 bekam sie den Titel »Periodico di Storia dell'Arte medioevale e moderna e d'arte decorativa«; die Schriftleitung hatte Adolfo Venturi. Verlag: Michele Danesi, Rom, und Ulrico Hoepli, Mailand. Die Zeitschrift erschien in wechselnden Zeitabständen. Im Jahr 1904 begann eine neue, zweimonatliche Folge unter derselben Schriftleitung und bei denselben Verlagshäusern. Von 1905 an wurde sie vom Verlag Casa editrice de l'Arte, Rom, herausgegeben. Im Jahr 1930 kam eine neue Serie unter der Schriftleitung von Adolfo und Lionello Venturi heraus, die bei Ajani e Canale,

Turin, gedruckt wurde. Ab Juli 1935 war Adolfo Venturi allein Schriftleiter, und mit der Januar-Nummer 1936 erschien die Zeitschrift vierteljährlich. Von Januar 1935 an wurde sie von Industrie Grafiche Italiane Stucchi, Mailand, herausgegeben. Ab 1943 kamen die Hefte in unregelmäßigen Zeitabständen heraus, so zwei im Jahr 1943, eines im Jahr 1944, kein Heft im Jahr 1945 und nur eines im Jahr 1946 mit Aurelio Minghetti als verantwortlichem Redakteur. Erst 1948 erschien das nächste Heft, sodann ein Zusatzheft im Jahr 1949, keines im Jahr 1950. 1951 war Giorgio Nicodemi Chefredakteur. Im Jahr 1952 erschien nur ein Heft, keines im Jahr 1953, eines 1954, keines 1955, und ab Januar 1956 erschienen die Hefte halbjährlich. Mit dem Januar 1958 wurde die Erscheinungsfolge vierteljährlich; von 1959 bis 1961 kamen jährlich drei Hefte heraus, und im Jahr 1962, mit dessen Ende die Zeitschrift eingestellt wurde, erschien sie wieder halbjährlich.

L'Edilizia moderna — Mailand
Monatliche Zeitschrift für praktische Architektur und Bauwesen im Verlag Arturo Demarchi, Mailand. Erscheinungsbeginn im April 1892 unter den Redakteuren Luca Beltrami, Andrea Ferrari, Federico Jorini, Carlo Mina und Gaetano Moretti. Später wurde die Schriftleitung von Carlo Formenti und Francesco Magnoni übernommen. Die Zeitschrift erlosch im Dezember 1916.

L'Industria italiana del Cemento — Rom
Monatszeitschrift, herausgegeben von der Gesellschaft zur Steigerung der Zementverwertung (SIAC) im Verlag der SIAC von Januar 1930 bis September 1943. Nach einer Pause von drei Jahren erschien sie im September 1946 wieder; Verleger war die Italienische Zement-, Asbestzement-, Kalk- und Gips-Industrie. Mit dem Januarheft 1962 erhielt das Blatt sein heutiges typographisches Aussehen unter der Schriftleitung von Gaetano Bologna, Rom, Via di Santa Teresa 23.

La nuova città — Florenz
Monatszeitschrift für Architektur, Städtebau und Inneneinrichtung; wird im Jahr 1946 zum erstenmal herausgegeben. Die Schriftleitung lag bei Giovanni Michelucci bis zum Jahr 1954, in dem die Zeitschrift ihr Erscheinen einstellte.

Lineestruttura — Neapel
Vierteljahreszeitschrift für Architektur, Design und bildende Künste. Sie kam im Mai 1966 unter der Schriftleitung von Lea Vergine heraus. Nino del Papa war für Architektur und Städtebau verantwortlich, Enzo Mari für Design und Lea Vergine für die bildenden Künste. Verlag Diaframma, Neapel.

Metron — Rom
Internationale Monatszeitschrift für Architektur, herausgegeben vom Verlag Sandron, Rom. Erschien erstmalig im August 1945. Schriftleitung: Luigi Piccinato (für Städtebau) und Mario Ridolfi (für Architektur). Im Jahr 1946 erschienen sieben, im Jahr 1947 zehn Hefte. Mit der Nummer 25, die 1948 herauskam, änderten sich Format und Umfang, wobei Leserdienst und Bebilderung umfangreicher wurden. Schriftleiter der neuen Zeitschrift waren Luigi Piccinato, Mario Ridolfi, Silvio Radiconcini und

Bruno Zevi. 1948 erschienen acht, 1949 sechs Nummern. Ab Juli 1950 erschien die Zeitschrift im Zweimonatsrhythmus im Verlag Comunità unter der Schriftleitung von Riccardo Musatti, Luigi Piccinato, Silvio Radiconcini und Bruno Zevi. 1951 und 1952 gab es je vier Nummern, eine im Jahr 1953, sechs im Jahr 1954. Mit der Nr. 54 vom November/Dezember erschien das letzte Heft.

Pagine d'Arte — Mailand
Verlegt von Alfieri e Lacroix mit Antonio Bonfanti als verantwortlichem Redakteur. Diese »Chronik und Rundschau der antiken und modernen Kunst« begann mit ihrem Erscheinen im Jahr 1913, zweiwöchentlich von Oktober bis Juni und monatlich von Juli bis September. Vom Januar 1917 an kam sie monatlich heraus, bis sie mit der Dezember-Nummer des Jahres 1919 ihr Erscheinen einstellte.

Pagine d'Arte (zweite Ausgabe) — Mailand
Erschien monatlich unter der Schriftleitung von Marisa Romano und Innocenza Papetti vom April 1951 an und wurde von Fattori, Rom, gedruckt. Später wurde die Zeitschrift in wechselnden Zeitabständen herausgebracht, bis sie schließlich ihr Erscheinen im Dezember 1952 einstellte.

Prefabbricare — Mailand
Zweimonatszeitschrift der Italienischen Gesellschaft zur Erforschung der Entwicklung auf dem Gebiet der Vorfertigungsmaterialien und -systeme. Sie erschien im Januar 1958 unter der Schriftleitung von Sergio Mulitsch. Mit der Nr. 3/4 vom Dezember 1958/Februar 1959 ging die Schriftleitung auf Ete Stucchi über. Von der Nr. 4 vom Oktober/Dezember 1959 an erschien das Blatt zweimonatlich; seit 1961 wird es bei der Italienischen Gesellschaft für Vorfertigung verlegt. 1964 übernahm Arardo Spreti, Mailand, Galleria Passarella 1, die Schriftleitung.

Prospettive — Mailand
Vierteljahres-Rundschau für Architektur, Inneneinrichtung, Ausstattung und Bühnendekoration unter der Schriftleitung von C. E. Rava im Verlag Görlich, Mailand. Sie erschien erstmals im Jahr 1953. Mit der Nr. 13 vom Dezember 1956 kam sie alle zwei Monate heraus. Das letzte Heft war die Nr. 26/27 vom Juni 1963.

Quadrante — Mailand
Monatszeitschrift für Architektur und Raumkunst unter der Schriftleitung von Massimo Bontempelli und Pietro Maria Bardi. Erschien von Mai 1932 bis Oktober 1936.

Rassegna di Architettura — Mailand
Monatliche Zeitschrift für Architektur und Innenausstattung, herausgegeben von der Verlagsgruppe der Rundschau für Architektur. Sie erschien erstmals im Januar 1929 unter der Chefredaktion von Giovanni Rocco. Die Schriftleitung ging dann von Januar bis Dezember 1940 auf A. Cassi-Ramelli über. Ende 1940 stellte die Zeitschrift ihr Erscheinen ein.

Rassegna d'Arte — Mailand
Monatszeitschrift im Verlag G. Martinelli & C., Mailand, mit Cesare Ostini als Chefredakteur. Erscheinungsbeginn: Januar 1901. Im Redaktionsausschuß befanden

sich bedeutende Persönlichkeiten des italienischen Kulturlebens jener Zeit, unter ihnen Luca Beltrami, Gaetano Moretti, Lodovico Pogliaghi und Virginio Muzio. Im Mai 1902 trat Amos Mantegazza an Ostinis Stelle, der im Juli 1902 von Emilio Magni abgelöst wurde. Zum gleichen Zeitpunkt übernahm der Verlag Menotti, Bassani & C., Mailand, die Zeitschrift. Im Januar 1903 konstituierte sich ein Redaktionsausschuß, dem Solone Ambrosoli, Guido Cagnola, Francesco Malaguzzi-Valeri, Corrado Ricci und G. B. Vittadini angehörten. Hauptverantwortlicher war Emilio Magni, an dessen Stelle im April Battista Biassoni trat. Im Januar 1904 wurde die neue Schriftleitung von G. Cagnola, Francesco Malaguzzi-Valeri und Corrado Ricci mit Battista Biassoni als Verantwortlichem gebildet. Ab Januar 1905 erschien die »Rassegna d'Arte« unter der Schriftleitung von Guido Cagnola und Francesco Malaguzzi-Valeri zusammen mit dem bisher Verantwortlichen, den im Juni 1906 Andrea Moretti ablöste. Von Januar 1908 an wurde sie von Alfieri e Lacroix, Mailand, mit Antonio Bonfanti herausgegeben, doch verblieb die Schriftleitung bei Guido Cagnola und Francesco Malaguzzi-Valeri. Von Januar 1915 bis Dezember 1916 hatte Guido Cagnola die Schriftleitung allein inne; danach verschmolz das Blatt mit der Zeitschrift »Rassegna d'Arte antica e moderna«.

Rassegna d'arte antica e moderna — Mailand
Erschien zunächst monatlich, erstmals im Januar 1914, unter der Schriftleitung von Guido Cagnola und Francesco Malaguzzi-Valeri im Verlag Alfieri e Lacroix, Mailand, mit dem Untertitel »Vita d'Arte«. Im Jahr 1917, nach der Verschmelzung mit »Rassegna d'Arte«, wurden in monatlichem Wechsel zwei Zeitschriften-Serien herausgegeben: »Rassegna d'arte antica e moderna — vita d'arte« und »Rassegna d'arte antica e moderna — rassegna d'arte antica«, diese unter Guido Cagnola, jene unter F. Bargagli-Petrucci. Im Jahr 1920 vereinigten sich beide Serien zur »Rassegna d'arte antica e moderna«; Schriftleitung: Corrado Ricci; Verlag: Alfieri e Lacroix mit Antonio Bonfanti, der die Verantwortung bis zum Januar 1921 behielt. Er wurde dann durch Carlo Zacchetti ersetzt, an dessen Stelle im April 1922 Cesare Castelli trat. Die Zeitschrift stellte im Dezember 1922 ihr Erscheinen ein.

Sele arte — Ivrea
Zweimonatszeitschrift für Kultur und internationale Kunstmitteilungen. Sie kommt seit Juli 1952 unter der Schriftleitung von Carlo L. Ragghianti im Verlag »Ufficio Stampa della Ing. C. Olivetti & C. S.p.A., heraus. Die Zeitschrift stellte mit dem Juniheft 1966 ihr Erscheinen ein.

Spazio — Rom
Monatliche Rundschau für Kunst und Architektur. Kam im Juli 1950 unter der Schriftleitung von Luigi Moretti heraus. Ab Februar 1953 stellte sie ihr Erscheinen ein.

Stile — Mailand
Unter dem Titel »Stile nella casa e nell'arredamento« erschien die Zeitschrift erstmals im Januar 1941 unter der Schriftleitung von Gio Ponti, herausgegeben vom Verlag Garzanti. Sie stellte ihr Erscheinen mit dem Dezemberheft 1947 ein.

Urbanistica — Turin
Erschien erstmals im Januar 1932 als »Bollettino della Sezione Regionale Piemontese Istituto Nazionale di Urbanistica« unter der Schriftleitung von Pietro Betta im Verlag F. Casanova & C., Turin. Im Juli 1932 ging die Schriftleitung auf Armando Melis über. Im Januar 1934 wurde sie zur »Rivista dell'Istituto Nazionale di Urbanistica«. Von Januar 1947 bis Dezember 1948 war Mario Zocca Chefredakteur. Ab Juli 1949 wurde sie zur Zweimonatszeitschrift — Schriftleitung: Adriano Olivetti — und nahm ihr heutiges typographisches Aussehen an. Seit Januar 1950 erscheint sie vierteljährlich. Im Dezember 1953 übernahm Giovanni Astengo die Schriftleitung.

Vitrum — Mailand
Erschien zunächst monatlich, erstmals im November 1949 als »Lastre di vetro e cristallo«, als Nachrichtenblatt der Informations- und Forschungszentrale für die Verwertung von Glas bei Bauten und Einrichtungen (CISAV) und unter der Schriftleitung von Giulio Benelli. Mit der Nr. 10 vom August 1950 übernahm Luigi Gandini die Schriftleitung, mit der Nr. 15 vom Januar 1951 erhielt sie den Titel »Vitrum — Lastre di vetro e cristallo«. Seit Januar 1959 erscheint die Zeitschrift zweimonatlich und nimmt ihr heutiges typographisches Gesicht an. Verlag CISAV, Mailand, Via Hoepli 5.

Zodiac — Mailand
Internationale Zeitschrift für zeitgenössische Architektur, gegründet von Adriano Olivetti. Kam im Oktober 1957 unter der Schriftleitung von Bruno Alfieri beim Verlag Comunità heraus. Seit 1964 liegt die Schriftleitung in den Händen von Pier Carlo Santini.

Index

Albini, Franco 20/21, 144
Angellnl, Luigi 12/13
Arata, Giulio 10/11, 12/13
Ashbee, Charles Robert 10/11
Azzolini, Tito 6/7

Balla, Giacomo 12/15
Banfi, Gianluigi 16/17, 18/19
Baroni, Nello 18/19
Basile, Ernesto 10/11, 12/13
Bassi, Carlo 100
Battaglia, Carlo 12/13
Bega, Melchiorre 158
Behrens, Peter 10/11
Belgiojoso, Lodovico Barbiani di 16/17, 18/19, 156
Berardi, Pier Nicolò 18/19
Bernasconi, Gianantonio 148
Boccioni, Umberto 12/15
Boggiano, Arnoldo 44
Boito, Camillo 6/7, 8/9
Bonamico, Sergio 110
Borzi, Ennio 38
Boschetti, Goffredo 100
Bottoni, Piero 16/17
Bozzetti, Gino 118
Brigatti, Dante 84
Brizzi, Emilio 132
Bruno, Giovanni 38

Calini, Leo 150
Carminati 18/19
Carrà, Carlo 12/15
Castiglioni, Enrico 80, 84, 86, 104
Cereghini, Mario 16/17
Chiodi, Giuseppe 46
Cocchia, Carlo 110
Colonnese, Vittorio 14/15
Cometti, Giacomo 10/11
Cosenza, Luigi 18/19
Covre, Gino 186
Crane, Walter 10/11
Crapiz, G. 164

Dall'Olio, Claudio 110
D'Andrade, Alfredo 6/7
Daneri, Luigi Carlo 56
Danusso, Arturo 18/19, 160
D'Aronco, Raimondo 10/11, 12/13
De Carlo, Adolfo 90
Dell'Orto, Egidio 160
Delmonte, Franco Enrico 44
De Simoni, Luigi 110
D'Isola, Aimaro Oreglia 106
D'Olivo, Marcello 60

Favini, Aldo 88, 170
Figini, Gino 14/15, 16/17, 18/19
Figini, Luigi 20/21, 70, 92, 180

Finzi, Leo 30
Fiocchi, Annibale 148
Fontana, Carlo 86
Fornaroli, Antonio 160
Frette, Guido 14/15, 16/17

Gabetti, Roberto 106
Galardi, Alberto 176
Gamberini, Italo 18/19
Gandolfi, Vittorio 54, 82
Gardella, Ignazio 20/21, 74
Ghedina, Mario 108, 110
Gori, Enzo 132
Gori, Giuseppe 132
Griffini, Enrico 16/17
Guarnieri, Sarre 18/19

Helg, Franca 144
Hoffmann, Josef 10/11
Horta, Victor 10/11

Larco, Sebastiano 14/15
Levi, Corrado 172
Levi, Laura 172
Libera, Adalberto 14/15
Ligini, Cesare 114
Linari, Attilio 110
Lingeri, Pietro 16/17, 18/19
Lusanna, Leonardo 18/19

Macchi, Giorgio 190
Maciachini, Carlo 6/7
Mackintosh, Charles Rennie 10/11
Magistretti, Vico 40, 52
Mangiarotti, Angelo 36, 88, 170
Marchi, Virgilio 14/15
Marinetti, Filippo Tommaso 12/15, 18/19
Michelucci, Giovanni 18/19, 20/21, 96
Migliasso, Antonio 74, 176
Minoletti, Giulio 46
Montalcini, Levi 16/17
Montuori, Eugenio 150
Mor, Andrea 90
Morandi, Riccardo 134, 184
Morassutti, Bruno 32, 36, 88, 170
Morassutti, Giovanni 170
Moretti, Carlo 22, 78
Moretti, Gaetano 8/9, 10/11
Moretti, Luigi 18/19, 26
Morozzo della Rocca, Robaldo 48
Morris, William 10/11
Muzio, Giovanni 14/15

Nalli, Riccardo 108
Nervi, Antonio 138
Nervi, Pier Luigi 18/19, 20/21, 122, 128, 138, 160, 186
Nichelli, Egizio 118
Nizzoli, Marcello 42, 148, 152

Nova, Edoardo 30
Novarin, R. 164

Olbrich, Joseph Maria 10/11
Oliveri, Mario 42, 152
Ortensi, Dagoberto 110, 114

Pagano, Giuseppe 16/17, 18/19, 20/21
Paniconi, Mario 50
Papini, Gian Luca 180
Pediconi, Giulio 50
Peressutti, Enrico 16/17, 156
Persico, Edoardo 17/18, 19
Piacentini, Marcello 12/13, 14/15, 18/19, 128
Poggi, Giuseppe 6/7
Pollini, Gino 14/15, 16/17, 20/21, 70, 92, 180
Ponti, Gio 14/15, 18/19, 160
Portaluppi, Piero 14/15
Predaval, G. 18/19
Procesi, Mario 110

Quaroni, Ludovico 90
Quarti, Eugenio 10/11

Raineri, Giuseppe 106
Rava, Carlo Enrico 14/15
Reale, Alberto 172
Ricci, Leonardo 132
Ricci, Silvano 114
Rogers, Ernesto N. 16/17, 18/19, 156
Rosselli, Alberto 160, 168
Russolo, Luigi 12/15

Sacconi, Giuseppe 6/7
Saliva, Ernesto 18/19
Sant'Elia, Antonio 12, 14, 15/16
Savioli, Leonardo 132
Severini, Gino 12/15
Severino, Renato 62
Sibilla, Angelo 90
Sommaruga, Giuseppe 12/13

Tamburini, Franco 38
Terragni, Giuseppe 14/15, 16/17, 18/19, 20/21

Uras, Francesco 108, 110

Valle, Gino 164
Valtolina, Giuseppe 160
Vietti, Luigi 18/19
Viganò, Vittoriano 30, 66
Villari, Pasquale 6/7
Viollet-Le-Duc, Eugène Emmanuel 8/9
Vitellozzi, Annibale 122
Voysey, Charles Annesley Francis 10/11

Wagner, Otto 10/11

Zorzi, Silvano 180, 190

Photo Credits · Fotonachweis

Allegri, Brescia 30 (2)
Aldo Ballo, Milano 31 (5), 55 (4), 82 (1), 83 (4, 5), 154 (5), 162 (6)
A. Cartoni, Roma 26 (1, 2), 27 (3), 28 (4), 29 (6), 150 (1, 2)
Foto-Studio Casali, Milano 40 (1), 41 (3), 76 (6), 77 (7), 80 (1), 81 (4), 148 (1), 156 (2), 169 (2)
G. Chiolini, Pavia 190 (1, 2), 191 (3, 4)
C-I-S-A-V 30 (1)
Cresta, Genova 56 (1), 58 (4), 59 (6)
Domus, Milano 158 (1)
Fotocielo, Roma 117 (6)
Fotocinetecnica s.r.l., Roma 127 (8)
Fotogramma s.r.l., Milano 66 (1), 67 (2), 102 (6, 7)
Fototecnica Fortunati, Milano 73 (7), 92 (1), 94 (5, 6), 95 (7), 104 (1), 105 (3)
G. Gherardi — A. Fiorelli, Roma 62 (1), 63 (4), 116 (4), 122 (1), 126 (7)
Martinotti, Milano 148 (2), 149 (3)
Mercurio, Milano 101 (4)
Moisio, Torino 143 (7)
Paolo Monti, Milano 101 (5)
Novelli, Busto Arsizio 84 (1)
Carlo Orsi 181 (3)
Perucca 179 (8)
Publicolor, Milano 55 (2)
Publifoto, Genova 65 (7)
Publifoto, Milano 47 (3), 74 (2), 76 (5), 118 (1), 120 (5, 6), 121 (7, 8), 156 (1), 162 (5)
Publifoto, Torino 172 (1), 173 (3), 174 (4)
Sala Dino, Milano 177 (4), 178 (5, 6)
Oscar Savio, Roma 38 (1), 39 (2, 3), 125 (5), 128 (1), 130 (4, 5), 131 (7), 144 (1), 146 (4, 5), 147 (6), 187 (2), 188 (6)
Vasari, Roma 50 (1), 126 (6), 187 (3)
A. Villani & Figli, Bologna 114 (1), 116 (5), 158 (2)
Orlando Zanichelli, Torino 100 (1)
Italo Zannier, Spilimbergo 164 (1), 165 (5), 166 (6, 7), 167 (8, 9)